SPIRITUAL CAPITAL

THE NEW CURRENCY OF CORPORATE GROWTH

Copyright Case ID: 1-14969529281

Library of Congress Control Number (LCCN): 2025916496

ISBNs:
E-book: 978-1-967894-00-0
Paperback: 978-1-967894-01-7
Hardcover: 978-1-967894-02-4
Audiobook: 978-1-967894-03-1

THE TWO WORLDS COLLIDE

I spent over 26 years at one of the world's leading IT services companies, navigating through leadership roles, managing strategic initiatives, and driving growth for global P&L. In July 2005, a select group of leaders flew into Delhi, India, for a pivotal three-day conference, which was named "Blueprint." Our newly appointed CEO, a seasoned veteran with the group, took the stage and shook the very foundation of our beliefs with one bold, disruptive statement: "Employees First, Customers Second."

I vividly remember the room falling into a stunned silence. A heavy, suffocating stillness blanketed the room. Eyes widened, pens froze mid-sentence over notepads, and even the hum of the projector seemed to fade, swallowed by a silence so dense it felt almost physical. There we sat, seasoned professionals, veterans of the corporate grind, with decades of experience in following the golden rule of customer-first strategies. We had been trained to see customers not just as clients, but as sovereigns—entitled to unwavering respect, their satisfaction, the axis around which every decision turned. This mantra was so well ingrained in our minds that questioning it felt almost sacrilegious. Skepticism ran through the air thick as fog—my own included. I remember thinking, "Is this really going to work? How will our customers react?"

But our CEO's vision was clear: if we, as a services company, truly wanted to deliver exceptional value, it would not happen in boardrooms or strategy decks, but in the moment of interaction between our employees and customers. Happy, empowered employees would naturally ensure delighted customers. This philosophy wasn't just a tagline; it was a revolution. And it worked. Our employees found a renewed sense of passion, pride, and purpose. What followed was a remarkable transformation—our rapid growth outpaced the competition and established us as the fastest-growing company in the industry, setting new benchmarks along the way. We had created something extraordinary. The entire ecosystem—our customers, industry analysts, partners, and even academic institutions—was intrigued, puzzled, and desperate to understand how a single shift in philosophy could yield such stunning results.

Now, fast forward to September 2024, and we are confronted with a jarring and heartbreaking reminder of the other end of the spectrum. A 26-year-old employee from a top consulting firm in Pune, India, tragically succumbed to work-related stress. The story quickly made headlines, serving as a stark reminder of the dark side of unchecked corporate pressure. But this was not just another statistic—it was a profound human tragedy.

Shattered and grieving, the mother wrote a heart-wrenching letter to the organization, accusing it of driving her daughter to the brink through relentless overwork. She recounted how the young woman labored tirelessly, sacrificing sleep and battling mounting anxiety to meet the company's unending demands. Just four months after joining, her daughter died—what the mother described as death by 'overwork.' In a final act of neglect, not a single representative from the organization attended the funeral. She hoped her daughter's tragic end would serve as a wake-up call, sparing other families from similar heartbreak.

The contrast couldn't be more glaring: on one hand, empowered employees drive organizational success; on the other, work-related stress claims lives—even young ones—becoming tragic symbols of a deepening crisis in today's professional world. Grueling hours, relentless pressure, sleeplessness, anxiety, and crippling stress are taking a toll in environments that leave little room for well-being. As we climb higher up the corporate ladder, this pressure only intensifies. Increasingly, CEOs and senior executives are facing the grim reality of burnout—some even dying on the job. According to *The Wall Street Journal*, more than 1,900 CEOs left their roles in 2023, and a record 19 died in office. A Deloitte study from August 2022, which surveyed over 1,100 senior leaders, found that 82% experienced exhaustion indicative of burnout, and 96% reported a decline in their mental health.

This growing crisis has led to a rising global awareness about the importance of *mental well-being*. Indeed, the corporate world is gradually waking up to the understanding that true success isn't simply about the financial gains or outpacing peers in career advancement. It's about achieving balance—external success paired with internal fulfillment. Leaders are beginning to embrace spiritual principles to cultivate lives that are not just successful but also deeply meaningful. This shift highlights an emerging belief that sustainability in success is most achievable when it is rooted in personal contentment, ethical practices, and a higher sense of purpose that transcends profits.

However, such examples are sporadic and few. To address this, the world doesn't need another cleverly packaged strategy but a true revolution—a disruption not of profits, but of purpose and meaning. The answer may not lie in another quarterly roadmap or performance metric; rather, it could be found in the *often-overlooked yet profound reservoir of human potential: spirituality.*

If organizations embrace spiritual principles—nurturing the inner well-being of their employees—then the ripple effect could be profound. Happy, content employees will naturally lead to higher productivity, better performance on all fronts, and ultimately, more sustainable success.

It may seem paradoxical—after all, the corporate world and spirituality are often seen as opposing forces. Business is driven by goals, profits, competition, and efficiency, while spirituality emphasizes inner peace, mindfulness, and personal growth. Looking at the list of Fortune 100 Best Companies to Work For® 2024, I found that Hilton, Cisco, and NVIDIA topped the list, distinguished by their focus on recognition, celebration, warmth, welcoming, supportive, respect, and equality. While I'm sure other companies on the list have their own unique policies fostering inclusive cultures, these examples are still relatively few. Despite such initiatives, more and more professionals are recognizing that the age-old markers of success—

wealth, power, and influence—often leave them feeling hollow and unfulfilled. Many reach the pinnacle of their careers, only to find themselves staring into the abyss of emptiness.

I have explored how integrating spiritual principles into the corporate world can foster lasting success, personal fulfillment, and a profoundly ethical approach to business. By embracing concepts such as mindfulness, empathy, detachment, and purpose-driven leadership, professionals not only excel in their careers but also cultivate richer, more balanced lives. When spiritual values and corporate objectives align, workplaces transform from mere spaces of labor into arenas of true human flourishing. Employees feel connected to a greater purpose, discovering meaning that transcends profits or titles and delving into a deeper sense of contribution.

Beyond personal growth, spirituality in business also encompasses critical dimensions such as *ethics and morality*.

Looking back at history, we see a series of corporate scandals. In 2000, PerkinElmer faced allegations of fraud. The Enron collapse rocked the world in 2001. In 2002, both WorldCom and Tyco were exposed for fraud. Then came the fall of Lehman Brothers in 2008. In 2015, Volkswagen faced an emissions scandal. Finally, Wirecard's downfall shook the market in 2020. A clear pattern emerges: across borders and industries, leading companies manipulate financial records, costing stakeholders hundreds of billions of dollars and eroding trust in the system.

When spirituality guides us toward inner fulfillment and authentic contentment, it awakens a new consciousness—one rooted in compassion and empathy for others. In this awakened state, people naturally move away from greed, conflict, and division, focusing instead on uplifting one another.

By incorporating spirituality into daily life, I sense a profound transformation is possible—one that could reshape the very fabric of our world and, perhaps, lay the foundation for global peace.

With this potential shift, I believe *we possess the power to create a more stable, harmonious world, united under the principles of peaceful coexistence.*

Contents

CHAPTER ONE

UNDERSTANDING
THE TWO WORLDS

The Backdrop

For decades, the relentless grind of corporate ambition, high expectations, stringent deadlines, and insatiable pursuit of profits has driven corporate employees and executives to burnout—a toxic cocktail of exhaustion that drains physically and mentally. Prolonged stress is a merciless predator, ravaging lives and wreaking havoc on the body. Chronic pain, sleepless nights, heart problems—these are not just words in a medical journal but the grim reality of millions, etched in the lines of weary faces and empty stares. The cost of stress is no longer confined to just the personal realm; it has metastasized into an organizational and societal epidemic. The physical and mental health of individuals impacts their productive hours at work. Productivity—both in terms of hours logged and quality of work with sparks of innovation—crumbles under this invisible weight.

A study by the World Health Organization (WHO) found that depression and anxiety cost the global economy an estimated $1 trillion annually in lost productivity. In the U.S. alone, nearly one in five adults experienced a mental illness in 2023, and work-related stress was cited as a major contributing factor. According to Gallup, a staggering 76% of employees report feeling burned out at least some of the time, highlighting the severity of the issue.

Decent work, coupled with a healthy environment, plays a vital role in sustaining mental well-being. As per the International Labour Organization, "Decent work sums up the aspirations of people in their working lives. It involves opportunities for work that is productive and delivers a fair income, security in the workplace and social protection for all, better prospects for personal development and social integration, freedom for people to express their concerns, organize and participate in the decisions that affect their lives, and equality of opportunity and treatment for all women and men."

Several companies recognized in the Deloitte Global Human Capital Trends Report and the Great Place to Work® Mental Health at Work list have adopted forward-thinking policies to promote employee well-being. For example, organizations like Salesforce, Adobe, and American Express have introduced initiatives like mental health days, flexible work options, access to professional counseling, and ongoing mindfulness programs. These companies also foster a culture where discussing mental health is encouraged rather than stigmatized. These initiatives align with the principles of decent work and are linked to higher employee satisfaction and lower burnout rates.

On the other hand, poor working environments—including discrimination and inequality, excessive workloads, low job control, and job insecurity—pose a risk to mental health. Globally, an estimated 12 billion working days are lost every year to depression and anxiety.

As the data points shown above highlight, the implications of poor mental health extend far beyond the individual. For businesses, the costs are staggering: decreased engagement, increased absenteeism, and rising turnover. According to the Center for Prevention and Health Services, untreated mental health concerns result in annual costs of $60,000 for a single organization—and a nationwide impact exceeding $105 billion.

Moreover, the stigma surrounding mental health often prevents employees from seeking help. According to the American Psychiatric Association, eight in ten workers with a mental health condition hesitate to disclose their struggles to their employers, fearing discrimination or judgment. This lack of openness exacerbates the problem, as untreated mental health issues escalate into crises.

The growing awareness of this epidemic has led to some progress, with forward-thinking organizations stepping up to address the crisis. Companies such as Delta Airlines, Accenture, Hilton, Cisco, NVIDIA, and American Express offer comprehensive mental health programs, including counseling services, employee assistance programs (EAPs), and mindfulness training. These efforts are not just altruistic but strategic; research shows that every dollar spent on mental health interventions can yield a return of up to $4 in improved health and productivity.

Addressing the mental health epidemic requires a fundamental shift in corporate culture. Leaders must prioritize mental health as a core pillar of organizational strategy, fostering open conversations and creating environments where employees feel safe seeking help. Simple yet impactful initiatives—such as flexible work arrangements and regular mental health check-ins, can significantly reduce stress and enhance overall well-being.

Mental health is no longer a personal issue but a collective responsibility. As organizations increasingly recognize the human and financial toll of neglecting mental well-being, the corporate world stands at a crossroads. By embracing proactive mental health strategies, companies can not only improve lives but also unlock the full potential of their workforce, driving innovation, resilience, and sustainable success in an increasingly demanding world.

This framing highlights the urgency of the mental health crisis in corporate environments, supported by compelling data and actionable solutions.

We now stand at a critical juncture. On one side, corporations funnel billions of dollars into well-intentioned HR programs and glossy leadership initiatives, hoping to stem the tide. On the other hand, this tidal wave of burnout and exhaustion continues to rise, sweeping away progress like a house of cards. Decades of tinkering with strategies and programs have done little to quell this storm.

The Corporate World

The corporate world is defined by the pursuit of external success—measurable targets such as revenue, margins, market share, efficiency, and growth. It operates within frameworks that emphasize competition, profitability, and productivity. Organizations are driven by metrics and goals, and employees are often encouraged to prioritize work achievements above all else. The relentless demands of the corporate world frequently leave little space for personal reflection, work-life balance, or emotional well-being.

To ground these complex realities in something more tangible, this book includes fictional narratives inspired by real-world patterns and experiences. These illustrative stories are designed to breathe life into the data and research, helping readers visualize how systemic issues unfold in everyday corporate settings. By stepping into the boardrooms and back offices of fictional companies like Zenyra Technologies, readers can engage with the emotional and organizational dynamics that statistics alone cannot capture.

The following scenario illustrates this. While fictional in form, the challenges it explores reflect truths drawn from hundreds of real-life conversations, cases, and corporate environments.

It is the third week of January 2023, and the 40th-floor boardroom of one of the world's largest multinational corporations, Zenyra Technologies, overlooking the sprawling New York City skyline, is abuzz with their quarterly meeting. The mood is tense, and the room is filled with senior executives and board members. Sleek leather chairs surround a massive glass table, and digital projections display the company's financial figures. A few notable team members in the room are:

» Rachel Sinclair: the CEO, sharp, ambitious, and in control.

» David Harris: the CFO, analytical, with a reputation for precision.

» Sophia Morales: Head of Strategy, brilliant but often at odds with others.

» Stan Miller: Chief Operating Officer, cautious and methodical.

» Mark Daniels: an aggressive board member pushing for a strategic acquisition.

» Other board members (unnamed but present in the background).

Rachel stood at the head of the table, a laser pointer in hand. Her posture was upright, commanding, her gaze steady as she scanned the room. When she spoke, her voice cut crisply through the tension.

"As you can see, our international revenue has increased by 8%, largely driven by the success in Southeast Asia. However, our domestic numbers have stagnated."

David gave a small nod, then reached for the spreadsheet in front of him. His brow furrowed slightly as he scanned the figures.

"We've been anticipating some slowdown stateside. Our operational costs have been rising, and we haven't seen the expected ROI from recent tech investments. In light of this, we need to reassess our overhead. We've kept the headcount steady, but we might need to reconsider... difficult decisions moving forward."

Sophia's eyes narrowed, a flicker of sharp recognition crossing her face.

"Are you suggesting cost-cutting measures, David?"

There was a pause before David answered. He looked up, his jaw set, voice measured but unflinching.

"Yes. Our current cost structure is unsustainable if domestic revenues don't rebound. This could include layoffs or reallocation of resources. We've been avoiding these discussions, but the time may have come to face reality."

Mark leans forward, his fingers tapping lightly against the polished conference table, a subtle staccato that slices through the uneasy quiet. His voice drops low, sharp, and edged.

"That's exactly why we should move forward with the acquisition of Orion Analytics. Their platform would give us the market edge we need to dominate the domestic market. We can't sit around while our competitors innovate—and frankly, layoffs might make us vulnerable."

A faint rustle swept the room—papers shifting, a pen clicking somewhere down the table. Faces turned toward Rachel, eyes searching for direction. She didn't speak at once. Her expression remained unreadable, gaze steady, as if weighing every word against an invisible scale. The silence hung heavy, broken only by the soft hum of the overhead lights. Then, after a deliberate exhale, she spoke—each word honed to precision.

"Mark, we've discussed this. Orion Analytics is a high-risk acquisition. Their financials are far from transparent, and we cannot afford to gamble on another shaky integration, especially with potential layoffs on the horizon."

Sophia leaned in slightly, voice calm but tinged with tension.

"Rachel's right. Orion's technology is promising, but they're hemorrhaging cash. If we add them to our existing cost burden, we could end up deeper in the red. And yes, David's right. We'll need to consider cost cuts—layoffs or streamlining operations—if our domestic performance doesn't improve."

Mark straightened abruptly, his voice rising with frustration.

"By the time your precious R&D finishes, we'll be outpaced by every major player in the industry. We need to act—now. Cutting jobs won't solve the larger issue; we need a bold strategy to grow, not just save pennies."

Stan sat still for a moment before speaking, his tone even and composed.

"Mark, the due diligence process has raised several red flags with Orion. We've identified potential regulatory issues, especially with their data handling practices. If we proceed hastily, it could expose us to serious compliance risks—and layoffs on top of that would send a very negative signal to both investors and employees."

Rachel's voice lowered, but the steel in it remained.

"Let me remind everyone that this isn't a decision we can afford to rush. We need to protect the long-term interests of this company. Yes, Mark, growth comes with risk, but reckless actions could jeopardize more than just short-term financials."

A few heads nod, while others trade uneasy looks; the atmosphere is still heavy with tension.

Mark's voice cut through again, harsher now, his composure slipping.

"Protect the company? Rachel, sometimes you're too focused on playing it safe. If you're not willing to make bold moves, maybe someone else should be leading."

A ripple moved through the room—sharp murmurs, darted glances. Rachel's eyes locked on Mark's. The air seemed still, saturated with challenge. Her voice was ice—controlled, exact, and deadly serious. "Are you questioning my leadership, Mark? Because if you want to have that discussion, we can. Right here. Right now."

The tension spikes as everyone waits for Mark's response. His jaw tightens, but he leans back in his chair, unwilling to escalate further.

"I'm just pushing for what's best for the company."

Rachel didn't look away.

"Good. So am I. But that doesn't mean reckless acquisitions or blind cuts to our workforce. We'll approach this with balance. We may need to make tough decisions, including layoffs, but they will be part of a broader strategy that secures our future—not one that mortgages it for the sake of a quick win."

She paused, her words settling over the room like falling ash. The others watched her, recognizing the gravity of her stance.

David finally spoke, breaking the silence with a tone of careful diplomacy. "In that case, I propose we review not just R&D but the entire cost structure. We should aim for efficiency where possible before any layoffs become necessary."

Rachel nodded. Her posture relaxed by a fraction, and her tone softened—but only slightly.

"Agreed. Let's reassess the expenditure of every department and look for areas where we can streamline without compromising our strategic goals. We'll come back with a comprehensive report at the next meeting. And regarding Orion, we'll keep them on the table, but we won't rush. Simultaneously, we will accelerate our efforts to assess additional acquisition opportunities."

The board members begin to relax, though the tension still hums beneath the surface. As the meeting comes to a close, Rachel remains standing, her gaze lingering on Mark, who, for the first time, looks slightly humbled.

"Meeting adjourned."

The executives slowly filter out of the room, leaving Rachel alone, gazing out at the skyline. The weight of leadership rests on her shoulders, but her expression shows resolve. She knows the fight for the company's future is far from over—and the hardest decisions may still lie ahead.

At age 47, Rachel embodies the very essence of a modern business leader—poised, razor-sharp, and relentlessly driven. She stands tall, exuding quiet authority, her tailored navy-blue power suit impeccable, the sharp pleats of her trousers mirroring her precision in decision-making. A platinum watch gleams subtly on her wrist, not as a statement of wealth but of discipline—she values every second.

Her dark eyes, intense and calculating, miss nothing. Framing them are sculpted features—an angular jawline and lips that hold a hint of resolve—lending her an air of both refinement and quiet authority. Even in solitude, there's an air of command around her, as if the very walls recognize her presence. Years of boardroom battles, market shifts, and high-stakes negotiations have honed her into an unshakable force—someone who doesn't just navigate chaos but bends it to her will.

Her accolades speak for themselves—*Best CEO Under 50*, *Forbes Top 10 Visionary Leaders*, and a keynote speaker at the world's most elite business forums. Yet, it's not the awards that define her; it's the way she walks into a room, and conversations still mid-sentence as people take note. Rachel

Sinclair has built a career turning struggling enterprises into market leaders. Highly data-driven, ruthless in execution, she thrives when the stakes are the highest.

Behind that steely focus lay sacrifices not found in press releases. Her rise came with a quiet cost—family moments traded for midnight flights, recitals missed for revenue calls, connection slowly fraying under the weight of ambition. Rachel had a husband, a son, and a daughter—each witnessing her ascent with a mix of pride and quiet longing. She had chosen excellence over presence, impact over intimacy, not out of neglect but necessity—what she believed was climbing her way up the corporate ladder.

And tonight, as she stands in her corner office overlooking the New York skyline, she feels something unusual—doubt. She had given everything—her time, her strategy, her disciplined hard work—and still, growth remained elusive.

Was it possible that what the organization needed now wasn't more analysis or sharper execution—but something deeper? Something she had never thought to factor into the equation?

Like Rachel's introspection, most boardroom discussions inevitably wade into similar territory at some point. The relentless pressure to deliver industry-leading, quarter-on-quarter growth in both revenues and margins is nothing short of staggering. Investors and board members demand this from executive management as if it were a mere baseline expectation—a given, not an achievement. Yet, in the unyielding pursuit of maximizing returns for stakeholders, one critical element is often sidelined: the employees.

The corporate personnel departments, being referred to as Human Resources, have long raised questions. What weight does the word resources truly carry in this context? On the surface, it acknowledges employees as indispensable contributors to an organization's success, comparable to financial or material assets.

But dig deeper, and you often find a stark reality: employees reduced to mere resources—tools in the relentless machinery of business goals. Is that all they are? Or should they be more?

The Spiritual World

Spirituality, on the other hand, is about the internal journey—a quest for self-awareness, purpose, and connection to something larger than oneself. It transcends religion, centering instead on personal growth, mindfulness, compassion, and the search for meaning. Spirituality encourages individuals to look beyond material success, emphasizing contentment, ethics, and inner harmony. To explore these ideas more vividly, let us step into a fictional story setting—one that captures the essence of spirituality in leadership by showing how stillness and introspection offer a powerful counterpoint to corporate urgency, and how inner clarity can illuminate organizational complexity.

In stark contrast to the polished boardroom in New York, where strategy buzzed through fluorescent air, the ashram nestled in the Himalayan foothills breathed in silence. High in the mountains, far from noise and ambition, a retreat session unfolded inside a meditation hall wrapped in stillness.

Sunlight streamed through tall windows, laying gold across the smooth wooden floor. Incense spiraled toward the beams above, mingling with the scent of fresh marigolds arranged in copper bowls. Outside, a breeze stirred the leaves of ancient trees and slipped quietly into the hall, cooling the foreheads of those seated in still rows.

Dozens of men and women—CEOs, founders, changemakers—sat cross-legged, robed in white. Their suits were folded away, their business cards irrelevant here. Titles, once worn like armor, seemed to dissolve in the stillness, unspoken but not forgotten. Some sat with their eyes closed, their brows furrowed in concentration; others simply stared ahead, as if waiting for something to loosen inside them. One man in the second row clenches his jaw as he stares at the floor, his white robes unable to mask the tension in his shoulders. Beside him, a woman presses her hands together as if in prayer, her eyes shut tight, lips trembling—not in sorrow, but in surrender. Silence bound them, not awkward but sacred, charged with unsaid things.

At the front of the hall, the Guru sat upright on a simple cushion. His presence didn't command the room—it calmed it. He wore the same white robes as the rest, but around him, stillness seemed to gather. His eyes, half-lidded, held a depth that was not distracted by thought. When he finally spoke, his voice was no louder than the wind outside.

"To know the self," he said, "one must first stop chasing what is not the self. But tell me—do you truly know who you are?"

His words fell gently, like water over stone, and the silence absorbed them. A woman in the third row exhaled, her breath shaky but slow, as if something unnamed had just eased its grip.

Many had come here burdened by unspoken regrets, by the grind of endless ambition, by the haunting sense that success had left something behind. Their stories were not shared, but felt. In the hush of the hall, pain was not confessed—it was witnessed.

The room did not demand transformation. It only offered space. And sometimes, space is the rarest gift of all.

One participant, eager to understand the relevance of spirituality in their professional lives, spoke up. "Guruji, we understand spirituality helps us personally, but how does it fit in a corporate setting?"

The Guru's gaze softened as he responded, "Spirituality in your boardroom is not about rituals. It is about intention, integrity, and inner clarity. It means leading not only with your mind but also with your heart."

Another participant, concerned about potential conflicts with company values, asked: "What if our company values clash with spiritual principles?"

The Guru offered a knowing nod, his gaze calm and reassuring. "Then it is your role to become a mirror to those values. Align your decisions with timeless principles. When your actions uplift others, you are already leading spiritually. When you perform *Seva*, where you serve without expectation, without ego, the act itself becomes a meditation. In serving others, if the intent is pure, you serve the Divine," he says, his words carried by the soft breeze into the hearts of those listening.

"The mind," Guru explains, "is like a storm. The more you fight it, the stronger it becomes. True peace is found not in battling the storm, but in resting within the eye of it. Many of you have come here seeking answers—answers to questions you may not even have fully formed. But the path forward is not through questioning; it is through surrender. It is in service, in stillness, and the quietness of your heart that you will find what you are seeking. Stillness is not the absence of movement but the presence of purpose; pause often to align your actions with your higher self."

From the back of the hall, a man in his early fifties raised his hand hesitantly. The simple tag pinned to his robe read "Samuel Hartman." Few here would know he led a global tech empire; fewer still would care. In this space, he was just another seeker, voice uncertain, heart curious. "Guruji," he asked, "we live in a world that rewards speed and constant results. How do we find this 'eye of the storm' when we're expected to keep moving, always delivering?"

The Guru smiled, his eyes crinkling with warmth. "Samuel, a tree grows silently, even in the middle of a storm. To move with purpose, you must first learn to pause with intention. In that stillness, clarity arises. When you cultivate calm within, your actions outside will have power without aggression."

Hartman nodded slowly, the words already beginning to reshape something within him.

Another hand went up. Leila Costa, a senior leader from a global consumer goods firm, spoke. "Guruji, you mentioned 'Seva' earlier. Can you tell us what that truly means in our world? Is it just about doing charity or volunteering? We're here to lead businesses. How does Seva apply to us?"

The Guru leaned forward slightly. "Ah, Seva. Service without expectation. In your world, you call it Servant Leadership. The role of a leader is not to sit atop, but to uplift. When you empower your team, when you listen with humility, when you support without seeking credit—that is Seva. It turns leadership from a position into a purpose."

"You mean we serve our teams, not just lead them?" Leila asked, intrigued.

"Precisely," the Guru replied. "When a leader seeks only control, trust fades. When a leader serves, people rise. Empower your teams, listen deeply, and remove obstacles for their growth. That, too, is *Seva*. You do not lose your authority. You elevate it. The soul of leadership lies not in control, but in connection—within yourself and with those you serve. True leaders are like rivers—they nourish those they pass through, without needing recognition."

The participants stirred. The message was beginning to land.

Oliver Grant, from the automotive sector, raised a skeptical brow. "But how does this kind of leadership drive performance?" he asked. "We're measured by quarterly results, not intention."

Guruji chuckled softly. "Let me ask you this, Oliver. What happens to a machine when it runs without oil?"

"It overheats, and ultimately it will break down."

"Exactly. And what is the oil in your organization? Its purpose, trust, and cohesion. *Seva* is not in conflict with performance—it is the lubricant that keeps your system running without friction."

There was a hum of agreement. Eyes met across the room with a silent recognition of truth.

The Guru let his gaze sweep gently across the room, then said,

"Many of you lead teams where certain individuals consistently deliver—not just what's asked, but more. You trust them because their performance is dependable, and their discipline is self-driven. You rarely need to follow up. They anticipate, they execute, they rise."

A few heads nodded—those faces lit with the quiet pride of recognition.

The Guru continued, "Now imagine if your *mind* worked with the same reliability. Imagine if, instead of resisting, it supported you—thinking with clarity, focusing with precision, and aligning with your higher purpose without constant struggle. This is not fantasy. It is training."

He paused.

"Raja Yoga meditation is that training. It is not about suppressing the mind—it is about elevating it. Just as a capable employee grows through trust, guidance, and consistent practice, your mind too becomes your most powerful ally when given the right direction. You lead teams in your outer world. Raja Yoga teaches you to lead the team within: your thoughts, your emotions, your energy. When they move in harmony, your potential is not just reached—it is multiplied."

The room fell into an even deeper stillness—nct of emptiness, but of comprehension.

Another participant, Daphne Grayson, from the financial sector, posed her question carefully. "How do we keep this alive once we're back in the world? How do we bring this stillness into the noise?"

Guruji folded his hands in his lap. "By creating small sanctuaries within your day. A moment of breath before a decision. A silent gratitude before a meeting. Encourage spaces where your people can pause—without guilt. Let well-being be woven into your culture, not added as an afterthought."

Daphne wrote something in her journal. Her expression softened.

Guruji continued, "A company guided only by profit will always be chasing. But one guided by purpose will attract success effortlessly."

The words hang in the air like a sacred mantra, each syllable resonating deeply with the global participants. The room seems to expand, as if the very walls themselves are breathing. The sound of birds outside blends seamlessly with the occasional chime of temple bells in the distance, creating an aura of timelessness, as though the present moment is the only one that has ever existed.

The Guru's gaze drifts slowly across the hall, then settles. He leans forward slightly, voice calm but clear. "Raise your hand if you've ever made a decision under stress that you later regretted."

At first, silence. Then, one hand rises. Another. Soon, a quiet forest of arms stands above folded laps—CEOs, strategists, advisors—all acknowledging a shared vulnerability. The Guru smiles—not amused, but knowing. "In business," he says, "you're taught to push through pressure. What if clarity doesn't come from effort... but knowing when to pause." A few furrowed brows remain—arms crossed, lips tight. But as heads begin to nod around them, something flickers behind their eyes. Not agreement. Not yet. Just...curiosity. As if they're wondering whether they've overlooked something important.

The Guru speaks in rhythms—short truths, spaced like breath. Each pause leaves room not just for silence, but for something to land.

Eyes closed, backs straight, they sit in stillness. For some, the silence is familiar—an old companion. For others, it's uncharted, strange, and oddly tender. But here, those differences vanish. The air carries no hierarchy, no homeland. Only breath. Only presence.

The participants sit with their eyes closed, allowing the teachings to wash over them. Some of them are seasoned meditators, familiar with the path of silence, while others are experiencing this depth of spiritual practice for the first time. And yet, the differences between them seem to dissolve in the stillness. Whether from Europe, North America, or India itself, they share the same journey of rediscovering the sacred within.

As boardrooms buzz with spreadsheets, quarterly metrics, and market expansions, a quieter revolution is gaining momentum—one not measured in KPIs or shareholder returns but in moments of intentional stillness. Across the globe, millions are stepping off the treadmill of constant doing to ask deeper questions of being. But here, those differences vanish. The air carries no hierarchy, no homeland. Only breath. Only presence.

Meditation, once confined to monasteries or yoga studios, is now a common item on executive calendars and mental health benefit plans. In 2022, 18.3% of U.S. adults reported engaging in meditation—a staggering increase from just a decade prior. That translates to over 60 million Americans turning inward regularly, seeking clarity not from caffeine or strategy off-sites, but from quiet reflection.

But this shift isn't only about managing stress or avoiding burnout, though those are certainly powerful motivators. The COVID-19 pandemic cracked open something deeper. In the eerie stillness of lockdowns and the shared uncertainty of global disruption, millions were forced into a pause—a pause not just from work, but from distraction. For many, it was the first time in years that the relentless forward march of career goals, financial targets, and social validations had been interrupted. And in that silence, a new question emerged: *What truly matters?*

The Great Resignation, a term coined in the aftermath, wasn't just about quitting jobs. It was about quitting autopilot. People weren't just leaving companies—they were leaving behind unsustainable definitions of success. A 2021 McKinsey report found that 70% of employees who left their jobs cited a lack of meaning or purpose as a key factor—often rooted in not feeling valued by their organization or manager, and a broader absence of belonging in the workplace. The pandemic prompted a widespread re-evaluation of life priorities, with many individuals reassessing what truly matters— personally, professionally, and spiritually.

One striking outcome of this re-evaluation was a global surge in spiritual exploration and mindfulness practices. Meditation app downloads soared during the pandemic—*Calm*, *Headspace*, and *Insight Timer* reported a significant surge in daily usage during 2020. According to research and public health trends highlighted by the American Psychological Association, interest in mindfulness, meditation, and overall well-being has significantly increased among working professionals in the post-COVID era, as employees seek ways to manage heightened workplace stress and burnout. Churches, temples, online satsangs, and virtual retreats saw record attendance— not from ritual-driven devotees, but from everyday individuals searching for stillness, meaning, and inner clarity.

It's as if the pandemic served as a collective mirror, reflecting how far we had drifted from ourselves while chasing things we never truly questioned. In those months of solitude, many came to realize: climbing the ladder means little if it's leaning against the wrong wall.

This is about rebalancing a worldview that has long celebrated intellect while undervaluing intuition, that has prized performance while neglecting presence. For years, corporate culture asked: *What can you produce?* Now, increasingly, we are learning: *Who are we becoming?*

The data clearly support this pivot. Meditation has shown strong links to improved memory, emotional regulation, and concentration—critical skills for leaders managing complexity. As per the statistics on finances online, a full 84% of meditators say the practice helps them reduce anxiety, while 53% report better cognitive focus and 52% perform better at work and/or school. In a business climate that demands both decisiveness and resilience, those numbers matter. More than just wellness, stillness is becoming a strategic asset.

We see it in the increasing number of executives attending silent retreats, joining mindfulness programs, or sponsoring meditation apps for their teams. Salesforce CEO Marc Benioff has spoken about the influence of spiritual teacher Thich Nhat Hanh on his leadership style. Arianna Huffington left a successful media career to build a wellness company rooted in ancient contemplative traditions. Even Wall Street, once the epitome of unrelenting hustle, now houses meditation rooms and offers breathwork sessions.

This is not to say that spiritual practice is replacing strategy—it's deepening it. The Guru in our previous fictional scene spoke of *Seva*—selfless service—as leadership without ego. In the corporate world, this translates into purpose-led decision-making, empathetic leadership, and cultures that nourish rather than deplete. Companies like Adobe and American Express are seeing the returns—not just in lowered absenteeism, but in employee engagement and long-term performance.

And yet, these shifts aren't without tension. As one executive in the ashram asked, "How do we bring stillness into the noise?" It's a real question, because the modern organization is designed for speed. Quarterly earnings don't wait for clarity to arise through meditation. Deadlines rarely pause for deep reflection.

But perhaps they should. Or at least, perhaps we should design our systems in ways that allow both speed and stillness to coexist. Meditation is not about doing less; it's about doing from a deeper place. Leaders who cultivate presence can respond with discernment instead of reactivity. Teams that rest can innovate more sustainably. And companies that align purpose with profit can weather storms that metrics alone cannot forecast.

As of 2025, between 200 and 500 million people around the world are practicing meditation. That number is expected to grow exponentially as mindfulness and conscious leadership continue to permeate the workplace. The spiritual world is no longer separate from the business world—it is becoming its foundation.

We are witnessing a paradigm shift—from burnout to balance, from ego-led leadership to servant leadership, from strategy-first to soul-aligned action. It's not a replacement for capitalism, but a re-centering of it around human flourishing. As the Guru said, "Stillness is not the absence of movement, but the presence of purpose."

The question before us now is not whether spirituality belongs in business, but whether business can thrive without it.

CHAPTER TWO

IS THIS DOABLE?

For decades, spirituality was viewed as too personal, too abstract—or even too unprofessional—for the workplace. But that perception is rapidly changing. From boardrooms to co-working spaces, a growing number of leaders are beginning to see what ancient traditions have long understood: inner clarity is the foundation of outer excellence.

A powerful example of this shift began in 2007 at Google, where an internal course called Search Inside Yourself (SIY) was launched. What started as a simple, free offering to employees became a pioneering movement in integrating mindfulness into professional life. Designed to enhance emotional intelligence through meditation and self-awareness, SIY taught skills such as empathy, compassion, focus, and resilience—all essential not just for personal growth but for high-performing teams and sustainable leadership.

The program's architect, Chade-Meng Tan, a Google engineer with a deep mindfulness practice, collaborated with neuroscientist Philippe Goldin and emotional intelligence expert Marc Lesser. Their success was so compelling that the initiative soon evolved into an independent global organization: The Search Inside Yourself Leadership Institute (SIYLI).

Today, SIYLI offers evidence-based programs to companies around the world, promoting mental well-being, conscious leadership, and emotional agility. Its continued growth underscores a profound truth: bringing mindfulness into the workplace is no longer a fringe idea—it's becoming a strategic imperative.

Salesforce founder Marc Benioff regularly cites mindfulness, meditation, and values-based leadership as strategic essentials. More than half of Salesforce's offices have created a "mindful zone" on each floor of their offices. Marc believes that when employees keep all distractions aside (including but not limited to mobile phones) in these zones, it helps with clear thinking and innovation.

During his tenure as CEO of LinkedIn, Jeff Weiner introduced daily group meditation and openly discussed "managing compassionately" as a leadership ethos.

The numbers affirm this evolution. The Global Wellness Institute's 2023 report forecasts the total global wellness economy to grow from $5.6 trillion in 2022 to $8.5 trillion by 2027, with an annual growth rate of 8.6%. The global personal growth industry, which includes retreats, coaching, and spiritual practices, has been growing substantially over the years. A lot of large U.S. companies now offer structured mindfulness or meditation programs under their Employee Assistance Programs.

Meditation itself is booming: 18% of American adults now report regular meditation practice, up from just 4% in 2012 (*CDC, 2022*). Apps like Calm and Headspace have seen over 150 million global downloads, with corporate partnerships becoming a major source of adoption.

Despite these encouraging signs, the corporate embrace of this is still surface-level in most cases. Many organizations invest in "wellness perks"—yoga sessions, mental health days, nap pods—but shy away from deeper changes in how business is done and led. As highlighted in a 2025 article by TruWorth Wellness, this contrast between *hype and reality* reveals that such perks often mask deeper systemic issues.

Spiritual principles like stillness, compassion, and presence are powerful, but they're often treated as optional extras—rather than essential competencies. However, the article "Corporate Wellness: The Ultimate Power Status Symbol of 2025" demonstrates how these qualities are rapidly becoming core competencies in leading organizations. In fact, the piece explains that today's most influential companies are being defined not just by revenue—but by how authentically they empower people, often embedding mindfulness and well-being directly into their workspace design, policies, and leadership practices.

This shift reflects a growing recognition that well-being and purpose are now strategic assets. Different researches consistently show that when employees find meaning in their work and feel aligned with their company's values, they are more likely to stay engaged, perform at higher levels, and remain with their employer longer. Purpose-driven workplaces foster stronger cultures, greater resilience, and better results—demonstrating that meaning at work fuels performance.

Examples: Spirituality Driving Strategic Results

The clearest signs of possibility come from companies that dare to go deeper.

Aetna, one of the largest U.S. insurers, reduced healthcare costs and improved productivity by $3,000 per employee after launching a mindfulness program (*Harvard Business Review*).

SAP, the German software giant, created a global "Compassionate Leadership" program led by its Chief Mindfulness Officer. Post-program surveys show significantly improved employee engagement and stress resilience.

General Mills introduced meditation and self-awareness training at the executive level, leading to higher strategic clarity and more inclusive decision-making.

Perspective: The Road Forward

Spirituality in the workplace is no longer a fringe idea—but its potential remains largely untapped. The challenge is not in access to tools, but in a deeper willingness to rethink the culture of leadership itself.

To unleash the full power of the human spirit at work, we must move beyond token gestures toward lasting integration. Leaders must be willing not just to offer mindfulness apps, but to embody mindful presence. Not just to fund wellness days, but to redefine success through purpose, compassion, and inner balance.

We stand at a crossroads: one path leads to more burnout hidden behind wellness branding. The other—more courageous—calls us to reshape the corporate world from the inside out.

But what happens when intentions are tested at ground level? Let's explore this by tracing the journey of five leaders who returned from the ashram carrying not just insights, but a quiet determination to lead differently. Inspired but untested, the five executives in this story now face their true challenge: translating spiritual insight into boardroom action. The corporate world—with its pressure, pace, and complexity—comes rushing back in.

As the leaders dispersed after the week-long retreat at the ashram, five executives—out of a larger group of twenty participants—made a deliberate choice to stay in touch, committed to exchanging notes on the changes they plan to implement in their respective organizations. During the retreat, they had formed a strong rapport, bonding over shared leadership philosophies, common challenges, and a mutual desire for growth and impact. Their connection, grounded in trust and camaraderie, is strengthened by the realization that their diverse industries offer valuable cross-sector insights. Once strangers to each other, they now share a quiet bond, as though their inner worlds have aligned with a common thread of understanding. They carried back with them more than just the serenity of the ashram. Their hearts are lighter, as if they've laid down the burdens and baggage. These five—Samuel Hartman, Leila Costa, Oliver Grant, Daphne Grayson, and Meera Anand—each return to their domains with a renewed sense of purpose.

At the Ashram, they had performed acts of *Seva*—tending to the earth, helping in the kitchen, or simply offering their time to those in need. These simple acts left them feeling humbled and grounded, generating a quiet but profound sense of fulfillment. Inspired by this experience, some of them later initiate a company-wide "Community Hour," where employees dedicate one hour each month to serve their local communities—whether by mentoring students, cleaning public spaces, or supporting social initiatives.

While the messaging from the Ashram was consistent for everyone, the interpretation and takeaway by the different leaders were contextualized for their own environment. The tech CEO, Samuel, envisions an innovation culture that thrives on clarity and mindfulness. The consumer goods executive, Leila, charts a path toward deeper employee engagement and broader societal impact. Automotive pioneer Oliver uncovers a unifying purpose that aligns people and profit. Financial leader Daphne reimagines her role as a bridge between capital and community empowerment. And Meera, the media visionary, begins to cultivate a culture of soulful creativity within her organization. These acted as a guide for transforming their industries—and perhaps, the world—through the stillness they have discovered. Their roles, though unique, are now illuminated by a common thread: the need to align their professional missions with inner peace and higher purpose. Their eyes, filled with quiet determination and newfound clarity, reflect a readiness to take these teachings beyond the ashram walls. Each of them now holds a roadmap for growth—one that intertwines professional success with spiritual depth. They understand that Guru's teachings are not an abstract ideal but a practical guide for leading with purpose, compassion, and authenticity. In embracing these principles, they see the potential for transformative growth within their corporations.

Together, they reflect a universal truth: when corporations align their missions with higher purpose and inner harmony, they not only navigate challenges with resilience but also pave the way for a future of sustainable, meaningful growth.

Each of these five leaders has carved a niche for themselves in their respective industries, shaping the future with their vision, resilience, and bold decisions. They are not just executives; they are pioneers—architects of change who have disrupted norms, built empires, and influenced industries at a global scale. Yet, despite their towering success, each of them now stands at a crossroads, seeking something deeper— an evolution beyond business metrics, towards a leadership that is not just *profitable*, but *purposeful*.

At 52, Samuel Hartman is the embodiment of structured brilliance—a tech CEO whose very presence commands attention. Tall and lean, with an air of effortless authority, he carries the disciplined posture of a man who measures his words as precisely as his decisions. With silver-streaked hair neatly combed back and a minimalist, no-frills style, he is a man who values efficiency in everything, from algorithms to attire. His sharp, wire-rimmed glasses rest lightly on his nose, framing eyes that have seen the rise and fall of industries, yet never lost their hunger for innovation. He speaks with a measured cadence, every word carrying the weight of experience. To his employees, he is both an enigma and a mentor—demanding yet deeply invested in their growth.

Rachel and Samuel initially crossed paths as peers in the technology space, quickly recognizing and respecting each other's expertise. Over the years, their professional acquaintance deepened into a genuine friendship, built on trust and shared values. While their respective organizations maintained a highly effective partnership, Rachel and Samuel cultivated a unique dynamic that went beyond corporate collaboration. They often turned to one another as sounding boards for their ideas, engaging in candid discussions where they invited honest feedback. Each brought a unique perspective, challenging assumptions, identifying blind spots, and offering valuable insights that enriched their strategic thinking and decision-making.

It was but natural that they exchanged notes on Samuel's spiritual retreat. She was very keen to hear and learn more from Samuel about it. Samuel's positive response intrigued her. She was still unsure of what might be accomplished via spirituality while dealing with some of the pressing needs of the business. Rachel was surprised to learn of the sheer exuberance and confidence being echoed by Samuel, and that too from just one retreat.

"Alright, Samuel, spill it," she said, eyeing him with a mixture of curiosity and skepticism. "What exactly did they do to you at that retreat? You're glowing like you've discovered some ancient treasure or something."

Samuel let out a warm laugh, his eyes crinkling at the edges. "Glowing? Really, Rachel? It wasn't anything mystical. It was... transformative. Eye-opening, even."

Rachel raised an eyebrow, her tone dry. "Transformative, huh? That's what they all say after these 'life-changing' retreats. Did they have you meditating in a cave or walking on hot coals?"

"No caves, no hot coals," Samuel replied, still smiling. "It wasn't gimmicky like that. It was more about introspection, letting go of baggage, and reconnecting with what matters."

Rachel leaned forward slightly, resting her elbows on the table. "Sounds suspiciously vague. Come on, give me specifics. What did they make you do?"

"Well, the first thing they did was strip away all distractions. No phones, no laptops. Just a group of us and a serene environment," Samuel said. "We started with silence—a whole day of it."

"A whole day of silence?" Rachel blinked, clearly baffled. "That sounds torturous. What did you even do?"

"At first, it felt unbearable," Samuel admitted. "My mind was racing with work thoughts, to-do lists, and random worries. But as the hours passed, it was like all that noise began to fade. I started noticing things—the sound of the wind, my own breathing, even my heartbeat. It was grounding."

Rachel gave a skeptical grunt. "Hmm, sounds a bit too Zen for me. What else? Did they lecture you on finding your 'true self' or something?"

"Not lectures, more like guided discussions," Samuel said. "One exercise stood out. We were asked to write a letter to ourselves—our younger selves, to be precise. The catch was, we had to offer forgiveness for any regrets or mistakes."

Rachel paused, her tone softening slightly. "Forgiveness? For yourself? That's... intriguing. What did you write?"

"A lot of things I didn't realize I'd been holding onto," he said, his voice quieter now. "Like not spending enough time with my dad before he passed, or some decisions I made early in my career that hurt others unintentionally. Writing it down was like lifting a weight off my shoulders."

She leaned in, her expression less teasing now. "Okay, that sounds... useful. But what about the practical side? Did it help with, you know, the real world? Work, decisions, that sort of thing?"

"Absolutely," Samuel said. "One of the facilitators introduced us to this idea of the 'power of pause.' They said that most of our decisions are made on autopilot—reacting rather than responding. By learning to pause, even for a few seconds, we can approach situations with clarity instead of impulse. I've already started using it, and it's a game-changer in meetings and negotiations."

Rachel smirked. "The power of pause? So now you're the Dalai Lama of boardrooms?"

Samuel's smile widened. "Not quite. But it's incredible how much it's helped me stay composed under pressure. It's like having a mental reset button."

Rachel tilted her head. "Alright, Samuel, but I've got to ask—what's the catch? These things always have a catch. Did they try to sell you some expensive follow-up program or declare that enlightenment comes with a subscription fee?"

He chuckled again, shaking his head. "No, nothing like that. It's not a cult, Rachel. They made it clear that the real work begins after the retreat. All the exercises, the reflections—they're tools. It's up to us to use them consistently."

She narrowed her eyes. "Hmm. And you really think it's worth it?"

"Without a doubt," Samuel said. "You know how we're always chasing the next big thing—the next milestone, the next deal? This retreat helped me realize that it's not just about the destination. It's about how we travel. And honestly, Rachel, I've never felt more clear-headed or... content."

Rachel raised an eyebrow, bemused. "Content? You?"

"It doesn't mean I've lost my ambition," he said. "It just means I'm approaching it differently. With balance."

She sat back, crossing her arms, studying him. "Well, I'm not sold yet. But you do seem... different. Lighter, maybe."

"That's the thing, Rachel," Samuel said softly. "You don't realize how heavy you've been carrying things until you let them go."

She let out a sigh, reluctant amusement flickering across her face. "Alright, maybe I'll consider trying one of these retreats someday. But don't think I'm going to start writing love letters to my past self anytime soon."

"No pressure," he said with a grin. "Just know that if you ever do, it might surprise you."

"We'll see," Rachel replied, shaking her head with a half-smile. "For now, I'll stick to poking holes in your newfound Zen approach. Someone has to keep you grounded."

"And for that," Samuel said, "I'll always be grateful."

They share a laugh, the conversation shifting to lighter topics, but Rachel's curiosity lingers as she watches the ease and calm in Samuel's demeanor, a stark contrast to the driven, restless man she's known for years.

This was the beginning of a series of dialogues between both of them on how spirituality within the corporate environment can help organizations and people to thrive.

They had just wrapped up a discussion on joint go-to-market strategies when Rachel leaned back slightly, tapping a pen against her notebook.

"Hey, Samuel," she said, her tone casual but curious, "do you really think Zenyra could tap into some of that... spiritual energy you were talking about? I mean—real momentum, not just some feel-good side note."

Samuel's face lit up instantly. "Absolutely. I wholeheartedly do."

Rachel studied him for a moment. "You're still figuring it out yourself, though, right? But you sound... sure."

"I am taking baby steps, yes," he admitted, "but even those have shifted something big for me. And it's not just me. Leaders from different industries are getting serious about this."

"Oh?"

"Yeah. Leila Costa, for instance—she runs a consumer goods empire, and views spirituality to energize employees while giving real meaning to their CSR programs. Then there's Oliver—the automotive guy—he's exploring how it could unify people and profits. Daphne Grayson, the finance powerhouse, wants to use it to empower folks at the grassroots and fuel real growth. And Meera Anand from the media industry—she's trying to reimagine her whole company culture around soulful creativity."

Rachel gave a slow nod, absorbing it all.

"I didn't realize people were thinking that expansively about it," she said. "It's more strategic than I thought."

Samuel smiled. "I could check with the group—see if they'd be open to you joining our conversations. We've been bouncing around ideas, learning from each other. You'd add a lot to that mix."

Rachel's brow arched. "You sure I won't slow you down?"

"Quite the opposite," he said. "You'd raise the bar."

A week after the retreat, the forum of leaders got together on a video call. They had agreed to do a weekly 30-minute call to exchange notes and ensure that they could keep building the momentum.

One transformative practice they adopted was beginning each call with a few minutes of meditation. This simple yet profound ritual acted as a reset button, dissolving biases and grounding everyone in the present moment. Conversations became more objective, free from knee-jerk reactions, and carried an air of detachment that allowed for clear, solution-oriented discussions. Productivity was no longer just a goal—it became the baseline.

Beyond maintaining clarity in discussions, a shared philosophy emerged among them: *keep moving forward*. No matter the roadblocks, the focus remained on *how* to make things happen rather than *why* they couldn't. One pivotal decision was to document their journey—capturing not just the insights gained from the retreat center but also the real-world challenges and breakthroughs they encountered along the way.

The idea had surfaced during one of the early calls when Meera shared a moment from her team's shift toward more soulful brainstorming sessions. Others chimed in with their own small wins and setbacks. It became clear that they were collectively charting unfamiliar territory.

By putting their experiences to paper—not just the polished takeaways, but the messy, imperfect steps too—they hoped to create something bigger than themselves. Their vision was bold: to create a living, breathing guide—a bible for integrating spirituality into the corporate world. A blueprint for those daring enough to redefine success in business and life alike. They weren't just capturing progress; they were laying the groundwork for a new paradigm—one that could outlast their companies and inspire a movement.

Post the spiritual retreat, each of them carried a sense of excitement tempered with caution, realizing that this journey would require more than just intellectual understanding; it would demand courage, patience, and unwavering commitment. The transformative insights they had gained—the power of stillness, humility, selfless service, and alignment with a higher purpose—were clear in theory. Yet, implementing these in the corporate world, where profits, metrics, and speed often dominated decision-making, felt like stepping into uncharted territory.

The first regroup call was scheduled amongst them to share the progress on their playbook of integrating spirituality in their respective organizations. Samuel sought permission to go first with his story and take input from everyone.

Samuel's organization was a multinational tech company with several breakthrough AI products and solutions that were in high demand. Not only were the customers flocking to get their hands on them, but leading hyperscalers like Amazon Web Services (AWS), Google, and Microsoft were all offering huge incentives to onboard these solutions. Each of them saw potential to maximize their cloud consumption by riding on these innovative AI-based solutions. These solutions, once deployed, delivered a unique outcome of positively impacting revenue as well as margins for the customer. It only needed a couple of weeks of additional effort to customize it to every organization's requirements.

However, the engineering team faced burnout due to a relentless cycle of product launches. The workplace culture had become extremely demanding, characterized by long hours, towering expectations, and intense performance reviews. During a critical product launch, a key engineer collapsed due to overwork, leading to a domino effect as other team members also fell behind. A highly talented project leader resigned, citing that he had "no space to think creatively." This led to key innovators resigning and critical projects being stalled as stress overshadowed creativity. Employees highlighted systemic issues during their exit interviews, one of the key issues being harassment. They claimed the higher-ups would frequently require employees to meet unrealistic deadlines, creating a highly pressured environment. For many on the team, this wasn't just a matter of tough expectations—it felt like a slow erosion of psychological safety. Over time, the pressure stopped being motivational and started feeling punitive. Some even described it as a form of harassment, not because of direct insults or overt mistreatment, but because the relentless pace and disregard for limits created a climate of fear and chronic stress. It became clear that when high expectations ignore human limits, they cross a line—from challenge into coercion.

Inspired by Guru's metaphor of calming the storm, Samuel piloted a Mindfulness for Innovation program. The leadership team underwent half a day of training to practice empathetic communication. They were encouraged to consider weekly mindfulness sessions and take reflective pauses before critical brainstorming meetings.

However, there was stiff resistance from senior managers who viewed mindfulness as a non-productive activity. Concerns about potential dips in productivity loomed over everyone.

Samuel finished presenting the challenges at his organization—the burnout, resistance to mindfulness, and the struggle to balance innovation with employee well-being. Now, he looked around the table at the other leaders, eager for their insights.

Samuel leaned forward, expressing intent. "You've heard the situation. I want to introduce mindfulness and holistic leadership values into performance metrics, but the pushback is strong. Senior managers fear it'll dilute productivity. They're worried that time spent on introspection or wellness practices means less time focused on tangible outputs—client meetings, deliverables, deadlines. How do I make this shift without compromising execution?"

Meera responded without missing a beat. "Samuel, I've seen this before. If you want these values—empathy, well-being, purpose—to be taken seriously, they need to be embedded into formal evaluations. Otherwise, they'll remain just 'nice-to-have' ideas. At my firm, we mapped these traits into leadership appraisals—literally adding them as performance indicators alongside things like revenue growth or team efficiency. For example, we assess how leaders foster psychological safety, support mental health, or create purpose-driven team cultures. We even trained managers on how to recognize and evaluate these behaviors. Eventually, we tied them to promotion criteria. Once people saw that emotional intelligence and mindful leadership impacted their career trajectory, they started taking it seriously."

Daphne nodded, her tone pragmatic. "I agree with Meera. But let's be honest—many leaders will still push back. When we introduced well-being as a leadership metric, some managers scoffed, saying we were 'going soft.' For them, the idea of prioritizing mindfulness or empathy felt impractical in the face of harsh market realities and relentless competition. There's this perception that soft skills can't coexist with hard decisions. That mindfulness might dilute the grit needed to navigate high-stakes environments."

She paused and then added, "But that's a misconception. In reality, mindful leaders often make better, more balanced decisions—because they're not operating from burnout or reactivity. One way we countered the skepticism was by starting small. We piloted mindfulness and well-being metrics in just a few teams. And sure enough, those pockets became poster children for success. We tracked engagement, retention, and performance over time. Once leaders saw those results in action—real outcomes from real teams—it shifted the narrative. The data didn't need to be universal from the outset. It just needed to be undeniable where it existed."

"That's exactly what you need, Samuel." Oliver's voice was calm and assured. "People in high-pressure industries— especially tech—are skeptical of anything that isn't directly tied to output. I'd recommend bringing in a neuroscientist or behavioral scientist to present the science behind mindfulness and cognitive performance. If your managers see how mental clarity drives better decisions, they'll be less resistant."

Resting her arms on the table, Leila leaned in. "I love that approach. And beyond leadership buy-in, you need structural support. We talk about work-life balance, but in reality, people are expected to be online all the time. If you're serious about well-being, put real boundaries in place. When we set strict 'no work beyond 7:00 p.m.' policies, it was chaotic at first—but over time, it forced teams to plan better and respect personal time."

Raising an eyebrow, Samuel replied. "That's a radical move in the tech space. We thrive on 24/7 responsiveness. What about urgent issues?"

Without missing a beat, Meera responded confidently. "We tackled that with automated messaging. Outside of work hours, employees received auto-responses with an emergency contact. For global teams, we structured transitions so there was always coverage without burning out individuals. It wasn't easy at first, but within months, stress levels dropped, and performance measurably improved."

A quiet moment followed as Oliver tapped his pen thoughtfully. "This makes sense. Right now, my engineers are constantly firefighting. They don't have the space to think creatively. If we set boundaries and track the impact on innovation, we could prove that deep work and balance drive better results than exhaustion."

"Exactly," Daphne said, nodding. "And once you have results, you'll change the industry narrative. It's not just about retaining talent—it's about attracting the best minds who left because of burnout. We had top performers return after seeing our commitment to a sustainable work culture."

The group paused, letting it sink in. Then Samuel smiled slowly. "Alright, here's the plan: We implement holistic performance metrics—not only KPIs linked to revenue, margin,

CSAT, or sprint velocity, but also indicators like psychological safety scores, team engagement levels, burnout risk indices, and leadership empathy ratings. Will bring in a neuroscientist to reinforce the science, and introduce structured work-hour boundaries with global team transitions. It's time to prove that innovation isn't fueled by exhaustion, but by clarity, balance, and purpose. I will also seriously evaluate the concept of *no work after office hours*."

With a dry laugh, Oliver added. "The irony is that we spent decades optimizing business processes but never questioned the burnout cycles we imposed on ourselves and our teams."

Daphne tilted her head. "Maybe leadership was never just about driving results, but about shaping environments where people—and ideas—can truly thrive."

Samuel exhaled, a sense of clarity settling in. They weren't just running companies anymore; they were crafting legacies. And perhaps, just perhaps, the future of leadership lies not in more control—but in more consciousness.

As the meeting drew to a close, Samuel pulled up a file on his screen. "Before we wrap, I wanted to share the profile of a fellow CEO—she leads Zenyra Technologies. She's expressed a strong interest in joining our weekly sessions. Though she wasn't part of the original retreat, she's keen to implement this model and go even further with it. Are we okay to include her?"

Meera was the first to respond. "One of the key insights from the retreat was the importance of helping others selflessly. That makes it an obvious choice. My only concern— are we ready to truly mentor someone else?"

Oliver, Leila, and Daphne chimed in, each echoing their support with thoughtful reflections. Within minutes, the group reached a unanimous decision.

They had no idea yet that this new member, inspired by their vision but unbound by its beginnings, would become the boldest force among them.

As the nature of work evolves, organizations are waking up to a vital truth: when people are supported in aligning their purpose, well-being, and work—performance becomes not just sustainable, but deeply human. This isn't just about how we structure our work; it's about how we treat our people. How we design our systems, and how purpose at work connects to personal meaning.

The journey of the business executive peers may be fictionalized, but the questions they wrestle with—and the transformations they seek—mirror a growing reality in today's business landscape. As organizations face relentless complexity, the call for more conscious, human-centered leadership has never been louder.

The old models—rooted in control, hyper-productivity, and competitive aggression—are no longer enough to sustain creativity, resilience, or meaningful innovation. More and more, leaders are realizing that success without soul is a fragile victory.

This reevaluation is closely tied to a growing recognition of the importance of work-life balance—or, more precisely, work-life integration. Leaders are beginning to understand that sustainable performance requires a systems view of well-being. According to a 2023 McKinsey Health Institute survey, Indian respondents reported the highest rates of burnout symptoms at 59%. For another metric on workplace exhaustion, Indians stood highest at 62% followed by Japan (61%), and Switzerland at 22% reported the least. The report quoted, "For most adults, the majority of waking daily life is spent at work. That offers employers an opportunity to influence their employees' physical, mental, social, and spiritual health."

Additionally, the World Health Organization estimated that in 2016, long working hours were responsible for over 745,000 deaths annually due to stroke and heart disease, underscoring the real cost of unsustainable work models. Needless to say, employees cannot thrive in environments that compromise their health and well-being— mental, physical, or emotional. The message is clear: organizations must move beyond surface-level initiatives and embed well-being into the very fabric of how work is designed and managed.

Arianna Huffington, founder of Thrive Global, emphasizes this in her leadership philosophy: "We need to abandon the collective delusion that burnout is the price we must pay for success." Satya Nadella, CEO of Microsoft, echoes this sentiment, advocating for empathy and flexibility in how people work: "The lived experience of our employees is the new scorecard." Salesforce CEO Marc Benioff similarly stated, "The business of business is improving the state of the world—and that starts with how we treat our people."

Importantly, this is not about limiting ambition or productivity— it's about creating environments that honor the cyclical nature of human energy. Meanwhile, Atlassian's multi-year internal study found that teams allowed flexibility in location and timing of work were more innovative and had lower attrition. In fact, their 2022 report revealed that location flexibility alone led to a dramatic drop in burnout—from 36% to just 14%—while positive perceptions of company culture soared from 47% to 83%, and the number of employees who saw their teams as innovative rose from 57% to 71%.

This isn't about shorter hours or remote perks—it's about reimagining the rhythms of work to support the whole human. When leaders model integration—such as setting boundaries, prioritizing recovery, and promoting psychological safety—it sends a cultural signal that well-being is not a trade-off, but a prerequisite for high performance.

Emerging neuroscience research is also shedding light on how subtle shifts in workplace dynamics can create profound benefits for employee well-being and performance. A joint study by the Wharton Neuroscience Initiative and global consultancy Slalom conducted a series of lab experiments with employees to better understand how the brain responds to workplace culture, collaboration, and communication. One of their key findings confirmed what many professionals intuitively feel: Zoom fatigue is real.

According to a 2021 report from Microsoft WorkLab, back-to-back virtual meetings significantly dampen brain activity associated with joy and motivation. However, inserting even short 10-minute breaks between meetings noticeably increased brain signals linked to reduced stress and deeper, more creative thinking. Integrating structured breaks—through tools like Microsoft's scheduling shortcuts or meeting buffers—can enhance cognitive recovery and boost long-term productivity.

Another important insight: workplace friendships matter, even in virtual teams. The study found that brains that "fire together, wire together." In other words, people who collaborate closely tend to develop similar neural patterns—showing that the same mechanisms that support friendship in real life also strengthen psychological bonds in remote or hybrid work environments. Regular team rituals, open dialogue, and pulse surveys can amplify this "brain synchrony," creating a stronger sense of belonging and engagement.

Finally, the research uncovered that internal messaging and communication efforts have a diminished impact on employees who are already disengaged. Using brain wave analysis to track moment-to-moment reactions, the researchers discovered that shared emotional resonance—not just the message itself—predicts engagement. This points to the importance of clear, emotionally intelligent storytelling, consistent brand alignment, and empathetic leadership communication in fostering employee alignment and trust.

Several pioneering organizations have already begun putting these principles into practice—reaping not just engagement gains, but measurable performance and innovation benefits:

Microsoft: As part of its "Thrive" initiative, Microsoft redesigned its meeting culture by promoting "30-minute default meetings" and embedding scheduled focus time into employee calendars through its Viva Insights tool. After piloting this across multiple teams, they observed reduced stress markers, improved productivity, and a significant increase in creative problem-solving. The initiative also responded to their own research showing that back-to-back meetings reduce brain activity linked to engagement and motivation.

Atlassian: This software company implemented "Team Anywhere," a remote-first model allowing employees to work from anywhere and design their own schedules. Rather than monitoring hours, the company shifted to outcome-based metrics. Internal studies revealed that meeting load had a clear link to burnout: teams with 15 hours of meetings per week experienced 23% burnout compared to 31% for those exceeding 20 hours. Atlassian introduced a "ritual rest" exercise to help teams intentionally balance synchronous and asynchronous work. Another key finding: teams that regularly expressed appreciation and encouragement fostered a more positive perception of the organization and showed stronger intent to stay. Psychological safety surveys further reflected this shift, with notable gains in employee trust and team cohesion.

Unilever: Unilever ran an internal pilot on "Agile Working" where employees could choose when and how they worked. Additionally, the company placed strong emphasis on 'Outcome-Based Performance', allowing flexibility across roles. To support this shift, Unilever invested heavily in technology and digital infrastructure. Reports indicated a boost in employee satisfaction, improved retention rates, and a noticeable advantage in attracting top-tier talent. As a further step, Unilever integrated well-being metrics into leadership KPIs and tied promotions to how leaders support team balance—not just business results.

Salesforce: As part of its Ohana Culture, Salesforce integrates employee well-being check-ins into regular team meetings. They have also created "well-being reimbursement budgets" and encourage mindfulness practice through their B-Well Together program. An internal study found that these programs led to improved employee retention, higher employee satisfaction, enhanced collaboration, sustained innovation, strengthened employer brand, and set a benchmark for best practices in corporate culture.

SAP: SAP has embedded emotional intelligence and mindfulness training into its global leadership curriculum. Their "Search Inside Yourself" program, co-created with Google, helped managers improve empathy, communication, and resilience. SAP reported not only stronger leadership effectiveness but also improvements in employee satisfaction and innovation output, as rated by team surveys.

Work-life integration becomes not a balancing act, but a design principle woven into organizational DNA. Recent research supports this shift. A *Deloitte's 2023 Human Capital Trends* report—drawing insights from over 1500 C-suite executives and board members—revealed that 87% of respondents believe that finding the right workplace model is critical to their organization's success. However, only 24% believe their organizations are truly prepared to meet this trend. Concurrently, the American Psychological Association has reported unprecedented levels of burnout among knowledge workers in the post-pandemic era, triggering a massive reassessment of leadership, culture, and well-being.

And yet—change is underway. Across industries, there is a growing shift toward leadership models that emphasize compassion, emotional intelligence, and mindfulness. This isn't sentimentality; it's strategic recalibration. The message is clear: *the way we work must evolve.*

However, when workplace cultures prioritize relentless productivity over human well-being, the consequences can be deeply harmful. Practices such as setting unrealistic performance targets can cross the line into harassment, leading to detrimental effects on mental health and organizational performance. What is often framed in some organizations as "high performance culture" may, under different legal systems or cultural norms, be interpreted as psychological harassment—or even constructive dismissal. Constructive dismissal occurs when an employee feels compelled to resign due to a hostile or unsustainable work environment— effectively making the resignation a dismissal. In such cases, relentless pressure, disregard for boundaries, or toxic leadership may legally be seen as a breach of trust and duty by the employer. In jurisdictions like the UK and parts of the EU, persistent pressure to meet unattainable goals, when combined with a lack of support or disregard for employees' personal limits, has been legally challenged by workers as bullying or workplace harassment. "It is not the intention of the perpetrator, but the deed itself and the impact this behaviour has on the recipient, which constitutes bullying or harassment," as explained by one of the employment law advisers. "The setting of unattainable targets can, therefore, constitute bullying, and could result in an employee feeling pressured enough to walk out of their job, later claiming constructive unfair dismissal."

As the fictional narrative in the preceding chapter illustrated, toxic intensity doesn't always arrive in the form of shouting or discrimination—it often comes cloaked in impossible deadlines, an always-on expectation, or the slow erosion of psychological safety. Over time, the pressure stops being a driver of excellence and instead becomes a source of trauma. In one widely cited case, a tribunal found that management's insistence on continuously raising targets without providing resources or support amounted to a form of indirect harassment, triggering chronic anxiety and burnout among staff.

This reflects a deeper truth: when high expectations ignore human limits, they cross a line—from challenge into coercion. And in today's evolving legal and ethical climate, this isn't just a moral failing—it can also be a legal and reputational risk for employers.

A tectonic shift is clearly underway. But as encouraging as the data and anecdotes are, they also underscore an inconvenient truth: most corporate environments still resist meaningful integration of spirituality. When introduced in business contexts, spirituality is often diluted—treated as a garnish to strategy rather than a foundational ingredient.

This hesitation is not without reason. The word *spirituality* itself can trigger discomfort, ambiguity, or skepticism. It evokes personal belief systems, cultural overtones, and sometimes a perceived lack of pragmatism. But what if we reframed spirituality not as doctrine or dogma, but as a science of inner development?

This is exactly the proposition offered by emerging frameworks such as Spiritual Intelligence (SQ), coined and studied by researchers like Danah Zohar. Building on the ideas of Intelligence Quotient (IQ) and Emotional Quotient or Intelligence (EQ), Zohar describes SQ as the "intelligence with which we access our deepest meanings, values, purposes, and higher motivations." Her work suggests that SQ is what enables leaders to reframe challenges, lead from purpose, and serve beyond ego. In other words, SQ could be the most underleveraged form of leadership capital in the modern organization. While mindfulness rooms and wellness perks are helpful, they are not substitutes for cultural courage. What's needed now is not just the availability of spiritual tools, but the embodiment of spiritual values—compassion, integrity, humility, and presence—at the highest levels of leadership. The idea of spiritual intelligence—once seen as abstract or esoteric—is now entering the mainstream vocabulary of progressive leadership. It's no longer just about KPIs and quarterly earnings; it's about creating spaces where people can show up whole, grounded in clarity, presence, and purpose. What the fictional leaders in this chapter demonstrate is not just a nice-to-have philosophy, but a blueprint for what forward-thinking companies are beginning to build: cultures where performance flows from well-being, not despite it.

Scientific advancements are increasingly validating the ancient wisdom that practices like meditation, breathwork, and intentional stillness are not just good for mental health—they directly impact executive functioning.

A 2022 meta-analysis published in *Frontiers in Psychology* examined 44 studies and found consistent evidence that meditation enhances attention control, emotional regulation, and cognitive flexibility—three traits essential to leadership under pressure.

Moreover, brain imaging studies from Harvard and Yale show that regular mindfulness practice reduces activity in the *default mode network*—the part of the brain associated with mind-wandering, worry, and rumination—while enhancing connectivity in areas related to empathy and insight.

This is why elite performers—from CEOs to athletes to Navy SEALs—incorporate mindfulness not as a luxury, but as a performance edge.

What we're witnessing is the gradual emergence of a new kind of leadership—one that integrates spiritual intelligence as a core capacity. It's about building environments where people show up whole—anchored in clarity, presence, and purpose.

In 2021, a study published in the *Journal of Business Ethics* by Stephen Anderson and Jodine Burchell examined how individual spirituality and situational moral intensity relate to ethical decision-making in the workplace. Contrary to expectations, the study found that workers with higher levels of measured spirituality actually made *less* ethical decisions than those with lower spirituality. This surprising result challenges common assumptions and underscores the importance of examining ethical behavior through both personal and contextual lenses—not just abstract ideals.

The fictional leaders in this chapter offer more than a symbolic arc. They reflect a larger truth: the workplace is becoming a frontier for inner transformation. Cultures that support authenticity, reflection, and meaning don't just feel better—they perform better. Not despite spirituality, but because of it.

Still, the road ahead demands more than inspiration—it demands integration. It calls on us to bridge the tension: between old expectations and new aspirations, between pressure and purpose. The way forward will not be easy—but as the data, stories, and shifts show, it is possible. And more than that, it is essential.

This isn't a passing trend. It's a turning point.

The question isn't just *"Is it doable?"* The evidence says yes. The data says yes. The experience of thousands says yes.

The real question is—*are we willing to do the inner work it takes?* To lead differently. To listen more deeply. To act more consciously.

If so, the possibilities—for our organizations, our people, and ourselves—are not only doable. They're transformational.

Another key question you need to ask yourself is: *"Are you brave enough?"*

CHAPTER THREE

RACHEL'S SPIRITUAL QUEST

The Playbook

Samuel invited Rachel to their weekly virtual meetings.

Rachel's experience at her first meeting with the *peer group* was interesting. The meeting started with a two-minute silent meditation. It was her first time attempting to sit by herself in complete silence in a meditative state. While she had no clue, Rachel closed her eyes, determined to try meditation. At first, she felt awkward, unsure of what she was supposed to do. Her mind raced all over: Is this going to work? Did I ask my assistant for that important investor meeting? She tried focusing on her breath, but the silence seemed deafening. Her shoulders tensed as she resisted the urge to check the time, wondering how two minutes could feel so long. Her thoughts were interrupted when she heard everyone exchange the phrase "Om Shanti." She exhaled deeply and slowly muttered, "Om Shanti."

With a hesitant smile, she looked at everyone to find a few people smiling gently. That sense of being out of place began to ease. An oddly satisfying feeling was brewing within her, post the two-minute meditation.

Since Rachel and the others had already been introduced virtually, they did not waste time on detailed intros and pleasantries.

Rachel thanked everyone for including her. Then, with a curious glint in her eye, she asked, "I've got to admit, that two-minute meditation felt like twenty. How do you all manage to quiet your minds? Are there techniques, or is it just practice?"

Leila was the first to respond, her voice warm and measured, like someone used to diplomacy across cultures. "It's both," she said, adjusting the vibrant silk scarf that peeked out from her blazer. "For me, focusing on breath is the anchor. Sometimes I silently repeat a phrase or question—it helps filter the noise. Like tuning into the signal beneath the static."

Oliver leaned forward, his presence grounded and assertive, like a man used to calling shots from both the floor and the boardroom. "I use sound. Gentle background chants or even just ambient tones. It helps me stay grounded without drifting."

Daphne, ever composed, spoke with the crisp precision of someone who once orchestrated billion-dollar trades before lunch. "Body awareness works for me. I scan from head to toe, noticing tension without judgment. It's subtle, but it centers me. Like rebalancing a portfolio—only internal."

Meera chimed in, her tone soft but vibrant, as if painting a picture with words. "I often visualize. A candle flame, a still lake—something that invites stillness without effort. The trick is not to force stillness but to create space for it."

Rachel scribbled mental notes, visibly more at ease now. "And what if my mind keeps racing? Is that a sign I'm doing it wrong?"

Samuel, who had been quietly observing, finally spoke—his voice calm, deliberate, and deeply grounded, like someone who calibrated his words the way he did his algorithms. "That *is* the practice. Meditation isn't about stopping your thoughts. It's about not chasing them. Letting them pass like clouds, without holding on."

Rachel exhaled, the tension in her frame softening. "Okay, that makes me feel a bit better. I've always assumed a clear mind was the goal, not just... noticing."

Samuel leaned forward, his silver-streaked hair catching the afternoon light. "Also—something our teacher emphasized: belief matters. You have to trust the process, not measure it every second. Meditation works, but only when you surrender to it."

Rachel nodded slowly. "I've still got questions, honestly. But I don't want to derail the meeting."

Oliver offered a reassuring grin. "Questions are part of the journey. We're working on a playbook—best practices, reflections, what's worked in different contexts. We'll send the draft version your way. It might help answer some of those questions... or lead to better ones."

Rachel smiled, her curiosity piqued rather than pacified.

Rachel was struck by the sheer energy pulsing through the virtual room. This wasn't the usual corporate dialogue filled with posturing or carefully curated opinions. Here, leaders spoke with raw honesty—laying bare their toughest challenges—and in return, were met with insight, empathy, and solution-driven thinking. There were no hidden agendas, no power plays, no need to impress. It felt as though each person was holding a piece of a shared mission, guided by something deeper—something almost sacred.

Despite their vastly different industries, there was an effortless harmony in the way the group collaborated, a flow that seemed too fluid to be accidental. Rachel could sense the invisible thread binding them: that one spiritual retreat. And yet, what had grown out of it felt much larger than a week-long experience—it was a movement in motion. She found herself silently wondering, *What kind of alchemy was at play here? What made this collective so special—and how could she tap into it?*

As the call neared its end, the group reaffirmed their next step: each leader would share their updated plans for infusing spiritual values into their organizations ahead of the next meeting. The session wrapped with a crisp sense of closure—ending not only on time but with a full minute to spare.

Rachel sat back in her chair, both stirred and still, knowing this was more than a meeting. This was a ripple of change—and she was now part of it.

Rachel thought to herself how effectively the meeting was conducted. She walked away from the meeting uplifted, tasked with reading the playbook.

The first thing she Googled was the phrase "Om Shanti," which was used by everyone. She had heard about it somewhere but was not sure of the exact meaning. She started reading on her phone:

Om Shanti is a Sanskrit phrase with deep spiritual significance and is believed to have originated from one of the oldest Hindu scriptures, the *Brihadaranyaka Upanishad*.

"Om" is considered the primordial sound of the universe, representing the essence of creation, consciousness, and the ultimate reality. It symbolizes unity and the infinite nature of existence, often chanted to align the mind, body, and soul.

"Shanti" means peace—specifically, a deep and lasting inner tranquility that transcends external circumstances.

Together, "Om Shanti" is a mantra that invokes universal and personal peace. It is often used in meditation and spiritual practices to calm the mind, bring harmony, and connect with a higher state of being. The repetition of "Shanti" (sometimes said three times) emphasizes peace on all levels:

- *Peace within oneself (mental and emotional balance),*
- *Peace in interpersonal relationships, and*
- *Peace in the natural and cosmic order.*

Saying or chanting "Om Shanti" is both a prayer and an affirmation of inner serenity and harmony with the world.

Rachel had never thought that these two short words would have such a deep meaning and implication. She was glad for checking out the real meaning of the phrase, in lieu of uttering it blindly. At that moment, something shifted. She felt this greeting like a window into a much deeper philosophy—one that centered on balance, clarity, and inner alignment. For someone often caught in the noise of decisions, deadlines, and deliverables, the meaning of "Om Shanti" offered her a quiet anchor. It reminded her that peace wasn't a luxury—it was a foundation. And perhaps, integrating just a bit of that stillness into her day could bring more clarity to the chaos. Rachel looked at her watch and proceeded to meet her CFO, David, to get his input on the various cost-cutting areas for the organization.

When she was done with her meetings, she grabbed a simple meal. For the last few months, she had made a conscious call to eat lightly in the evening and was religiously sticking to it. This helped her with better digestion and improved sleep patterns. Her mornings were more energetic.

Post her dinner, she took a warm shower and was all fresh. Time for my homework, she thought to herself, and with a smile, she clicked the link for the playbook on her laptop. She was told that the content was a work in progress, but it still looked very polished. She started reading the first part, which explained what spirituality is. She thought to herself that she possibly didn't need to go through this, but still decided to read it. The playbook started with:

Spirituality?

In this playbook, spirituality will show up not as philosophy but as practice: in how we handle conflict, design meetings, build culture, and measure what matters. It is not an abstract ideal—it is a daily discipline.

And perhaps most importantly—it's a reclamation: of clarity, of connection, and of the courage to lead from within.

One of the ways this daily discipline shows up is through inner alignment. When employees experience a sense of purpose that transcends job titles and quarterly targets, their work becomes more than transactional—it becomes transformational.

For leaders, this is not about lofty ideals—it's a call to shape cultures where meaning and performance reinforce each other. Where inner clarity becomes a competitive advantage. Spirituality also fosters emotional intelligence, enabling individuals to better navigate challenges, manage stress, and maintain healthy relationships. Through mindfulness and compassion, professionals develop a balanced approach to problem-solving and decision-making—leading to both personal effectiveness and healthier team dynamics.

A cornerstone of this approach is self-reflection. When professionals take intentional moments to pause and introspect, they better understand what drives their actions, how they impact others, and where growth is needed. Whether through journaling, meditation, or quiet review of the day, this ongoing internal dialogue cultivates accountability and purpose across both personal and professional spheres.

Beyond the workplace, spirituality provides strength during adversity. It helps individuals meet uncertainty with resilience and grace, shifting challenges into opportunities for growth. Gratitude and acceptance anchor this mindset—helping us appreciate the present while staying focused on what truly matters.

One of the simplest yet most profound ways this inner clarity manifests in everyday leadership is through the practice of gratitude. It's where the abstract becomes actionable—where values like presence and purpose take shape in ordinary moments

This attitude of gratitude isn't merely a positive outlook; it's a deliberate shift in awareness. And the good news is, it can be developed through simple, repeatable actions. Start by paying attention to everyday moments that are ripe for gratitude—mundane yet meaningful instances that often pass unnoticed:

1. *A colleague who stays late to help you wrap up a deadline.*

2. *A family member quietly taking care of household chores.*

3. *A customer service agent who patiently resolves your issue.*

4. *A friend who picks up your coffee without being asked.*

5. *A stranger who lets you merge into traffic during rush hour.*

6. *A partner or friend offering emotional support during tough times.*

7. *A compliment received that you forget to acknowledge.*

8. *A mentor whose advice changed your path.*

9. *A habitual giver whose kindness you've come to expect.*

10. *A co-worker or neighbor who always greets you warmly.*

The Practice: To cultivate this attitude, take five minutes daily to reflect on such moments. Write them down in a gratitude journal or mentally acknowledge them before bed. Take it one step further by expressing your appreciation—through a message, a verbal thank-you, or a simple gesture of acknowledgment. Over time, this shifts your internal focus from scarcity to abundance, from stress to perspective.

In an increasingly fast-paced and competitive world, spirituality—anchored in practices like gratitude—offers a counterbalance to the relentless pursuit of external success. It reminds us that true fulfillment lies not in the accumulation of accolades or possessions, but in the quality of our relationships, the impact of our contributions, and the peace we carry within.

Embracing spirituality as part of our daily lives allows us to navigate complexity with clarity, find joy in simplicity, and create a legacy that resonates far beyond professional achievements. It is not about retreating from the world; it is about engaging with it fully— with purpose, presence, and a deep sense of connection to a wisdom that transcends the self.

Rachel had several thoughts running through her mind. She was aware of spirituality at a high level—concepts of mindfulness, inner peace, and moral values often came to mind when the term was mentioned. But these ideas had always felt abstract, like distant ideals that were somehow separate from the hustle and grind of the corporate world. She had never invested the time to dive deeper, believing spirituality was something personal, even private, and perhaps unrelated to the goals and challenges of running a fast-paced organization like Zenyra.

Yet, as she read the opening section of the playbook, something shifted within her. The words didn't just describe spirituality; they redefined it in a way she hadn't considered before. Spirituality wasn't framed as an escape or an abstract ideal. Instead, it was presented as a practical way of thinking and being—a mindset and way of life that could enhance clarity, resilience, and purpose in any context, including the workplace.

Rachel paused to reflect. Could spirituality be more than just personal fulfillment? Could it hold the key to creating a culture where employees thrive—not just as professionals but as people? Was spirituality the missing ingredient for a better world?

The last line from the playbook resonated deeply with her. What if all the employees engaged with a *"sense of connection to a higher wisdom that transcends the self"* could redefine Zenyra as an organization? The key would be to connect the dots between individual aspirations or purpose with the organization's mission. Or was it the other way around? Could Zenyra become a platform for employees to express themselves individually?

This reframing struck a chord. Rachel realized that spirituality wasn't just about individuals—it was also about fostering a collective consciousness.

She also realized that spirituality could provide a framework for decision-making that is aligned with integrity and empathy, a way to navigate complexity with calm and focus, and a foundation for deeper connections between people, even in a corporate setting.

Her thoughts shifted to the potential impact this could have on Zenyra. She imagined a workplace where employees were not only productive but also genuinely happy and fulfilled. A place where innovation stemmed not from pressure but from inspiration, and where collaboration was driven by mutual respect and a shared purpose.

The next chapter aimed to dispel common misconceptions about spirituality, a topic Rachel found both intriguing and timely. As she glanced at the heading, she thought to herself, *"This should be interesting,"* and eagerly continued reading:

Misconceptions about Spirituality Clarified

Spirituality, while deeply personal and enriching, is often misunderstood. Here are some common misconceptions:

1. *Spirituality Equals Religion: While religion can be a pathway to spirituality for some, spirituality is broader and can exist independently. It focuses on personal growth, connection, and inner peace rather than organized practices or doctrines of any particular religion. Its broad canvas encompasses all religions and applies to people of all faiths, without discriminating based on color, caste, creed, age, nationality, or language.*

2. *It Requires Renouncing Material Life: Spirituality is about balance and perspective. One can live a materially successful life while being spiritually aware by aligning actions with purpose and values.*

3. *It's Only for the Elderly or Troubled: Spirituality is not about pursuing it during crises or later in life. Spirituality can benefit individuals of all ages and circumstances, helping to cultivate mindfulness, emotional resilience, and a sense of purpose.*

4. *Spiritual People Are Always Calm and Perfect: Spirituality is a journey, not a destination. Spiritual individuals also experience emotions and challenges, but strive to grow and learn from them.*

5. *It Requires Following a Guru or Teacher: While mentors can provide valuable insights, spirituality is ultimately about one's personal journey and experiences.*

6. *It's All About Meditation or Yoga: These are tools for spiritual growth, but spirituality encompasses a broader spectrum, including compassion, gratitude, service, and self-awareness.*

7. *It's Mystical and Inaccessible: Spirituality can be simple and practical, involving daily acts of kindness, mindfulness, and living with intention. It is also available for all.*

8. *It Conflicts with Science or Logic: Spirituality often complements science, exploring questions of meaning, connection, and consciousness that science doesn't address directly.*

9. *It Solves All Problems Instantly: Spirituality provides tools to navigate life's ups and downs more gracefully, but it doesn't eliminate challenges. It helps us respond to situations in life much better and increases our resilience. However, it's important to understand that spirituality is a long, evolving journey—not a magic wand. Real transformation takes time, reflection, and consistent practice.*

Understanding spirituality as a dynamic and inclusive concept allows individuals to explore it in ways that resonate personally and authentically.

When she finished reading this section, each misconception clarified in the passage felt like a revelation, not just for her personally but for the journey she envisioned for Zenyra. It struck her that for years she and maybe most people in the corporate world had been shackled by a narrow understanding of spirituality, treating it as either irrelevant or impractical. But this playbook was attempting to shatter those limitations, presenting spirituality as a unifying force, a bridge between personal purpose and collective ambition.

She thought about the people of Zenyra—engineers, marketers, strategists, and support staff—each carrying their own aspirations, struggles, and stories. Many had likely dismissed spirituality, assuming it required renouncing ambition or confusing it with organized religion. Yet, if reframed as a tool for balance, resilience, and deeper connection—to one's work, self, and others—it could become a source of strength rather than conflict.

The idea of spirituality being both practical and accessible resonated deeply. Rachel envisioned team meetings infused with moments of gratitude, negotiations shaped by empathy, and innovations emerging from a place of clarity and purpose. She imagined the collective potential of employees who viewed their work not as a routine obligation, but as an expression of personal values and meaning. Leadership, she believed, had the power to set this tone—not by embodying perfection, but by modeling intentional progress and self-awareness.

As these thoughts played out in her mind like scenes from a movie, her fingers instinctively began tapping rapidly against the armrest—a telltale sign of tension that those who knew her well would instantly recognize. The weight of the potential challenges ahead pressed on her, reminding her that integrating spirituality into a profit-driven organization would demand not just persistence but also vulnerability and a readiness to confront skepticism head-on. Yet, the more she reflected, the stronger her conviction grew. What if they could redefine spirituality—not as something mystical or exclusive, but as a universal human experience? One that harmonized with science, welcomed logic, and championed authenticity.

Feeling the swirl of thoughts building, Rachel paused, closed her eyes briefly, and practiced a simple breathing technique she had picked up from the peer group's meditation ritual. Just two minutes of silence. Her shoulders softened, her heartbeat slowed, and the mental fog began to lift. Meditation, she realized, was becoming her quiet anchor—a way to reclaim calm and clarity when everything felt overwhelming.

Her finger tapping gradually faded as clarity took hold, strengthening her resolve. She could now see a clear path forward—designing workshops to dispel misconceptions, weaving moments of mindfulness into the fabric of daily work, and amplifying the voices of employees who were already finding deeper meaning through the initiative. But above all, she knew she had to lead by example—sharing her own journey and vulnerability, showing that spirituality wasn't a lofty ideal but a grounded, personal pursuit.

A rare sense of optimism washed over Rachel, bringing a quiet smile to her face. This was no longer just a strategy to boost engagement or retention; it was a mission to humanize the workplace. To transform Zenyra into more than just a corporation—into a symbol of balance, purpose, and conscious leadership in a world that desperately needed it.

With renewed energy, she turned to the next section:

The Great Divide

The perceived gap between corporate ambition and spiritual well-being stems from long-held assumptions about what each represents.

This binary view still lingers, shaping how we define what belongs in the workplace—and what doesn't.

A few pointers on why these two worlds have been perceived as extremely different:

1. *Materialism vs. Inner Fulfillment: The corporate world is fueled by external achievements and financial gain, whereas spirituality encourages inner fulfillment and detachment from material rewards.*

2. *Metrics vs. Meaning: One of the most persistent divides between the corporate and spiritual worlds lies in how success is defined and measured. The corporate domain thrives on tangible, quantifiable outcomes—revenue, margins, market share, productivity, shareholder value— where everything is tracked, compared, and optimized. Spirituality, on the other hand, operates in the realm of the intangible: inner peace, compassion, empathy, integrity, and mindfulness—qualities not easily captured by dashboards or KPIs. This fundamental mismatch in measurement has led to a perceived incompatibility, reinforcing the belief that what cannot be measured doesn't belong in the boardroom. But what if we reimagined success to include both? What if the inner well-being of people became a legitimate driver of material outcomes?*

3. *Traditional Leadership Models: Most leadership models in the corporate world have favored power, control, and short-term gains, leaving little space for the introspective nature of spirituality, which often advocates humility, service, and long-term thinking.*

4. *Fear of Vulnerability: Spirituality often requires vulnerability, self-awareness, and admitting one's limitations—traits not traditionally associated with corporate*

leadership, where confidence and decisiveness are celebrated.

5. *Additional thoughts:*

- *The age-old management philosophy, "What you can't measure, you can't improve," has traditionally kept spirituality out of the equation in the corporate world. Spirituality may have subjectivity and sometimes can be deeply personal, however, if there was a way to connect the dots on interdependencies, that would help bridge the gap.*

  > *What if one of the ways to prevent unethical decisions by leaders could lie with spirituality?*

- *Time and again, corporations have suffered due to unethical decisions made by a few individuals in positions of power—damaging reputations, eroding stakeholder trust, and in some cases, contributing to financial collapse. These outcomes highlight the need for a values-based foundation in leadership. When grounded in spirituality—not in a religious sense, but as a framework for self-awareness, empathy, and integrity— leaders are better equipped to align their actions with a broader sense of purpose. By integrating reflective practices and considering the human impact of their choices, decision-makers can move beyond short-term gains and adopt a more ethical, sustainable approach. This shift encourages leadership that values accountability and the long-term well-being of the entire ecosystem alongside financial performance.*

  > *What if vulnerability and emotional intelligence can be used to develop trusted, authentic relationships between the various stakeholders, internal as well as external, to an organization?*

- *Organizations have struggled to generate true trust within their ecosystem (employees, partners, customers, and regulating bodies). While vulnerability and emotional intelligence have often been looked down upon in the corporate world, a study by Catalyst in 2021 involving 900 U.S. employees found that those with empathetic leaders reported higher levels of creativity (61%) and engagement (76%) compared to those with less empathetic leaders (13% and 32%, respectively). This research underscores the critical role of empathy in fostering an innovative and committed workforce. These traits help individuals connect with others on a deeper level as their foundation is built on patience and reflection.*

> *What if the focus on inner fulfillment, emotional balance, and ethical alignment can directly lead to growth in an organization's revenue and margins?*

- *Organizations have always struggled to keep all their employees energized, enthused, and plugged into the organization's mission and growth. Employees, when they feel they are contributing meaningfully and aligned with their personal purpose, will always go the extra mile to do wonders for their employers. Spirituality helps accomplish that.*

As Rachel delved into the playbook's section titled "The Great Divide," a wave of recognition swept over her. The words encapsulated the unspoken tension she had felt for years—how spirituality and the corporate world seemed like polar opposites, separated by an invisible wall. One stood for profits, targets, and competition; the other for purpose, introspection, and connection. Yet, the playbook challenged this dichotomy, arguing that the divide was an illusion, perpetuated by misconceptions and fear of the unknown.

Rachel couldn't help but reflect on her own career. How often had they sacrificed empathy for efficiency, or sidelined values in the pursuit of results?

Rachel vividly recalled a major restructuring she led early in her career as a regional head. The decision to downsize a struggling department was made purely on financial metrics, with little regard for the human toll. She recalled how her team member, a diligent employee and single parent, had pleaded for clarity and compassion during the process. At the time, Rachel had maintained a strictly professional demeanor, reassuring herself it was "just business."

Now, she reflected on how spirituality—anchored in empathy and transparency—could have transformed the experience. She could have fostered open dialogue by holding private, uninterrupted one-on-one conversations in a neutral office setting... offered more emotional support by bringing in an external counsellor or employee assistance professional... or by providing mental health days and peer support groups...

Rachel remembered a senior team member, Claire, who had shown signs of burnout but was delivering exceptional results. Rather than addressing Claire's obvious exhaustion, Rachel had praised her performance, inadvertently reinforcing a culture of overwork. Six months later, Claire resigned unexpectedly, citing stress and lack of work-life balance.

Reflecting on this, Rachel felt a pang of regret. She realized that fostering mindfulness and encouraging emotional openness could have helped Claire articulate her struggles earlier. Rachel could have introduced regular well-being check-ins during team meetings, offered flexible work schedules, or created designated quiet zones for decompression. Even the presence of a dedicated wellness officer or rotating "mental health ambassador" could have normalized conversations around stress and self-care.

She realized that this divide wasn't just conceptual; it was a barrier embedded in every decision, meeting, and metric at Zenyra. The section's assertion that spirituality could harmonize rather than conflict with corporate goals sparked a glimmer of hope. What if bridging this divide wasn't just possible, but essential for the future of work?

For Rachel, the message was clear: the path forward required courage—not just to embrace spirituality, but to reimagine the very DNA of corporate culture. The divide wasn't a wall; it was a bridge waiting to be built. And she was determined to lead the way.

As Rachel turned the page, a sense of anticipation grew. The questions swirling in her mind seemed to align with the themes that the playbook had been gradually unfolding. She found herself hoping that the next section might offer insights—perhaps even affirm her emerging belief that spirituality could hold value in navigating the complexities of the future workplace.

Even before reading further, a quiet sense of affirmation stirred within her—as if she were on the cusp of discovering that spirituality wasn't just a personal journey, but a vital foundation for building resilient, purpose-driven organizations.

Intrigued, Rachel eagerly turned to the next page:

Spirituality for Corporations: Relevance and Benefits

In the high-pressure world of modern business, spirituality offers more than solace—it provides a compass for navigating complexity with clarity, integrity, and balance. By grounding corporate life in spiritual principles, we enable growth that advances both profit and purpose—creating success that is sustainable and deeply human.

With this backdrop, let's dive into some of the potential benefits:

1. *Building Resilient Leaders and Teams: In today's fast-paced, volatile corporate environment, stress and burnout are widespread. Spirituality offers tools such as mindfulness, reflection, and self-awareness to manage these pressures effectively. By cultivating emotional resilience, organizations can create a workforce capable of navigating challenges with clarity, composure, and calmness, ensuring long-term sustainability. Leaders can build emotional resilience by normalizing regular mindfulness check-ins, encouraging practices like journaling or silent reflection before meetings, and modeling vulnerability through open conversations. Creating spaces for employees to pause, process, and realign—such as digital detox periods or purpose-led huddles—can foster a culture of inner balance and collective strength.*

2. *Enhancing Employee Engagement and Well-Being: A spiritually aligned workplace nurtures a culture of trust, respect, and inclusivity. When employees feel connected to a greater purpose and aligned with their organization's mission, they often report higher job satisfaction and engagement. Engaged employees are more productive, innovative, and loyal—directly impacting revenue, profitability, and reducing turnover costs.*

3. *Driving Ethical Decision-Making and Sustainability: Corporate scandals and short-termism have tarnished*

reputations and led to severe financial losses for many organizations. Short-termism—the tendency to prioritize immediate gains over long-term value—often drives risky decisions, undermines innovation, and erodes trust among employees, customers, and investors. Spirituality nurtures ethical decision-making by encouraging leaders to consider the broader impact of their actions on society and the environment. This not only mitigates risks but also strengthens the brand integrity and stakeholder confidence. Leaders can foster this mindset by embedding purpose into performance metrics, rewarding integrity over just outcomes, and creating safe spaces where teams can discuss values alongside goals. Ethical leadership thrives when values are not only stated but consistently demonstrated in everyday decisions.

4. *Boosting Creativity and Innovation: Creativity thrives in environments where employees feel empowered, valued, and mentally unencumbered. Spiritual practices like meditation and introspection enhance cognitive clarity and foster innovative thinking. Leading organizations like Google and Apple have incorporated mindfulness programs, recognizing their role in sparking groundbreaking ideas. In business, creativity fuels problem-solving, drives product innovation, and creates a competitive edge in rapidly evolving markets. To harness it, leaders must foster a culture of psychological safety—where experimentation is encouraged and failure is viewed as part of the learning process. Encouraging practices like mindful pauses, journaling, or walking meetings can unlock deeper insight and divergent thinking. When employees feel mentally centered and purpose-driven, they're more likely to contribute bold ideas that shape the future of the organization. Leaders can nurture this by modeling vulnerability and curiosity, creating space for reflection and open dialogue, and actively listening without judgment.*

Structured creativity rituals—such as hierarchy-free brainstorming sessions or occasional "idea sabbaticals"—send a powerful message: innovation isn't just welcomed, it's expected.

5. *Aligning with Modern Workforce Expectations: Millennials and Gen Z increasingly seek purpose-driven work and employers that align with their values. According to Deloitte's 2024 Gen Z and Millennial Survey, nearly nine in 10 Gen Zs (86%) and millennials (89%) say having a sense of purpose at work is key to their job satisfaction. Spirituality in the workplace helps fulfill this expectation, enabling organizations to attract and retain top talent by promoting meaning, personal growth, and societal contribution. Leaders can accomplish this by articulating a clear organizational purpose beyond profit, integrating social and environmental impact into business goals, and giving employees opportunities to engage in meaningful initiatives. Purpose shouldn't just be a slogan—it should be reflected in daily decisions, values, and company culture.*

6. *Fostering Inclusive and Emotionally Intelligent Leadership: Spirituality encourages leaders to lead with compassion, vulnerability, and emotional intelligence. This approach cultivates authenticity and psychological safety, allowing teams to express ideas freely, collaborate openly, and innovate without fear of judgment. Leaders can accomplish this by practicing active listening, seeking diverse perspectives, and regularly checking in with team members—not just on performance, but on well-being. Creating forums for open dialogue, offering emotional intelligence training, and modeling humility and empathy in everyday interactions help embed these values into the culture. When leaders show up as fully human, it gives others permission to do the same—*

fostering deeper trust, stronger relationships, and more inclusive innovation.

7. *Promoting Diversity and Inclusion: By valuing inner awareness and shared humanity, spirituality reinforces the importance of respecting diverse perspectives. Inclusive workplaces not only drive higher innovation but also perform better financially, as diverse teams bring varied problem-solving approaches and richer insights. According to a McKinsey report (Diversity Wins: How Inclusion Matters, 2020), companies in the top quartile for ethnic and cultural diversity on executive teams were 36% more likely to outperform their peers on profitability. This suggests that inclusive, values-driven environments aren't just morally grounded—they're strategically sound. Leaders can foster this by creating safe spaces for self-reflection and open dialogue, where individuals feel seen and heard beyond their roles. Embedding spiritual values such as empathy, humility, and non-judgment into leadership practices can help bridge cultural divides and strengthen team cohesion.*

8. *Bridging Personal and Professional Growth: Spirituality supports the integration of personal purpose with professional goals. When employees feel their personal development is aligned with organizational objectives, they experience deeper fulfillment, which reduces burnout and absenteeism and increases retention. A study by Imperative and LinkedIn (2016) found that employees who viewed their work as purposeful were 54% more likely to stay at a company for five years and 50% more likely to be in leadership positions—highlighting that alignment between personal meaning and professional contribution directly impacts engagement and retention. Leaders can enable this by incorporating purpose-alignment conversations into performance reviews and by encouraging employees to define*

how their work connects with their personal values. Structured frameworks like purpose workshops, career mapping, and mentorship programs can serve as effective tools.

9. *A Strategic Advantage: Embracing spirituality is not an added complexity—it's a strategic enabler to unlock the full potential of human capital. By weaving spiritual principles into leadership and workplace culture, organizations can foster a harmonious, purpose-driven, motivated, and high-performing workforce—an advantage that directly contributes to achieving both financial and social goals. This approach doesn't just create better employees; it creates better people in the entire ecosystem, laying the foundation for a legacy that transcends the bottom line. A Harvard Business Review study (2015) found that employees who worked in "purpose-driven organizations" were three times more likely to stay and 1.7 times more likely to be satisfied with their jobs—showing that when inner meaning meets strategy, performance naturally follows. Leaders can activate this by embedding practices such as mindful leadership training, purpose-alignment frameworks, and reflective rituals into daily operations. These approaches humanize work while driving resilience and clarity across teams. When leaders nurture the soul of the organization, performance becomes a natural outcome—not a forced pursuit.*

10. *Enhancing Revenues, Brand Equity, Strategic Vision, and Long-Term Thinking: Spirituality encourages leaders to think beyond immediate metrics, focusing on sustainable growth. This visionary approach strengthens brand equity, drives revenue growth, attracts top talent, and aligns with global sustainability goals. According to a January 2025 article by the Society for Human Resource Management (SHRM), companies that invest in social purpose initiatives generate*

20% more revenue. For instance, Cisco's social impact programs led to a 12% reduction in employee attrition, while Bumble Bee Foods achieved a major sustainability milestone three years ahead of schedule—demonstrating that purpose and profit can go hand in hand. Leaders can achieve this by embedding spiritual principles—like stewardship, integrity, and long-term responsibility—into strategic planning, brand storytelling, and KPIs. When purpose becomes part of the strategic agenda, not just the HR narrative, it shapes decisions that deliver both financial returns and societal value.

Incorporating spirituality into the workplace isn't just a moral or cultural imperative—it's a business one. It aligns human potential with organizational purpose, creating a culture of resilience, innovation, inclusion, and ethical leadership. In doing so, it lays the foundation for enduring success—financially, socially, and humanely.

It was becoming increasingly clear to Rachel that incorporating spirituality into the corporate world wasn't just a paradigm shift—it was a strategic imperative for long-term growth and well-being. By fostering a culture grounded in mindfulness, empathy, and purpose, organizations could transcend traditional success metrics—driving stronger revenues, healthier margins, and greater brand equity—while also increasing satisfaction among employees, customers, and the broader ecosystem. Just as importantly, it helped create humane environments where people could thrive both professionally and personally.

Yet a restless thought gnawed at her: if the benefits were so clear, why hadn't more organizations embraced this approach?

She pondered the disconnect. Perhaps it was fear—of appearing too idealistic, too unmeasurable, too "soft" for the hard edges of business. Maybe it was inertia—the deep grooves of habit that made quarterly results feel more urgent than long-term resilience. Or perhaps leaders simply hadn't experienced the transformation themselves. After all, how could they champion what they hadn't yet understood?

Rachel realized the problem wasn't a lack of evidence, but a lack of exposure. Spirituality had remained at the margins of leadership discourse—misunderstood, minimized, or dismissed as a personal pursuit rather than a strategic asset.

A sense of moral urgency swelled within her. This wasn't just an opportunity—it might be a responsibility. Rachel resolved to become a voice that could awaken more leaders to these truths and help spark a transformation capable of redefining the very fabric of corporate life.

The next heading, *Cultural Dynamics in the Workplace*, immediately caught Rachel's attention. As a leader managing a vast, globally dispersed team, the topic felt not just relevant but deeply personal. Her mind wandered briefly to the daily challenges she faced—navigating diverse perspectives, bridging cultural gaps, and fostering collaboration across time zones. Now, with the thought of incorporating spirituality into the corporate world, this topic seemed extremely relevant.

She glanced at her watch. It was already 9 p.m., and the soft glow of her desk lamp seemed to accentuate the stillness of the room. Most would have called it a day by now, but Rachel felt a pull she couldn't ignore. The promise of new insights for growth was too compelling.

With a resolute breath, she settled back into her chair, determined to uncover strategies that could help her unite her team in ways she had only dreamed of.

Cultural Dynamics in the Workplace

Another intriguing angle at play is the cultural nuances spanning the globe. Broadly speaking, each country and sometimes even several regions within the same country—possess their own unique ethos. Below is an overview of how some regions and cultures may view the relationship between corporate life and spirituality:

1. India

It tops the list with a long, rich history of spirituality, meditation, and yoga. Not only is it one of the oldest civilizations, but it also ranks among the top five economies globally, with vast potential, while holding the title of the world's most populous nation.

India has a long-standing tradition of integrating spirituality into everyday life, including business. Many Indian leaders and organizations believe that business and spirituality are not mutually exclusive. Concepts like dharma (duty), karma (actions and their consequences), and ahimsa (non-violence) often inform corporate decisions.

Narayana Murthy, co-founder of Infosys, has often emphasized the importance of integrity, humility, and purpose in leadership, drawing from India's spiritual traditions. He encouraged transparent governance and wealth creation that serves society.

Kiran Mazumdar-Shaw, founder of Biocon, also blends purpose with business, often speaking about "business as a force for good" and advocating ethical, inclusive innovation.

Spirituality is often integrated into the workplace, with many leaders practicing meditation, yoga, or other forms of mindfulness and encouraging similar practices among employees. Large conglomerates like the Tata Group emphasize ethical responsibility, a form of corporate dharma. They have institutionalized this philosophy through actions such as:

- *Voluntary Codes of Conduct and a group-wide ethical charter rooted in transparency and compassion.*

- *Investment in employee well-being initiatives, including emotional wellness and mindfulness training.*

- *A strong legacy of philanthropy, where over 60% of Tata Sons' profits are directed toward societal development through the Tata Trusts.*

- *Decisions like pulling out of potentially profitable but ethically questionable business ventures reflect a long-term, values-based worldview.*

Indian culture encourages a holistic view of life where business success is seen not just in terms of revenues and profit but also in social responsibility and the spiritual integrity maintained. Many corporate leaders in India feel that spiritual growth can enhance leadership and decision-making. That said, while India offers a fertile ground for integrating spirituality into business, the extent to which this is practiced varies widely across organizations and leadership styles. The growing pressures of global competition and short-term financial metrics can still challenge the consistent application of these ideals.

2. United States

The United States has been the undisputed leader of the world for decades as a superpower. It is the pinnacle for corporate culture, as approximately one-third of the top global 2000 companies per the Forbes G2000 list are based in the USA.

In the U.S., the corporate world is traditionally seen as driven by capitalism, competition, and financial success. However, in recent years, there has been a growing interest in spirituality and mindfulness within corporate settings, largely focused on enhancing personal well-being, productivity, and leadership.

Spirituality in the U.S. corporate sector is typically secularized, often in the form of mindfulness or wellness programs. Leaders like Marc Benioff (Salesforce) and Arianna Huffington (Thrive Global) integrate mindfulness practices into their companies, but often without overt religious connotations.

The U.S. culture places a strong emphasis on individual success and self-reliance, and spirituality is often seen as a personal matter. While there is growing acceptance of spiritual practices like meditation in the workplace, there is still a clear delineation between spirituality and business objectives in many companies.

3. Japan

Japan is home to some iconic corporate houses and ranks third for being the base to 192 companies in the global G2000 by Forbes. The Japanese people are known for their humility, modesty, and respect for others, which also happen to be cornerstones for spirituality.

In Japan, the integration of spirituality and business is often subtle and tied to traditional philosophies like Zen Buddhism and Shintoism. There is a focus on kaizen (continuous improvement), harmony, and collective well-being, which can be seen as spiritual principles guiding corporate behavior.

Japanese companies like Toyota and Sony emphasize respect, humility, and mindfulness in business operations, often influenced by Zen principles. However, spirituality is usually not explicitly discussed but rather embedded in corporate culture through rituals, respect for nature, and a focus on social harmony.

Japanese culture highly values group harmony (wa) and modesty, which are spiritual concepts that influence corporate behavior. The idea of meishi (business card exchange) is a ritual that shows respect and reflects a deeper cultural reverence for order and tradition in business.

4. China

Yet another example of an ancient civilization with a great blend of industrial growth and spirituality. China stands at number two after the USA per the G2000 list by Forbes.

Traditionally, Chinese culture emphasizes a balance between material success and spiritual well-being, deeply influenced by Confucianism, Taoism, and Buddhism. However, rapid industrialization and economic growth have, in some ways, overshadowed spiritual aspects in corporate life.

In contemporary China, the focus is more on material success and economic growth, and spirituality tends to play a secondary role in the corporate world. However, there is a resurgence of interest in ancient philosophies like Confucian ethics, which emphasize moral conduct and social harmony in business.

Confucian values of respect, hierarchy, and ethics still permeate Chinese business culture. The corporate world is often viewed as a reflection of one's Ren (virtue) and Li (ritual propriety), but modern corporate practices tend to prioritize economic achievements over spiritual values.

5. Western Europe (UK, France, Germany)

This region holds extreme relevance in world history, socio-economic, and political context. It has been the cradle of major global transformations—from the Enlightenment and the Industrial Revolution to the development of modern democracy, capitalism, and human rights. These nations have historically influenced global governance, economic models, and cultural norms, shaping how business and society interact worldwide.

Western European culture, influenced by the Enlightenment, tends to separate the secular from the spiritual. The Enlightenment, an intellectual movement of the 17th and 18th centuries, emphasized reason, science, and individualism over tradition and religious authority. It laid the philosophical foundation for modern democracy, capitalism, and the scientific method—prioritizing logic, empirical evidence, and rational thinking as the basis for decision-making. This legacy continues to shape the corporate world in much of Western Europe, where business is often viewed as a secular, results-driven pursuit rooted in rationality, science, and economics. As a result, spirituality is typically considered a personal matter, not a part of organizational culture.

In much of Western Europe, spirituality and the corporate world are largely seen as separate spheres. Business is viewed as a secular pursuit, and spiritual practices are generally personal, rather than being part of corporate culture.

There are some efforts, especially in progressive companies, to integrate well-being practices like mindfulness and meditation. However, these are usually framed in terms of improving efficiency and mental health rather than a deeper spiritual purpose.

That said, there is a growing shift. In recent years, some progressive companies have begun integrating practices like mindfulness and meditation—though usually framed in terms of improving efficiency, mental health, or productivity rather than fostering deeper spiritual growth. Alongside this, an increasing awareness of the need for work-life balance and emotional well-being is prompting conversations about more human-centered leadership models, even in traditionally rational and secular corporate environments.

6. Middle East

In many parts of the Middle East, Islamic values play a significant role in business and corporate governance. Spirituality and corporate ethics are often intertwined, with Islamic principles like Zakat (charity) and Taqwa (God-consciousness) influencing corporate behavior.

Sharia law, the Islamic legal framework, not only governs personal conduct but also offers detailed guidance on ethical business practices. It prohibits exploitative practices such as interest-based lending (riba), promotes risk-sharing in transactions, and mandates transparency and fairness—principles that form the foundation of Islamic finance. Businesses operating under Sharia compliance are expected to align profits with social good, reinforcing the connection between spirituality and economic activity. Specific restrictions include bans on investment in industries such as alcohol, gambling, or pork-related products, which are considered haram (forbidden). Companies frequently integrate spiritual routines like daily prayers and often structure workdays around religious observances. In some interpretations and regions, gender-related restrictions also shape workplace norms. For instance, in more conservative contexts, women may face limitations around dress codes, segregation in workspaces, travel without a male guardian (mahram), or holding senior leadership positions. While this varies significantly between countries in the region, such rules often stem from cultural-religious interpretations of modesty, guardianship, and gender roles.

Middle Eastern culture, deeply influenced by Islam, often views corporate success as intertwined with spiritual values. Ethical business conduct is seen as part of one's duty to God, and there is a strong emphasis on social responsibility and community welfare. However, within the region, spiritual concepts tend to gain broader acceptance when they are framed explicitly through the lens of religion rather than as secular or standalone philosophies. This suggests that even modern expressions of spirituality may resonate more deeply when anchored within the traditions of faith.

7. Latin America

In Latin American countries, there is a rich blend of indigenous spiritual practices and Catholicism, the latter being a dominant cultural and religious force across the region. While corporate life is typically secular, personal spirituality often shapes how leaders perceive responsibility, authority, and human connection in business.

There is a growing interest in mindfulness in Brazil, where corporate leaders are exploring ways to integrate personal well-being and social responsibility into business. Similarly, in countries like Mexico, Argentina, and Colombia, spirituality is often intertwined with Catholic values, influencing leadership styles and ethical decision-making. Catholic principles such as service, humility, stewardship, and moral accountability frequently guide leaders' approaches to social justice, employee welfare, and corporate ethics. Practices like prayer, attending Mass, and religious holidays also subtly reinforce a moral framework within which many executives operate. However, overt spiritual practices are not widely integrated into corporate life.

Latin American culture is influenced by community values, religion, and a sense of "familismo" (family-first), which often creates an environment where compassion, loyalty, and ethics play a significant role in business practices. This cultural emphasis on interpersonal relationships and moral duty reflects deeply rooted Catholic teachings about the dignity of the person and the importance of caring for others.

8. Africa

African business culture often blends spirituality with commerce, shaped by a dynamic mix of indigenous beliefs, Christianity, and Islam. In many African societies, indigenous spiritual traditions emphasize harmony with nature, reverence for ancestors, and the interconnectedness of all life. These belief systems—such as Ubuntu in Southern Africa, which promotes the idea of "I am because we are"—strongly influence leadership, ethics, and decision-making.

In this context, success in life and business is not measured solely by profit but by how well one uplifts the community and honors spiritual obligations. Ancestral guidance, ritual practices, and a respect for elders and spiritual leaders are often woven into business operations. In some regions, entrepreneurs consult traditional healers or spiritual elders before making major decisions, blending intuition and cultural wisdom with strategy.

Businesses influenced by these values often emphasize community development, ethical practices, and social responsibility. African culture places high importance on collective well-being, and leaders who embody these values tend to prioritize long-term communal prosperity over short-term individual gains. This integration of spirituality creates a business ethos grounded in responsibility, resilience, and reverence for life.

In essence, corporate leaders must remember that culture plays a crucial role in determining how spirituality and corporate life intersect. Corporate leaders in spiritual traditions often integrate ethics, community values, and well-being into their organizations, while more secular business environments might adopt mindfulness or well-being practices without a deeper spiritual foundation. At a high level, corporate leaders should keep in mind the following:

- *In collectivist cultures (e.g., India, Japan, the Middle East), acceptance of the intersection of spirituality and corporate life may be higher.*

- *In individualistic cultures (e.g., the U.S., Western Europe), spirituality is often seen as a personal journey, with less potential integration into corporate governance.*

As Rachel absorbed the passages, her mind was alive with imagery—faces of global leaders and teams from across her organization flashed before her, each one a detailed frame in a mental reel. She could almost hear their voices, feel their energy, and anticipate their reactions as she imagined introducing this topic. She already knew from earlier discussions that some of her team might meet this with quiet skepticism or guarded curiosity. So the question wasn't whether cynicism existed—it did. The real question now was: how could she overcome it? She began to imagine what might shift minds: authentic leadership examples, inviting dialogue rather than prescribing beliefs, and allowing room for doubt rather than suppressing it. The possibilities played out like a vivid montage in her thoughts.

While the insights outlined were broadly relevant and undeniably helpful, Rachel instinctively knew they would need careful tailoring to fit the unique rhythm of her organization. The challenge wasn't just about implementation; it was about resonance—making these ideas feel authentic and actionable in her team s diverse cultural tapestry.

She scribbled a note on her ever-growing playbook document, a repository of thoughts and strategies she planned to share with the group. A new section, tentatively titled "Bridging Doubt and Discovery," was already forming in her mind—dedicated to handling the emotional nuance of introducing spirituality in secular corporate settings. The flicker of determination in her eyes hinted at the weight of her responsibility.

Her attention then shifted to the next topic: *Perceived Risks and Mitigation Strategies*. The very mention of risks sent a ripple of tension through her, but it was accompanied by a spark of curiosity.

This wasn't just a chapter; it was a mirror to the unspoken fears that could either hinder progress or, when addressed wisely, pave the way for transformation.

Perceived Risks and Mitigation Strategies

Implementing spirituality in corporations can bring numerous benefits, but it also presents certain challenges if not approached thoughtfully. Below are some potential risks and strategies to mitigate them:

1. Risk of Perceived Favoritism or Exclusivity

If spirituality is introduced in a way that aligns too closely with specific beliefs or practices (e.g., Hindu meditation practices, Christian prayer circles, or Buddhist philosophies), it may alienate employees with different views. This can create divisions or lead to perceptions of favoritism. Some may feel pressured to conform to a dominant worldview, leading to disengagement or internal conflict.

Mitigation:

- *Adopt a Neutral Approach: Frame spirituality as a universal concept emphasizing shared values like integrity, empathy, and mindfulness, rather than specific religious or cultural practices.*

- *Inclusive Design: Encourage employees to explore spirituality in ways that resonate with their personal beliefs, offering multiple pathways for engagement (e.g., mindfulness workshops, gratitude practices, or personal reflection exercises).*

2. Risk of Misinterpretation or Resistance

Employees may perceive the introduction of spirituality as intrusive, unnecessary, or a form of indoctrination, especially if it's implemented without proper explanation. In culturally diverse or secular organizations, some might question whether spiritual efforts mask a deeper ideological agenda.

Mitigation:

- *Clear Communication: Emphasize that participation in spiritual practices or initiatives is entirely voluntary and designed to promote well-being and personal growth. Provide clear FAQs or internal memos that explain the 'why' behind such initiatives, ideally backed by science and case studies from successful companies as well as individuals.*

- *Leadership Example: Ensure leaders model the intended benefits of spirituality, such as emotional resilience and ethical decision-making, to build trust and credibility.*

3. Risk of Diluted Focus on Business Goals

An overemphasis on spirituality may shift attention away from key business objectives, potentially affecting productivity or bottom-line performance.

Mitigation:

- *Balance and Integration: Integrate spirituality with organizational goals, highlighting how practices like mindfulness, self-awareness, and empathy enhance professional outcomes like innovation, teamwork, and client satisfaction. For instance, McKinsey & Company integrated short mindfulness practices—such as 10-minute breaks—into high-stress project teams. This led to measurable improvements in decision-making clarity, emotional intelligence scores, and client satisfaction, according to their internal leadership development research.*

- *Regular Assessment: Continuously evaluate the impact of spiritual initiatives on employee performance and organizational goals to maintain alignment.*

4. Risk of Superficial Implementation (Tokenism)

Spirituality programs that are seen as shallow or performative may lose credibility and fail to deliver meaningful impact.

Mitigation:

- *Depth and Authenticity: Ensure that initiatives are thoughtfully designed and rooted in genuine intent, with opportunities for feedback and customization.*

- *Long-Term Commitment: View spirituality as a continuous process rather than a one-time program. Provide resources, training, and ongoing support to embed it authentically in the workplace culture.*

5. Risk of Blurring Boundaries

Encouraging employees to explore spirituality at work may inadvertently encroach on personal boundaries or create discomfort, especially when discussions touch on identity, values, or existential beliefs. While some may welcome the opportunity for reflection, others may feel pressured to disclose aspects of their inner lives they prefer to keep private—or may interpret such initiatives as overstepping the line between professional and personal domains. For instance, guided group reflections or values-based discussions, even when framed as secular, can evoke emotional responses or raise sensitive issues related to grief, trauma, or cultural beliefs. This may potentially trigger anxiety among employees, leading to disengagement. Additionally, employees from backgrounds where spirituality is deeply intertwined with religion may feel conflicted or excluded if workplace practices do not align with their worldview.

Mitigation:

- *Respect Privacy: Allow employees to engage with spiritual practices privately, offering optional resources such as mindfulness apps, journaling prompts, or quiet spaces—without mandating participation or personal disclosure.*

- *Professional Facilitation: Collaborate with trained facilitators or certified coaches who understand workplace boundaries and can guide spiritual initiatives with empathy, cultural sensitivity, and discretion. Communicate that participation is voluntary and that no personal sharing is required or expected.*

6. Legal and Ethical Risks

Incorporating spirituality into workplace practices might raise legal concerns, especially in regions with strict regulations on religious neutrality in professional settings. Even well-intentioned programs can be challenged if perceived as indirectly promoting particular ideologies. For instance, in the United States, Title VII of the Civil Rights Act prohibits employers from endorsing or imposing religious beliefs, which can lead to litigation if employees perceive spiritual programming as coercive or exclusionary. Even if the intent is secular—focused on mindfulness, purpose, or well-being—employees may still perceive such initiatives as aligned with particular faith traditions, potentially triggering discomfort or legal scrutiny. In 2019, a school district in West Virginia faced a lawsuit for promoting a Christian-based mindfulness program disguised as stress relief— highlighting the blurred boundaries between spirituality and religion in institutional environments. In European countries like France, where laïcité (secularism) is enforced by law, even subtle expressions of spirituality in the workplace can be challenged as breaches of public neutrality. In such contexts, introducing concepts like "soulful leadership" or "inner awakening" may inadvertently be seen as promoting ideological bias.

Mitigation:

- *Compliance Check: Work closely with legal and HR teams to ensure that spiritual initiatives comply with all regulations and policies regarding inclusivity and discrimination. This includes careful wording, voluntary participation, and ensuring offerings are presented in secular, values-based language.*

- *Open Feedback Channels: Create safe spaces for employees to voice concerns or suggest improvements, ensuring the program evolves in line with ethical standards. Anonymous surveys, inclusion councils, and external audits can all help monitor perception and adjust course when needed.*

7. Risk of Not Being Able to Measure Impact

The inability to measure and report will further fuel questions about the effectiveness of spirituality within the corporate world. Without tangible evidence, skeptics may dismiss it as an abstract concept, unsuitable for driving real-world business outcomes, risking its credibility as a viable strategy.

Mitigation:

- *Define clear objectives, metrics, and a structured framework for assessing job satisfaction, stress reduction, emotional intelligence, and work-life balance. Translate these into concrete business outcomes such as lower attrition, increased client retention, and improved innovation metrics.*

- *Leverage data analytics and technology along with the HR team. Start with small pilot programs and publish success to win trust by regularly communicating such metrics. Additionally, empower the champions within the organization who can share their experiences and observations to build organic support for spiritual initiatives.*

Rachel closed the section with a sense of accomplishment, yet her mind buzzed with unresolved thoughts. The playbook had been an enlightening guide—rich with insights and practical strategies—but it also stirred deeper questions that lingered like shadows in her mind.

Each topic felt like a puzzle piece, crucial yet incomplete:

» Assessment: How could the intangible aspects of spirituality be evaluated in a way that resonated with data-driven decision-makers?

» Measuring Impact: What tools or frameworks could translate emotional resilience, ethical alignment, or enhanced collaboration into quantifiable outcomes?

» Implementation Strategy: How would these principles be seamlessly woven into the fabric of day-to-day operations without overwhelming teams or diluting the essence of the message?

» Alignment and Communication: What would it take to inspire a unified belief in this vision across a globally dispersed workforce with varied cultural lenses?

» Role of Management: Could the leadership truly embody and champion these principles, or would this risk becoming just another check-the-box initiative?

» Long-Term Vision: Most pressing of all, how could this be tied to a purpose so profound, so aspirational, that it transcended short-term gains and anchored the organization in a higher goal—a true north?

» Success Stories: Are there any existing examples of successful implementation of spirituality in the corporate world? Any testimonials from professional leaders or from organizations?

She looked at her watch to realize it was already twenty minutes past eleven. Technically past her bedtime, but the questions stirring in her mind—and the quiet thrill of discovery—kept her going. She flipped the pages to the next chapter dedicated to:

Spiritual Trailblazers in the Corporate World

Several leaders have successfully integrated spiritual principles into their organizations, promoting mindfulness, empathy, and a higher sense of purpose alongside traditional corporate goals. These are not theoretical models or fictional scenarios—each example below is drawn from real-world leadership practices that have been implemented at the highest levels of global business. Here are some notable examples, with details on how their approach impacted their companies:

1. Satya Nadella – CEO of Microsoft

Spiritual Principle: Empathy and mindfulness

> *Implementation: Since becoming CEO in 2014, Satya Nadella has transformed Microsoft's culture by infusing empathy and emotional intelligence into the leadership approach. Nadella, who practices meditation and mindfulness, encouraged Microsoft's employees to adopt a growth mindset—focusing on continuous learning and the innovation potential. He began by reshaping leadership training, embedding Carol Dweck's growth mindset principles into performance reviews and goal-*

setting frameworks. Nadella personally modeled emotional intelligence through his communication—emphasizing listening, humility, and inclusive language. He also launched company-wide empathy initiatives, including disability-inclusive product design and internal dialogues on bias.

Impact:

- *Cultural Shift: Nadella helped move Microsoft away from a combative, competitive culture to one centered on collaboration and innovation. His emphasis on empathy helped nurture a more inclusive environment. Empathy training and EQ modeling from top leadership led to more psychologically safe environments where employees were more open to sharing ideas and challenges.*

- *Financial Growth: Under his leadership, Microsoft's market capitalization increased from about $300 billion in 2014 to over $2.5 trillion by 2023. His spiritual approach to leadership, focusing on long-term impact and building meaningful relationships with customers and employees, played a significant role in this success.*

- *Product Innovation: Nadella's leadership also enabled innovations in cloud computing and artificial intelligence, leading to Azure's growth as a dominant player in the cloud services industry.*

2. Ray Dalio – Founder of Bridgewater Associates

Spiritual Principle: Transcendental Meditation and Radical Transparency

Implementation: *Ray Dalio has been a proponent of transcendental meditation for decades and credits the practice with giving him clarity and calm in decision-making. He also created a corporate culture around the principle of radical* *transparency, where employees are encouraged to be brutally honest in giving and receiving feedback. Dalio views this culture as a form of "corporate mindfulness," where openness, truth, and self-reflection are encouraged. This was operationalized through daily peer reviews, recorded meetings, and a proprietary app called "Dot Collector,"—which allows team members to rate each other in real time across dozens of values and behaviors. To prevent emotional fallout, feedback is depersonalized and framed as data to identify blind spots, not to judge character.*

Impact:

- *Cultural Strength: Bridgewater's unique culture of transparency has allowed employees to better understand their strengths and weaknesses, leading to personal and professional growth. This environment also fosters a high level of trust and accountability.*

- *Financial Success: Bridgewater Associates became one of the world's largest hedge funds, managing over $150 billion in assets. Dalio attributes the firm's sustained success to its transparent culture and his own meditation practices, which help him approach challenges with equanimity.*

- *Personal Growth: Dalio's spiritual practices are central to his leadership approach and decision-making process. He also captured these leadership principles in a series of books, offering readers valuable insights into his philosophy. The firm's success is a testament to the power of introspection and honesty in a highly competitive field like hedge fund management.*

3. Marc Benioff – CEO of Salesforce

Spiritual Principle: Mindfulness, philanthropy, and compassion

Implementation: The 1-1-1 model is a philanthropic framework pioneered by Salesforce, in which the company donates 1% of its equity, 1% of its product, and 1% of its employees' time to charitable causes. Marc Benioff, a long-time advocate of mindfulness and meditation, has integrated spiritual values into Salesforce's corporate philosophy. Benioff introduced meditation rooms, on-site mindfulness sessions, and EQ coaching as part of leadership development. He personally advocates pausing before major decisions to reflect and center values—a mindfulness-based leadership behavior now part of Salesforce's internal training. Benioff's spiritual approach also emphasizes equality, inclusiveness, and purpose-driven work.

Impact:

- *Culture of Giving: Salesforce's 1-1-1 model has contributed millions of dollars in donations, products, and volunteer hours to various causes globally. This philanthropic focus aligns the company with the spiritual principle of compassion and giving back to society.*

- *Employee Well-being: By encouraging mindfulness, Salesforce promotes a work environment where employees can maintain balance and mental well-being. The company regularly hosts wellness programs, including mindfulness sessions. Surveys show higher resilience scores and lower burnout in teams that participate in the mindfulness initiatives.*

- *Business Growth: Under Benioff's leadership, Salesforce grew into one of the world's most valuable cloud computing companies, with a market capitalization exceeding $200 billion by 2023. Benioff's spiritual values have shaped a compassionate corporate culture, contributing to high employee engagement and customer loyalty.*

4. John Mackey – Co-founder of Whole Foods Market

Spiritual Principle: Conscious Capitalism

Implementation*: John Mackey is a leading advocate of Conscious Capitalism, a business philosophy that integrates ethical leadership, stakeholder orientation, and a higher purpose. Mackey believes that businesses should exist not just to make profits but to improve the well-being of everyone involved, from employees to communities to the environment. He embedded purpose into every leadership decision—from transparent pay structures to in-store values-based messaging. Leaders were trained to think beyond profit, aligning strategy with mission.*

Impact:

- *Corporate Culture: Whole Foods embraced the concept of Servant Leadership, where leaders serve the interests of employees, customers, and suppliers. This approach, rooted in Mackey's spiritual beliefs, created a strong community-focused culture within the company. Employee empowerment was seen in the autonomy given to individual store teams and the inclusion of team members in hiring decisions.*

- *Financial Performance: Whole Foods' emphasis on ethical sourcing and organic products helped it build a loyal customer base. The company's purpose-driven business model led to its acquisition by Amazon in 2017 for $13.7 billion, showcasing the commercial viability of spiritual principles in corporate strategy.*

- *Industry Impact: Mackey's leadership inspired a broader movement toward Conscious Capitalism, which encourages other businesses to pursue long-term value creation for all stakeholders, not just shareholders.*

5. A.G. Lafley – Former CEO of Procter & Gamble

Spiritual Principle: Mindfulness and emotional intelligence

Implementation: *A.G. Lafley, former CEO of Procter & Gamble, was a proponent of emotional intelligence (EQ) in leadership. Lafley integrated mindfulness practices into his leadership style, fostering self-awareness, empathy, and conscious decision-making. He used reflective pauses before key decisions, held silent thinking time during executive meetings, and trained senior leaders in EQ through custom coaching programs.*

Impact:

- *Leadership Effectiveness: Lafley's focus on EQ enabled him to lead P&G through significant transformations. His emphasis on empathy and listening helped P&G align better with consumer needs, driving product innovation. Leaders were encouraged to practice active listening in team huddles, which improved interdepartmental trust and agility.*

- *Business Growth: Under Lafley's leadership, P&G saw a resurgence in market dominance, with new product lines and a significant increase in revenues. His mindful leadership style helped guide the company through complex challenges while maintaining employee morale.*

- *Cultural Transformation: Lafley's approach helped shift the corporate culture at P&G to one that valued emotional intelligence and mindfulness as key elements of effective leadership.*

Rachel recalled reading that mindfulness and meditation were both important parts of the daily routine for some of these leaders. The answer had been there all along: the leaders who made the deepest impact weren't just doing more—they were being more. Mindfulness and meditation weren't side habits; they were daily anchors. And suddenly, her earlier question about what drives lasting success didn't seem so unclear anymore.

Due to having some crucial meetings scheduled early in the morning, Rachel decided to stop reading and hit the bed.

As Rachel lay in bed, her thoughts lingered on the passages she had just read. How mindfulness and meditation were not just occasional practices, but integral parts of the daily routines for some of the world's most accomplished leaders. It suddenly dawned on her—the connection between personal mindfulness and professional impact was undeniable.

Feeling a wave of clarity, Rachel jolted out of bed to grab her notebook and a pen. She made sure to jot down a quick note to revisit this insight with her team. It wasn't just about integrating mindfulness into leadership—it was about embedding it into the fabric of the organization itself.

She glanced at the clock. It was well past midnight, and the realization of her early-morning meetings snapped her back to reality. "Time to call it a day," she murmured to herself. She stood, stretched her arms toward the ceiling, feeling the satisfying pull in her muscles, and let out a deep, contented yawn.

Even with her eyes closed, her mind continued to race ahead, imagining the possibilities tomorrow could bring. But for now, she allowed herself the luxury of rest—a brief pause in an otherwise relentless pursuit of purpose. She knew that to lead with clarity, she needed to start with herself.

From Inner Clarity to Organizational Alchemy

Rachel's evolving perspective reflects a broader awakening that is now rippling across global boardrooms. No longer confined to spiritual retreats or wellness seminars, the integration of mindfulness, empathy, and values-based leadership is becoming a strategic imperative. A growing body of research underscores what Rachel was only beginning to intuit: that inner clarity, emotional resilience, and a sense of shared purpose are not soft skills—they are foundational to hard results.

A 2022 study by Harvard Business Review reported that companies with highly engaged workforces are 21% more profitable and 17% more productive. Employee engagement, in turn, is directly correlated with emotional well-being and purpose alignment—two outcomes significantly improved through spiritual and mindful practices. This suggests that the most forward-thinking companies are no longer asking *if* inner work matters, but rather *how best* to scale it across leadership and culture.

The Mercer's 2022 report on employees thriving and being more resilient when they feel a "sense of belonging" with "work that fulfills me" and "organizational purpose I am proud of". Rachel's realization—that spirituality could be the bridge connecting personal purpose with corporate mission—is increasingly being echoed by data-driven leaders across industries.

The transformation Rachel sensed from her two-minute meditation was not an isolated experience. Neuroscientific studies from institutions like MIT and UCLA have shown that mindfulness practices, even in short durations, can reduce cortisol levels (a stress hormone), improve focus, and enhance emotional regulation. Google's "Search Inside Yourself" program, which incorporates mindfulness and emotional intelligence training, is now cited globally as a benchmark for corporate mindfulness initiatives.

Aetna, one of the largest health insurers in the U.S., implemented mindfulness and yoga programs across its workforce. The result? A 28% reduction in stress levels and a productivity gain valued at $3,000 per employee annually. The hard metrics matched the soft transformation—creating a case study that bridges both worlds, one that Rachel has begun to navigate.

One of the most poignant reflections is the role spirituality could play in ethical decision-making. This is not theoretical. A 2018 report by the Ethics & Compliance Initiative (ECI) found that when organizations prioritize integrity, employees are significantly more empowered and protected: they feel less pressure to compromise ethical standards, witness less misconduct, are more likely to report wrongdoing, and face less retaliation when they do. When values such as empathy, integrity, and service are internalized—as they are through spiritual introspection—decisions tend to consider the long-term good of all stakeholders, not just short-term shareholder gain.

Companies listed on Ethisphere's "World's Most Ethical Companies" list consistently outperform the large-cap sector over five years, demonstrating that ethics and profitability are not mutually exclusive. Spirituality—rooted in self-awareness and connectedness—acts as a silent governor, guiding leaders toward the greater good even in uncertainty, and increasingly, research shows it can also contribute to stronger organizational performance and long-term profitability.

The global landscape offers compelling examples. In Japan, the fusion of spirituality and business is deeply embedded in tradition.

Corporate culture draws from Zen Buddhism and Shintoism, which emphasize simplicity, mindfulness, and reverence for nature. These principles are not overtly discussed but manifest through rituals, such as seasonal purification ceremonies or the respectful exchange of meishi (business cards), which are treated almost as sacred objects.

Equally important is the principle of kaizen—continuous improvement—rooted in spiritual self-cultivation. This philosophy drives innovation not through pressure, but through persistent, mindful progress. Underlying all is 'wa'—group harmony—a spiritual-social ethic that guides decision-making toward consensus, mutual respect, and balance. Japanese companies like Toyota and Sony embed these values into daily operations, cultivating an atmosphere where humility and harmony support performance.

Meanwhile, in China, ancient philosophies continue to shape corporate life—even amid rapid modernization. Confucianism remains a silent scaffolding in many businesses, emphasizing hierarchy, ethical conduct, and social harmony. Concepts like *Ren* (virtue) and *Li* (ritual propriety) inform everything from leadership behavior to negotiation styles. Taoism, with its principle of *wu wei* (effortless action), encourages leaders to remain adaptive, calm, and aligned with natural rhythms—rather than forcing outcomes. Chinese Buddhism, though less visibly corporate, influences attitudes toward compassion and detachment from ego. Though economic goals have often taken center stage, there is a growing resurgence of these philosophies as companies seek more ethical and human-centric models of growth.

Catholic traditions, too, offer valuable insights for corporate leadership—particularly through their emphasis on conscience, reflection, and service. The Ignatian practice of the "Examen," for example, is a daily spiritual reflection tool that invites individuals to review their thoughts, actions, and motivations—something that can easily be adapted as an executive mindfulness practice. The Catholic concept of 'servant leadership'—rooted in Christ's model of humility and care—has profoundly influenced leadership models around the world. It encourages decision-makers to prioritize the well-being of their people, especially the most vulnerable, aligning closely with stakeholder capitalism. Additionally, Catholic social teaching emphasizes the dignity of work, the common good, and ethical stewardship—values that, when translated into workplace policies, promote fairness, equity, and long-term trust. In environments where bottom lines dominate boardroom conversations, Catholic spirituality can act as a compass that reorients success toward justice, compassion, and community.

But how exactly does spirituality help build good character in leadership and employees? At its core, spirituality fosters self-awareness, humility, and a deepened sense of accountability. Practices like meditation, journaling, and ethical reflection cultivate a habit of pausing before reacting—an inner checkpoint that enables individuals to align actions with values rather than impulses. According to a 2021 study in the *Journal of Applied Psychology*, leaders who engaged in regular mindfulness practice demonstrated significantly higher levels of ethical awareness and prosocial behavior. These leaders were more likely to consider the ripple effects of their decisions, display fairness under pressure, and prioritize the collective good. By cultivating qualities such as patience, empathy, and moral courage, spirituality functions not as an abstract ideal but as a practical tool for character development.

The cost of ignoring this inner development is sobering. Consider the 2015 Volkswagen emissions scandal, where senior engineers and executives orchestrated software manipulation to cheat environmental tests. The fallout wiped out billions in shareholder value and severely damaged the company's reputation. Or the case of Theranos, where charisma and ambition were unchecked by introspection or moral compass—leading to fraudulent practices that endangered lives. In both cases, a culture focused solely on performance and optics might have been tempered by one that encouraged ethical reflection, inner alignment, and shared accountability. Had those leaders been equipped with the tools of spiritual awareness—such as regular self-inquiry, values-based decision frameworks, or even guided ethical dialogues—it's possible the warning signs would not have been ignored or rationalized away.

Perhaps the most groundbreaking shift Rachel sensed was in the meeting dynamics: vulnerability over posturing, authenticity over performance. This shift from transactional to transformational cultures is gaining traction in progressive organizations.

Research from Gallup found that when employees strongly agree that their company's leadership makes them "feel enthusiastic about the future," productivity increases by 29%, and profitability rises by 19%. That enthusiasm is less about polished PowerPoints and more about inspired leadership—leaders who are guided by values, open about their journeys, and committed to creating a safe space for others to flourish.

What Rachel witnessed in her peer group was a live case study of conscious leadership: a collective operating not from ego, but from ecosystemic thinking. From systems engineers to brand marketers, each voice was equal in the circle—not because of hierarchy, but because of shared humanity.

As Rachel read the playbook draft, it began to dawn on her that this wasn't just a manual for inner growth—it was a call to reframe leadership itself. In a world riddled with complexity, volatility, and existential uncertainty, the leaders of tomorrow will not just be strategists or technologists—they must also be wisdom-keepers. Spiritual intelligence (SQ), a term gaining momentum in leadership psychology, is now considered the third critical quotient after IQ and EQ.

According to research from the Journal of Business Ethics, leaders with high SQ are better equipped to navigate ambiguity, handle crises with composure, and inspire teams with vision—not fear. They do not seek control through dominance but offer stability through self-mastery.

Rachel's journey—while deeply personal—mirrors a broader cultural inflection point. The future of work is not about squeezing more output from already overburdened teams. It's about building environments where wholeness, wisdom, and purpose are not exceptions but norms. And whether it's a Toyota factory floor practicing kaizen, a Chinese CEO guided by Confucian ethics, or a Catholic leader drawing daily insight from the Examen, the global signal is clear: spiritual integration is a strength, not a soft spot. When organizations honor the inner lives of their people, they unlock a kind of exponential magic—where well-being becomes a growth strategy, ethics become brand equity, and stillness becomes the wellspring of innovation.

And so, the playbook isn't a doctrine. It's an invitation. To leaders like Rachel. To all of us. To pause. To breathe. And to imagine what business—and the world—could look like when guided not only by strategy, but by soul.

CHAPTER FOUR

CRISIS, CLARITY, TRANSFORMATION

Hard Choices: CFO's Report

The conference room was quiet except for the faint hum of the projector. Rachel sat at the head of the long oak table, her eyes fixed on the screen where the CFO's presentation lit up in stark white and red. The title was unassuming—Cost Optimization: Departmental Insights—but the contents beneath it carried weighty implications.

Rachel had been to countless meetings like this in her career, but something was different this time. As she prepared for the conversation, ideas from *The Spiritual Handbook for Leaders* echoed in her mind—reminders about conscious decision-making, human dignity, and leading with awareness.

David, the CFO, stood beside the screen, his clicker in hand. His voice was calm, but the gravity in his tone made everyone lean in. "We've identified several areas where costs can be optimized," he began, advancing to a slide that listed procurement efficiency, vendor overlaps, and contract renegotiations.

Rachel listened, nodding politely—but her thoughts were elsewhere. It wasn't that the numbers didn't matter. They did. But something in the room felt unbalanced, too reminiscent of the old ways she had begun to question.

Then came the departmental slide. "The sales team's bottom 20%—consistently underperforming even with coaching—may need to be let go," David continued. "It's a difficult call, but we believe it's necessary."

Rachel felt a pang. This was the same language she had used years ago during a painful restructuring—just business, just numbers. She remembered the single parent on her team who had pleaded for more time, more clarity. And how she had hardened herself in response.

Today, something inside her resisted that instinct.

She glanced around the table. Clara, the VP of Marketing, had tensed. John, the COO, leaned forward, brows furrowed. There was apprehension in the room—but also space.

Rachel cleared her throat. "Before we move forward," she said, keeping her tone calm, "I'd like to reframe how we approach this conversation."

David paused, surprised. A few others looked up, curious.

Rachel sat straighter. This was her moment to apply what she had been learning—not just about leadership, but about presence, mindfulness, and responsibility. "I understand the data, and I agree we need to be prudent," she continued. "But let's not forget these decisions impact people's lives. We're not just managing costs—we're shaping culture."

She looked at David. "Have we spoken with Amit and his direct reports? Have we explored reassignments or retraining options for that bottom segment?"

David hesitated. "Not yet. We prioritized modeling for the board."

Rachel nodded slowly. "Then let's do both. Let's gather those inputs before finalizing. If someone is willing to grow, let's give them that chance. Where that's not possible, let's be transparent and humane."

Sophia, the Head of Strategy, leaned forward. "This feels different," she said softly. "Not just the message, but the intent."

Rachel smiled. "It is. If we lead with empathy, we may not change the outcome—but we can change how it feels. And that matters."

The tone of the room shifted.

Clara spoke next, her voice more grounded. "On marketing—if cuts are inevitable, could we focus on consolidating campaigns instead of canceling them outright? Keep the strategic intent, even if scaled back."

Rachel nodded. "Exactly. Let's ask: what's the minimum we can preserve to maintain momentum, brand equity, and morale?"

As David clicked to the next slide, outlining automation and restructuring in operations, John spoke up. "Automation makes sense. But we need to do this with care. If we don't communicate clearly, we risk losing trust."

Rachel met his gaze. "Then let's communicate early and honestly. Offer support—internal mobility, skill-building, coaching."

She paused, then added: "We often say people are our greatest asset. Now's our chance to prove it."

A thoughtful silence followed.

Then Sophia returned to an earlier point. "David, the plan seems to treat each department in isolation. That risks weakening interdependencies—like cutting marketing might hurt sales, or streamlining ops could delay product development."

Rachel leaned in again. "She's right. Let's move away from isolated thinking. Let's hold this process with more integration and reflection."

David nodded slowly. "Understood. I'll revise the proposal to account for cross-functional impacts."

The meeting continued—still intense, still difficult—but now underpinned by a different tone: not just urgency, but intentionality.

When it finally adjourned, there was no celebration—but there was cohesion. A sense that something had shifted.

As Rachel walked back to her office beside David, she exhaled. "This is harder than I expected," she said. "But it's also an opportunity—a chance to show that we can lead with integrity and innovation, even in tough times."

David offered a faint smile. "Leadership is tested in moments like these, Rachel. And if anyone can guide this team through the storm, it's you."

She nodded quietly.

This was the real work of transformation—not in strategy documents or keynote speeches, but in the courage to pause, to listen, to lead with presence. Her daily meditation practice, which she had started recently, gave her space to reflect on the day—on moments of grace, missteps, and quiet course corrections.

This meeting, she realized, had been one of them.

Rachel's next engagement was just an hour away—a one-on-one with a key client who had specifically requested to speak with her alone. There was an air of mystery surrounding the interaction, as no formal agenda had been shared, leaving Rachel to prepare for the unexpected.

She had all the data from her team working with this customer. This included insights on the client's business performance—revenue and margin growth compared to past results and competitors, as well as feedback from their end clients. She also had data on how Zenyra Technologies was performing with this customer—revenue growth, progress against targets, changes in customer satisfaction, new connections made within the account, the quality of those connections, the current organization chart, and Zenyra's share of business in the account as compared to competitors.

With approximately an hour at hand, Rachel was evaluating her next steps, and there was too much at stake. One wrong move could make the organization, which was already under a lot of stress, crumble.

Unexpected blow

At the appointed time, Rachel and Rahul faced each other across a video call. He was immaculately dressed, as always—measured, polished, every inch the CEO of Catalyst Corp. They had known each other for two decades, built a strategic alliance that had scaled exponentially, and become trusted allies through crises and milestones.

Rahul, a seasoned leader, had grown Catalyst's market share significantly and was now aiming to make it the industry's top player within three years. Under his leadership, Catalyst launched a cutting-edge digital marketplace—connecting skilled volunteers with nonprofits, community groups, and governments in need. The platform quickly stood out for its tech-enabled reach and social impact, positioning Catalyst as a purpose-driven market leader. Zenyra was a key strategic partner in this journey, helping scale offerings that delivered a differentiated experience to end customers. The two companies often made joint announcements, presenting a unified front to the broader ecosystem.

But as soon as pleasantries ended, Rahul exhaled deeply— a sigh that seemed to pull the air out of the room.

"The board has made a decision," he said slowly. "After months of debate, they've decided to move our business away from Zenyra."

Rachel froze. For a second, she thought she'd misheard. "Wait—what?"

Rahul's gaze dropped. "It's not about you. Or Zenyra. The pressure came from our private equity backers. They want to consolidate with a company in their portfolio. I fought it, Rachel. But the board overruled me."

She stared at him. "Rahul, we built this brick by brick. We didn't just deliver—we co-created your vision. We invested in each other."

"I know," he said, voice rough. "You're more than a partner. You're family. But this is out of my hands."

Rachel's voice stayed steady, though her knuckles were white. "Do you realize what this will mean for both of us? For your teams relying on us? For mine, who has poured everything into this?"

The silence on the line was thick. History, trust, and disbelief hung between them.

After a beat, Rachel drew a breath. Her voice was calm but resolute.

"How much time do we have?"

"I am just fresh out of our board meeting, and I reached out to you as a heads-up," he explained, choosing his words carefully. "We will have the teams look at various elements at play, including transitioning, completing the in-flight projects, etc., and then revert. As of now, no one else apart from our board members knows about this decision."

"I need a favor, Rahul." The request hung in the air with quiet intensity.

Rahul, unsure of what was coming, still responded, "Sure." It was an eager response as if he were trying to make up for the bad news that he had to break.

"Give me 72 hours," she said. "Till then, let's keep the news between us, without the teams on the ground being made aware of it."

Rahul knew he could manage that and accepted Rachel's request. Before ending the call, he assured her that he would be available for her to discuss or strategize about anything. Rachel nodded in acknowledgement.

As the call ended, Rachel's mind was racing. Zenyra had not only lost a client but also a trusted partner. This wasn't just a business decision—it was also personal for her as she had invested so much time and energy in maintaining this relationship.

Rachel felt as if the weight of every challenge was descending on her all at once. First, the sluggish growth in domestic markets; then, the tense board meeting that had left her on edge. Next came the grueling cost-cutting discussions with her team, and now, this intense conversation with Rahul. It seemed as though the storm had finally caught up to her.

But it wasn't just the boardroom battles and market pressures gnawing at her—it was the silent war at home that no one saw. Her husband, once her biggest supporter, now barely looked up from his phone when she walked in late at night. Their once-warm conversations had turned into cold exchanges of logistical details. Her teenage son had stopped waiting up for her, his goodnight messages growing fewer, then disappearing altogether. And tonight, she had forgotten—again—it was her daughter's school recital. By the time she checked her phone, there were no missed calls. No angry texts. Just a single picture from her husband: their daughter on stage, smiling under the spotlight, performing for a crowd that did not include her mother.

The weight on her chest tightened. The storm outside was nothing compared to the one raging within her.

Sitting in her corner office, Rachel stared out at the city skyline. The towering buildings mirrored the immense responsibilities that rested on her shoulders. The corporation she led was grappling with some stiff challenges.

Rachel stood and walked to the whiteboard, but instead of rushing to solve things as she once would have, she paused. Breathing deeply, she recalled the stillness she had touched earlier that morning. This time, her strategy wouldn't be built on urgency—it would be guided by clarity. She realized that just as she had transformed her circumstances before, she could do it again. Her past wasn't just a memory; it was a reservoir of strength, proving she was capable of leading through even the most turbulent storms.

And as she fought her emotions, she resolved to one thing: Zenyra wouldn't crumble. If anything, this would be the fuel for their next chapter—a story of resilience and reinvention.

She asked her selective leadership team to reconvene this afternoon and messaged Amit separately, requesting that he attend the meeting in person.

But even as she outlined her next moves, a strange heaviness lingered—like a storm still swirling just beneath the surface. Logic, planning, and execution—her trusted tools—

suddenly felt insufficient. They had brought her this far, but now, they only seemed to skim the surface of a deeper unrest.

For the first time, the questions weren't external—they were within.

And in that vulnerable moment, and to her surprise, she felt the urge to do something she had never attempted on her own—meditating. She had once scoffed at the idea of meditation—dismissing it as the kind of thing other leaders turned to when they couldn't think clearly. She had always trusted sharp thinking over stillness. Until now. Sitting cross-legged, Rachel closed her eyes. The chaos of the day swirled in her mind—Rahul's call, the shock of their board's decision, the weight of two decades of partnership slipping away. Her chest tightened as she struggled to silence the relentless thoughts.

Then, as she took her first deep breath, something shifted. The breath felt like a bridge, anchoring her in the present. With each exhale, the tension began to ebb, like waves retreating from the shore.

For the first time in what felt like ages, she noticed the stillness within her—a quiet strength she had forgotten existed. It wasn't that the problem had disappeared; it was still there, waiting. But now, it felt like she could face it with clarity, not chaos.

As Rachel opened her eyes, the room seemed brighter, her resolve sharper. Meditation had not solved the problem, but it had given her the space to see beyond it. And that, she realized, was exactly what she needed.

The emotional chaos of Rahul's call slowly began to organize itself. The betrayal wasn't personal, but the consequences were deeply personal—two decades of shared triumphs now hanging by a thread of corporate strategy and portfolio real gnment.

The faint sketch of a counter-strategy emerged. It wasn't fully formed, but certain truths began crystallizing: the dependency of Catalyst's initiatives on Zenyra's support, the deep integration of their platforms, the board's limited visibility into ground-level realities, the goodwill Zenyra still commanded in the ecosystem—and perhaps, a compelling carrot to draw them back. Maybe—just maybe—there was still room to turn this around.

Not with desperation, but with precision. With presence. With purpose. And perhaps, for the first time, with trust in something deeper than strategy—a quiet knowing that when *intention is aligned with clarity*, the path forward begins to reveal itself.

She stood slowly, letting the clarity linger a moment longer. The weight on her shoulders felt lighter now—more manageable. For a brief moment, her eyes returned to the quiet corner of the room where she had just been sitting cross-legged—not with skepticism this time, but with something closer to trust.

The stillness hadn't fixed anything, but it had rearranged everything. The noise in her mind had softened, and in its place, something steadier had taken root. Glancing at the time, she smoothed her blazer, grabbed her notes, and stepped out of her office. Each step toward the conference room now carried renewed intention. She didn't have all the answers yet, but she had found her footing. The fog had lifted just enough to move forward. And though the challenge ahead remained as daunting as ever, Rachel felt anchored—no longer reacting, but responding. The corridor to the boardroom felt unusually quiet, almost reverent, as if the building itself sensed the gravity of what was to come.

Rachel sat at the head of the conference table, not just as a CEO, but as a leader now grounded in something more than urgency. The clarity she had accessed earlier flowed into her tone—firm, but anchored. "What we discuss here cannot leave this room..." The room buzzed with nervous energy as her core team—Amit, David, Clara, Sophia, and Uday—settled into their seats. The air was thick with anticipation. Uday was responsible for customer satisfaction and their success. Anything related to the entire lifecycle of the customer, right from their onboarding till their retirement, was the responsibility of him and his team.

Rachel's voice broke the silence, firm but tinged with the weight of her words. She began, locking eyes with each team member. "This is bigger than just a customer decision. It's about the survival of a partnership we've nurtured for twenty years. We have one chance to turn this around, and failure is not an option."

She outlined her conversation with Rahul, the crushing news of their board's decision to pivot away from Zenyra, and her frustration at the lack of foresight that had blindsided them all. "The real question," she said, her voice steady, "is not just how we can make them reconsider, but why they would choose us again? What can we do to remind them why we've always been their trusted partner?"

The room fell silent for a moment, her words sinking in. Then, like the strike of a match, the brainstorming began.

The initial moments were chaotic—a flood of ideas ranging from bold to improbable. Before diving deeper, Rachel paused. Energized by her morning meditation, she decided to do something unconventional. She invited the team to embrace a moment of stillness—not as a break, but as a space to reconnect with what truly mattered. "Let's stop for five minutes," she said, surprising the team. "Not to think harder—but to get quiet, so we can hear what matters." This moment of silence wasn't just a pause—it was a spiritual intervention. An opening for aligned action.

It felt awkward at first, but the effect was immediate. When they resumed, conversations were more focused, listening sharper, and the energy less frantic. Rachel also offered a new lens for shaping their pitch: 'connection over persuasion.' Presence is our competitive advantage," she added. "Let's pitch from a place of inner alignment—not desperation. She believed that trust would be won not just with logic, but through presence, clarity, and authenticity. Her stillness had become contagious, and it was starting to guide the team. Re-centered and more grounded, the team returned to the task with renewed clarity and cohesion. Amit leaned forward, sketching out strategies on the whiteboard, while Clara chimed in with messaging angles that could strike an emotional chord. Sophia worked to distill the ideas into a cohesive narrative, and David crunched numbers to strengthen the financial viability of their pitch. As they worked, her influence was evident—not in commands, but in the centered way decisions unfolded. The room felt less like a war room and more like a circle of intention.

Rachel reminded them that the pitch wasn't just a business case—it was a reaffirmation of shared values. "Let's speak to their purpose, not just their priorities," she said. "We've been their backbone in times of growth, their shield in times of crisis, and we need to make them feel again. Let's remind them not only of what we do, but why we do it—with integrity, with impact."

The hours ticked by unnoticed. Texts were fired off to family members, apologizing for late dinners and missed goodnights. Coffee cups piled up as determination replaced fatigue.

By the fifth hour, the chaos began to take form, coalescing into a three-pronged strategy for Rahul, his board, and the private equity team:

1. Data-Driven Storytelling

   David and Sophia outlined a compelling narrative backed by two decades of data, demonstrating Zenyra's undeniable impact on the customer's growth and resilience.

2. Strategic Alliances

   Clara and Uday proposed engaging the client's internal advocates—department heads who had benefited directly from Zenyra's solutions—to become their voice in the boardroom.

3. An Unassailable Value Proposition

   Amit sketched out an innovative offer: outcome-based pricing, a dedicated innovation team, and a joint venture with the private equity firm to co-develop solutions that would future-proof their business.

"This isn't just a presentation," Rachel said as the plan crystallized. "This is a battle for trust, and we're fighting with every weapon we've got."

Amit volunteered to reach out to Rahul to secure a meeting, emphasizing the urgency and the stakes. Uday was consolidating the voice of the customer. Clara began drafting the emotional core of their pitch, while David prepared financial projections to back their claims. Rachel was thinking that one good initiative which their team had taken was to capture the voices of different stakeholders on an ongoing basis.

As the team dispersed to execute their parts of the plan, Rachel stood by the whiteboard, looking at the skeleton of their strategy. It wasn't just about saving a client; it was about proving Zenyra's resilience and the strength of relationships built over decades. She traced a few lines on the whiteboard, realizing they mirrored thoughts that had surfaced earlier—quietly, during her meditation. Ideas she hadn't forced but simply received. Strange how stillness had offered what sleepless nights never could. For the first time, she wasn't just trusting her instincts—she was learning to listen to where they came from. Rachel paused and silently set an intention—not to win through pressure or persuasion, but through clarity, authenticity, and service. Her spiritual practice had begun to shift her leadership from being goal-driven to being purpose-aligned. She wasn't just leading to save a deal; she was leading to honor what had been built.

She thought to herself, *they may have made a decision, but we're about to make them rethink it*.

On her drive home, Rachel's thoughts churned relentlessly, each replay of the day's events making the knot in her stomach tighten further. Even as she prepared for bed, brushing away the day's fatigue, the nagging feeling wouldn't let go. Something was missing—a critical piece of the puzzle, the punch that could make their solution irresistible.

As sleep enveloped her, she clung to the hope that clarity would somehow emerge. A line on subconscious intelligence and creative problem-solving drifted into her mind—one she'd read years ago but never forgotten: "Go to sleep with an unresolved problem, and your subconscious mind will work on it while you rest. By morning, clarity will find you."

The next morning, Rachel decided to meditate, seeking solace in the silence of the early hour. She sat cross-legged, closed her eyes, and focused on her breath. The swirling chaos in her mind began to settle, like silt sinking to the bottom of a stream.

Fifteen minutes later, as she opened her eyes, the world seemed sharper, brighter. A cascade of thoughts poured into her consciousness, like sunlight breaking through a stormy sky. Ideas that had eluded her the night before now appeared with striking clarity. It was as if her subconscious had untangled the web overnight, then meditation stepped in to illuminate the threads. Together, they had cleared a path she hadn't seen before.

But it was more than mental clarity. Through meditation, Rachel had tapped into something deeper—a stillness that made space for awareness, not just of solutions, but of herself. The silence wasn't empty; it was instructive. It helped her hear the signals beneath the noise—the emotional fatigue she'd ignored, the subtle needs she'd buried. In the space between her breaths, she felt not just relief, but a kind of remembering.

This is what her spiritual practice had begun teaching her: that true leadership starts with inner alignment. Meditation helped her become less reactive, more anchored. It wasn't about escaping the storm—but learning to be calm within it.

Rachel felt a surge of energy, a renewed sense of purpose. The power of meditation, of stillness, and the subconscious mind had delivered its quiet brilliance. What had felt like insurmountable uncertainty now revealed itself as a puzzle with edges she could finally grasp.

More importantly, she was learning to distinguish between urgency and importance. Her meditation practice helped her shift from a constant state of doing to a space of being—from autopilot to conscious presence. This shift had been subtle, but profound. It was the foundation on which she now wanted to rebuild her life.

She jotted down her thoughts in a flurry, determined to infuse this newfound clarity into their plan. Today, she was ready to face the challenge—not just as a leader, but as someone who had unlocked a deeper wellspring of strength within herself.

She texted Rahul requesting a chat. Rahul was quick to respond, and they agreed to speak at noon today. She had jotted down her points to cover in the upcoming discussions. In addition to the meeting with Rahul, her mind was focused on her upcoming internal meeting just before it.

At 10 a.m., Sophia, Stan, and Cathy, the Head of HR at Zenyra, were in Rachel's office, on her request. Rachel wanted these key leaders to understand the full scope of the spirituality initiative and take the lead in implementing it across the organization. Rachel started the discussions by setting the context.

"Good morning, everyone. Thanks for joining on such short notice," she began, her tone warm but purposeful. "I've been reflecting deeply on how we can continue evolving as an organization—not just in terms of profits but in creating a workplace that truly nurtures our people." She paused briefly before continuing, "I believe we're at a pivotal moment where we can introduce a concept that's often overlooked: spirituality in the corporate world. Now, before you jump to conclusions, let me clarify—this isn't about religion but about creating a culture grounded in mindfulness, empathy, and purpose."

Sophia leaned forward, intrigued. "This sounds intriguing, Rachel. But can you help us understand—why now? And how would it align with our strategic goals?"

Rachel nodded. "Great question, Sophia. Think about the challenges we face: employee burnout, disengagement, and the constant pressure to innovate. Research consistently shows that practices like mindfulness and empathy can significantly boost productivity, creativity, and even decision-making. By integrating spirituality, we're not only addressing these issues but also building a resilient and innovative culture that aligns with our long-term vision."

As Cathy's question settled in, the room quickly came alive with a cascade of follow-ups—from practical concerns about inclusion and metrics, to legal compliance, cultural readiness, and operational impact.

Rachel welcomed the barrage of questions. She had expected them. Each one mirrored the pages she'd pored over in the playbook earlier that week. And rather than feeling challenged, she felt affirmed. The team was asking the right things. She took time to address each concern with clarity— grounding her responses in data, practical frameworks, and a clear sense of intent.

The resistance wasn't resistance at all—it was curiosity, laced with caution. And to Rachel, that was the perfect starting point.

When the discussion had run its course, she moved to closure with clarity.

"Cathy, I'd like you to lead on the cultural and communication aspects—how we position this initiative to employees. Sophia, please outline how this aligns with our strategic objectives and can drive measurable business impact. And Stan, you'll focus on identifying potential legal risks and developing mitigation strategies."

She took a breath, then continued, "Let's collaborate on a comprehensive approach document that covers assessment, implementation, adoption, and sustainability. This should include quantifiable metrics at every stage and a clear roadmap for success. I want this to be our bible for implementing spirituality in Zenyra."

"Got it," Sophia said, her tone energized. "This could be transformative if done right."

"Absolutely," Cathy agreed. "I'll start mapping out the cultural touchpoints and employee engagement strategies."

Stan gave a confident nod. "Consider it done. I'll make sure we have all the legal safeguards in place."

Rachel stood, looking at each of them with a sense of pride and urgency.

"Fantastic. Let's make this a game-changer for our organization. Time is of the essence here. Let's regroup later today with your thoughts collated in one place."

With a shared sense of commitment, Stan, Cathy, and Sophia exchanged glances, nodded in agreement, and walked out of her office—ready to begin.

After the team left, Rachel called her secretary to help shuffle and reprioritize her calendar. There were meetings she could delegate, reviews that could wait, and time she needed to carve out—for something far more urgent than another quarterly forecast.

The clarity she'd found in meditation that morning hadn't just illuminated Zenyra's path forward—it had quietly turned a mirror toward her personal life as well. After all, it wasn't just the professional front that needed transformation—there was much to address on the personal front as well. The silence at home had sharpened into something she could no longer ignore. Meditation hadn't fixed it, but it had stripped away the noise. No more excuses, no more hiding behind late nights and packed calendars. For the first time, she saw the cracks clearly—not as failures to be ashamed of, but as invitations to begin again. If she was to truly lead with presence and purpose, it had to begin where it mattered most: at home. She was determined to find holistic success on all fronts. Not balance in the conventional sense, but harmony—a life where fulfillment wasn't compartmentalized but integrated. It had to start right away, and it couldn't wait any further.

Personal Transformation

Rachel sat in her home office long after midnight, staring at the framed family photo on her desk. It was from years ago— before the late nights, the missed birthdays, the silent dinners. Her son had his arms wrapped around her neck, her daughter beamed with unguarded joy, and her husband stood beside her, his hand resting on her shoulder. That warmth... It felt like a lifetime ago.

For years, Rachel, like so many senior executives, had prioritized professional work over personal life whenever there was a clash. She was thinking that her sacrifices were justified, and this was the norm of the industry. But now, as she watched the empty hallway outside her home office, she realized that in chasing success, she had left behind the very people she was working so hard for. It was time to change.

The next morning, Rachel started with her newly found routine of daily meditation, which she had committed herself to. She sat in silence, closed her eyes, and let herself breathe. True, uninterrupted breath. No phone. No notifications. Just stillness. It was uncomfortable at first, but as she focused on her breathing, a strange clarity emerged. *She had spent years managing boardroom crises with strategy and precision—what if she approached her personal life with the same mindfulness?*

Drawing from the same principles of spirituality she had begun implementing at work—*presence, detachment from ego, and conscious listening*—she decided to rebuild her relationships with intention. Presence meant being truly there—not just physically, but mentally and emotionally—with her family, her team, and herself. Detachment from ego reminded her that not every conflict needed to be a battle won or a point proven. It wasn't about being right; it was about being real. And conscious listening, she realized, was perhaps the hardest: hearing others without interrupting, judging, or preparing a response. Just receiving. Just witnessing.

These weren't leadership tactics—they were human truths. And they had the power to heal what ambition had unknowingly fractured.

That evening, instead of rushing straight to her emails after dinner, she joined her husband on the patio. He glanced at her, surprised. "No calls tonight?" he asked, a mix of sarcasm and curiosity in his tone.

She shook her head. "No calls. Just us."

He raised an eyebrow, as if testing her sincerity. For a moment, silence stretched between them—thick, familiar, and a little uncomfortable. Then he leaned back in his chair and said, "You know, I used to wait up. Every night. Hoping you'd come home and want to talk. Eventually, I stopped."

Rachel looked down, her fingers nervously tracing the rim of her tea mug. "I know," she said quietly. "I kept telling myself it was temporary. Just one more quarter, one more client... but the truth is, I stopped showing up where it mattered most."

He didn't respond right away. Instead, his eyes wandered to the night sky above them. "You built an empire, Rach. But somewhere along the way, we lost the foundation."

She took a slow breath. "I've been meditating," she said, almost hesitantly. "It's helped me hear what I've been drowning out—including you."

He turned to her, a flicker of surprise in his eyes. "You're really trying, huh?"

Rachel reached for his hand. "I'm not just trying. I'm here. And I want to rebuild—slowly, honestly. Not with perfect answers, but with presence."

Her husband finally sighed. "It's not just about missing events, Rach. It's about missing *us*."

The words hit hard. She reached and squeezed his hand. "I know. But I want to change that. And I will."

With her son, it was harder. He had built a wall of indifference—one-word replies, distracted nods, barely any eye contact. *Rachel knew she couldn't undo years of distance overnight. But she also knew the power of small, consistent efforts.*

Instead of trying to force deep conversations, she started showing up. She joined him for breakfast instead of rushing out with coffee in hand. She asked about his favorite games, even played a round with him—badly, but with enthusiasm. Slowly, his guard dropped. The one-word replies became sentences. One evening, as they sat on the couch watching a movie, he casually leaned against her. It was small, but it was everything.

Her daughter, too, had been disappointed for too long to trust words. Rachel decided that actions would speak louder. She cleared her schedule for the next school recital—not just to attend, but to help her practice. When her daughter looked up, stunned, Rachel simply said, "I'm here now. And I'm not going anywhere."

For the first time in years, she felt the warmth of a hug that wasn't rushed.

Later that night, Rachel sat alone in the quiet of the living room, the soft glow of a lamp casting long shadows across the floor. The house, once just a stopover between meetings and flights, now felt alive again—filled with pauses, laughter, and conversations that weren't scheduled. She smiled, not at a grand breakthrough, but at the quiet rhythm returning to her days. The silence she used to avoid now felt like home.

Rachel began shaping her life the way she had structured her company's turnaround—*with clarity, discipline, and a commitment to balance.*

» Mornings were sacred—she started her day with meditation and affirmations, grounding herself before the storm of work began.

» Boundaries were non-negotiable—no late-night calls unless it was truly urgent.

» Presence was everything—when she was with family, she was *with* them, not just physically but mentally and emotionally.

Through spirituality, Rachel learned *detachment from guilt*—she stopped carrying the weight of past mistakes and instead focused on the present. She practiced *forgiveness*, not just towards her family but towards herself. One evening, she followed an exercise Samuel had once shared—writing a letter of forgiveness to her former self. As the words poured out, something softened. It didn't erase the past, but it released her from it. For the first time, she felt free to move forward—light, unburdened.

It wasn't just time that softened things—it was practice. Through meditation, she had learned to pause before reacting, to breathe before speaking. Her spirituality taught her to release control, to stop managing every moment like a crisis and start witnessing it like a teacher. She began showing up not as a fixer, but as a listener. And slowly, the gaps that had once felt impossible to bridge began to close.

One night, as she tucked her daughter in, her little girl whispered, "I missed you, Mommy."

Rachel felt a lump in her throat. She had faced boardroom wars, market downturns, and betrayal from within her own company—but nothing had ever felt as powerful as this moment.

She kissed her daughter's forehead and whispered back, "I missed me too. But I'm here now."

Turning the Tide Professionally

Back in the office, Rachel turned her attention to an earlier message sent to the core team regarding her noon call with

Rahul. This team, which had regrouped with her yesterday to strategize on bringing Rahul's organization back as a customer, had provided responses outlining specific pointers for the conversation. The pitch draft was still a work in progress, but they had a meeting scheduled with Rachel later this evening to review and finalize it together.

At precisely noon, Rachel dialed Rahul. His voice carried a lingering hint of regret over the previous day's revelations. Rachel, in her composed yet determined tone, began by expressing her gratitude for his unwavering support over the years. "Rahul, I've been reflecting," she said. "Do you believe in the quote, 'In the middle of adversity lies great opportunity?'"

Rahul paused briefly before affirming, "Absolutely, Rachel. I do."

Without missing a beat, Rachel went straight to the point. "Then tell me this—if my team were to create a proposition so compelling that it becomes impossible to refuse, would you back us in front of the board?"

The conviction in her voice seemed to catch Rahul off guard. It wasn't the tone of someone resigned to loss; it was the presence of a leader ready to fight. "Rachel," he said, "you know I've done all I could to push back. But if you have something transformational, I'm open to revisiting this with the board."

Despite having earlier insisted that the door was nearly closed, something had shifted. The certainty in Rachel's words—combined with the promise of meaningful impact and the weight of their shared history—gave Rahul pause. For the first time in the last few days, he felt a glimmer of possibility. And that was enough to give it one more push.

Rahul went on to mention Amit's request to present to the board at the next monthly meeting.

Rachel didn't hesitate. "Rahul, I'm afraid I need a bigger favor. We can't wait until next month. We need that meeting within days. Time is our biggest adversary here."

"Days?" Rahul echoed, his tone shifting to one of cautious optimism. "I can try, but I'm assuming you'll have something ready by then?"

Rachel didn't miss a beat. "Absolutely, Rahul. My team and I are already on it."

There was a moment of silence before Rahul asked, "And the second favor?"

Rachel laid out her request with clarity and urgency, detailing her vision and the role she needed him to play. For ten intense minutes, they strategized, rebuilding their bridge of mutual trust. By the end of the call, Rahul reassured her, "I'll do everything I can to get you in front of the board as soon as possible. You have my word."

Rachel thanked him, her resolve even stronger now. "We'll be in regular touch over the next couple of days to ensure that we iterate over the propositions. Together, we'll turn this around."

The call ended on a positive note, and Rachel felt a surge of purpose. This was more than a battle for a client—it was a test of their collective resilience and ability to turn adversity into opportunity.

Rachel dropped a note to the team on her positive dialogues with Rahul, and further details to be shared in their call later today for reviewing the propositions. The team reconvened in the evening and went through the pitch. It was getting refined delicately with every input.

Armed with this strategy, Rachel requested a meeting with the board of Catalyst, including representatives from the private equity firm—now scheduled to take place within days.

As the day arrived and she stepped into the boardroom, Rachel took a quiet breath—not to calm her nerves, but to anchor herself in presence. She wasn't there to convince, but to *serve the truth of their shared journey*.

Rachel opened the presentation not with numbers, but with a moment of reflection.

"Before we dive in, I want to say this: This isn't just about reversing a decision. It's about realigning with what's always defined our relationship—shared intention, service, and long-term impact. What follows is not just a business case—it's a values case. Because that's where real, lasting growth begins."

The presentation was a masterclass in persuasion:

» Rachel began with a heartfelt message about the 20-year journey Zenyra and the client had shared—a partnership not only built on delivery, but on shared values, trust, and a deeper sense of purpose. "At every milestone," she said, "we weren't just executing—we were co-creating something meaningful."

» She framed the next section not just as metrics, but as manifestations of values translated into real-world action—how purpose, trust, and shared intent had consistently translated into tangible business gains like faster delivery, greater agility, and accelerated growth. These weren't just guiding principles—they were operational levers that had moved the needle for

Catalyst. She then unveiled the data-driven story, showing how Zenyra's contributions had been indispensable to their success.

- Operational Excellence: How Zenyra had consistently delivered projects ahead of schedule, saving Catalyst Corporation millions in downtime costs. Rachel highlighted that these weren't isolated wins—they reflected a shift in how her teams prioritized clarity, accountability, and proactive collaboration. Their operating model, shaped around shared intent rather than rigid timelines, made agility a built-in advantage.

- Revenue Growth: Case studies highlighting how Zenyra's innovations had directly contributed to the customer's top-line growth. Rachel emphasized that this growth stemmed from co-creation, not just solution delivery—aligning deeply with the client's emerging needs and industry shifts. These innovations were a direct outcome of restructuring her team's mindset from "project-focused" to "purpose-driven."

- Resilience During Crises: Stories of how Zenyra stepped up during economic downturns and global disruptions, ensuring the client's operations never faltered. Rachel explained that their ability to remain steady in chaos wasn't accidental—it was the outcome of internalizing trust as a core operating value. This enabled faster decisions, deeper alignment, and mutual confidence even in moments of ambiguity.

This wasn't just data—it was a story. A story of partnership, trust, and shared success. Along with support from Rahul and his team, she had strong internal champions who reaffirmed her points, and all the data presented was validated by Rahul's team.

» Finally, she outlined the new proposal, emphasizing how it addressed both the customer's and the private equity firm's strategic objectives. The best part was that each of the propositions was backed by quantified dollar numbers which were validated by Rahul and his team. Rachel and her team developed a bold proposal tailored to the private equity firm's priorities:

- Cost-Reduction Guarantees: Zenyra offered outcome-based pricing that aligned with Catalyst's goals to optimize its cost structure. This was more than a financial promise—it was a reflection of Zenyra's commitment to shared risk and reward, grounded in mutual trust.

- Innovation Incubator: A dedicated team to co-develop new solutions—not just to stay ahead of industry trends, but to evolve together with intentionality, responsiveness, and a shared vision for impact. Rachel made it clear: this incubator was a manifestation of Zenyra's shift toward collaborative, co-owned innovation, rather than vendor-driven solutions.

- Risk Mitigation Strategy: Zenyra highlighted the risks of switching vendors, including delays, compliance challenges, and the steep learning curve for a new partner. Most importantly, the dollar impact due to interdependencies with top customers, where Catalyst and Zenyra's solutions were integrated. The team's ability to map these complexities and communicate them clearly was itself a product of Rachel's focus on presence, precision, and foresight.

- Growth in the Asia Pacific (APAC) Region: Rahul had shared that the big focus for his team was to expand their global footprint, especially in APAC. Zenyra was already riding high on its exponential growth in the APAC region over the last few quarters. Rachel had introduced Rahul to two of their largest customers in the APAC region, who had shared their openness to evaluate the offerings from Rahul's team. Additionally, Zenyra rolled out a thoughtfully designed outreach program for Zenyra's current as well as new customers in APAC. Rachel's early engagement and ecosystem thinking weren't just strategic— they were an example of how values like intentionality, foresight, and proactivity could lead to business acceleration.

Rachel finished covering the strategic section by drawing the board's attention to the deeper foundation beneath the numbers.

"We're not just proposing a set of deliverables—we're offering a renewed commitment to grow together with clarity of purpose and mutual empowerment," Rachel said. "This partnership has always stood for more than transactions—it's stood for transformation."

○ Joint Investment: Initiatives between Zenyra and the private equity firm to co-create cutting edge solutions, giving the firm a stake in Zenyra's innovations. Rachel presented this not just as a tactic, but as an invitation—to be part of a future built on co-ownership, shared learning, and trust-led innovation.

As she concluded, Rachel paused briefly, letting the numbers and strategies settle. Then she looked around the room and said,

"What we're presenting today isn't just a proposal—it's a reflection of what this partnership has always stood for. Yes, it's built on results over the last couple of decades, but more deeply, it's rooted in shared purpose, trust, and resilience. We've always shown up not just with deliverables—but with intention. We didn't just want Catalyst to grow—we wanted it to matter. And that's the mindset we bring into this next chapter."

The boardroom fell silent. The private equity representatives exchanged glances, clearly impressed by Zenyra's proactive approach and the new joint investment proposal.

Rahul, his voice steady but emotional, spoke up:

"Rachel is right. This isn't just about metrics. Zenyra has always brought something more—an alignment of intent, a clarity of purpose. That's rare. And that's why they've always been more than a vendor."

Rahul called Rachel later in the day and reassured her that this was one of the best pitches he had seen. While the decision was still not made, the board's mood was positive. He affirmed that they would get back to her in the next couple of weeks after further internal deliberations. However, the decision makers saw tremendous value in the propositions and, rather than taking more time, swiftly reached a consensus, expediting their decision-making process.

A couple of days later, the customer announced their decision to retain Zenyra, citing the strength of the new joint initiative and the risks of disrupting a proven partnership.

As Rahul called Rachel to share the news, his voice was filled with admiration. "You didn't just save this relationship, Rachel. You made it stronger. This is why we've trusted Zenyra for twenty years."

Rachel realized this wasn't just a win in business terms. It was proof that inner clarity could lead to outer impact—that when leadership flows from presence and purpose, even the most daunting challenges can be transformed into breakthroughs.

Rachel hung up with a quiet smile, aware that Zenyra's true strength wasn't just its innovation or execution—it was the consciousness behind its leadership. What had brought them this far wasn't just strategy, but a growing alignment with purpose, presence, and people. And this, she now believed, would be the foundation of everything they would build next.

Blueprint for Spirituality at Zenyra

Rachel was sincerely looking forward to the follow-up session with her team regarding the modus operandi for implementing spirituality at Zenyra. Over the last few days, there were a few iterations amongst them. Rachel also shared the playbook with her team just a day back, citing that she didn't share it initially as she didn't want their thought process to get biased. She was hoping that the team's approach would blend with the playbook and deliver a great outcome.

Cathy, Clara, Sophia, and Stan joined her later in the afternoon. There was an unmistakable sense of anticipation in the room—each of them carried the quiet confidence of having contributed to something innovative and meaningful.

"Everyone's looking energized," Rachel observed, glancing around the table.

Clara smiled. "We are. This has been more than just another project—it's felt like we're shaping something with real purpose."

"We've made strong progress," added Stan, "and we're excited to walk you through the high-level structure today."

Rachel nodded. "Perfect. I'm really looking forward to it. I'll hold my questions until the end—let's hear the flow first."

Sophia opened her laptop and cast the first slide to the screen. "We've structured the framework into six stages. Today, we'll walk you through the overarching design, including a section that explores how Zenyra's mission can align with individual purpose—and another on how management plays a pivotal role in bringing this to life."

Rachel leaned in, intrigued. "Sounds promising. Let's get started."

Framework for Spirituality, Mindfulness, and Purpose Alignment in Organizations

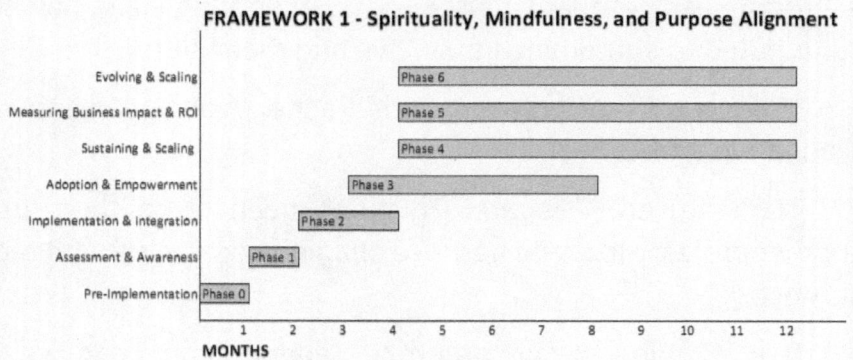

FRAMEWORK 1 - Spirituality, Mindfulness, and Purpose Alignment

Looking at the framework on the screen, Rachel was struck by its simplicity. *Could something that looked this straightforward really hold the key to such a critical and innovative initiative?* The simple six-phased approach felt almost too elegant for the complexity they were preparing to navigate—but perhaps that was the point. She knew, of course, that *further clarity would only emerge as they started peeling back the layers—like an onion revealing its core.*

"As you can see, Rachel," Sophia said, her eyes lighting up as she leaned forward, "we've carved out the first four weeks as dedicated prep time before we go live with the initiative." *Her voice carried the kind of energy that made the room lean in slightly, sensing the importance of what was to come.*

"This phase is packed with activities, but it neatly breaks down into three key buckets," she continued, gesturing toward the screen. "First, Compliance—we'll confirm alignment with all local HR and legal teams to cover every statutory, regulatory, and policy mandate. Second, Readiness—we'll make sure our internal teams are fully equipped and confident." *She tapped the screen with purpose.* "That means onboarding and training key stakeholders, drafting airtight FAQs, and proactively

138

mapping out how we'll handle any resistance or roadblocks before they surface."

The next 35 minutes were taken by the team to walk Rachel through the detailed plan. Each phase was supported by a clearly articulated objective and expected outcome. It was also broken into specific steps with metrics and specific time stamps/milestones. The team spent additional time on the new metrics like empathy index, ethical decision score, conflict resolution matrix etc. explaining the underlying rationale behind them and how they plan to accomplish it.

Sophia elaborated further, reinforcing how the A^2 HARMONIZE framework—a unified model combining *Aspire & Align* with *Head, Heart, and Hands*—would enable employees to map their personal aspirations to Zenyra's mission. This wasn't just about inspiration, she explained, but operationalizing purpose in a way that was intentional, measurable, and enduring. The framework had been designed to move from trust-building and self-discovery to role alignment, empowerment, and ultimately, cultural integration—making purpose alignment not just aspirational, but deeply actionable.

To support this, the team had already taken the liberty of fine-tuning Zenyra's mission statement to embed spiritual and human-centric elements—purpose, mindfulness, and holistic well-being—as foundational to its next phase of growth. This wasn't done in isolation. The team had built on the outcomes of an earlier organization-wide initiative, facilitated by an external consultant, where employees across levels shared what kind of mission and values they wished to see in Zenyra's future.

"That earlier work gave us the raw material," Sophia explained. "What we're presenting now is shaped by real stories, genuine aspirations, and collective intent. The revised mission statement isn't a top-down mandate—it's a reflection of who we're becoming."

The new proposed mission was shared on screen:

Zenyra's Revised Mission Statement:

"We empower individuals to thrive by fostering a culture of purpose, mindfulness, and inclusivity—driving innovation and delivering success through holistic well-being."

Clara then walked Rachel through the A² HARMONIZE framework, presenting it as a cohesive journey—starting with leadership readiness, moving through personal discovery, and culminating in sustained impact. Each phase of the framework—Foundation, Discovery, Alignment, Empowerment, and Sustaining—was tightly linked back to the mission, ensuring it was not just declared, but continuously activated through systems, behaviors, and storytelling.

Rachel nodded thoughtfully. This wasn't just a change initiative—it was a shift in consciousness, with a clear structure to support it.

Cathy touched on *Management as Catalyst*, explaining how Zenyra's transformation would succeed not through top-down directives, but by leaders showing up differently—as stewards of meaning, coherence, and care. This wasn't another HR initiative or a surface-level cultural refresh. It was an invitation—to lead with presence, to model purpose in motion, and to redefine success not just by revenue, but by resonance.

Leaders, she explained, would act as catalysts by actively participating in purpose-driven programs, embedding spiritual values into how decisions were made, how teams were managed, and how priorities were set. Leadership alignment wasn't a checkbox—it was the ignition point. Zenyra had committed to 100% leadership participation in spiritual alignment training within the first month, ensuring that the change began not at the edges but at the center.

Cathy highlighted how the revised mission—centered on purpose, mindfulness, and inclusivity—would be reviewed regularly, not just displayed on walls but reflected in one-on-one conversations, team goals, and company rituals. Leaders would help their teams map personal aspirations to Zenyra's evolving purpose using the A² HARMONIZE framework—revisiting this alignment quarterly to ensure it stayed real, not rhetorical.

She also emphasized that management transparency would be non-negotiable. Open channels such as a "Purpose Pulse" newsletter, Slack groups for well-being, and quarterly town halls would allow stories, data, and learnings to flow freely—reinforcing shared ownership rather than passive rollout. Feedback loops, including anonymous inputs, would allow employees to co-shape the journey.

And then came the resources—real investment in time, budget, and space. Zenyra had committed to dedicating up to 3% of its annual HR budget and up to 4% of work hours toward wellness and spiritual development. This signaled seriousness—an organization backing intent with infrastructure.

Finally, Cathy made it personal. "We're not just asking people to *believe* in purpose. We're asking our leaders to *live it*. Through recognition programs, spiritual mentoring, case stories, and consistent modeling—we'll make purpose visible and actionable, every single day."

In essence, management's role wasn't just to approve programs. It was to embody the change, creating the psychological and structural scaffolding for a culture that puts humanity back into business. Rachel listened carefully, aware that this moment marked a deep shift—not just in how Zenyra would operate, but in how it would *lead*.[1]

Rachel leaned back in her chair, scanning the room.

"Team, I'm impressed. The structure is solid, and I love the revised mission statement—especially how it connects back to individual purpose and aspiration. That's the key. Let's move forward with internal approval as per our process."

She paused for a moment.

"The plan is good, but execution is where we often stumble. We've seen ideas start with a bang, then fizzle out because departments aren't aligned, or employee buy-in is half-hearted. I don't want this spirituality initiative to end up the same way. So let's get critical. I'll play devil's advocate and ask some pointed questions."

Her gaze shifted toward Clara.

"Let's start with you. How do we make sure the survey responses are honest? That people aren't holding back out of fear? And how do we build trust?"

In a thoughtful but confident tone, Clara responded. "Good question," she said. "We can't just send out a survey and hope people spill their guts. If there's even a hint of fear, the whole thing falls flat. So, yeah—an outside consultant helps with anonymity, sure. But what really matters is what happens after. This is where Phase 1 of the A² HARMONIZE framework—

---

[1] For detailed framework, refer to the appendix

142

Foundation of Trust—becomes critical. It's not just about what we ask, but how we respond. That's what creates the safety people need to speak honestly. People will watch how we respond more than what we ask."

She glanced around the room. "And if they see leadership brushing off tough feedback or cherry-picking the good stuff, game over. That's why we need follow-ups—focus groups, open sessions. And not staged ones. Real conversations."

Clara paused, then added, "And stories help. Not the polished, HR-approved kind—but real ones. From people who doubted this at first, struggled through it, maybe even rolled their eyes... until something shifted. That's what makes it relatable. That's how we build trust."

Rachel nodded.

"Alright. How do we make sure this isn't seen as fluff? Something nice but disconnected from who we are?"

Clara replied.

"Honestly, this is where the frameworks—co-creation and aspiration-alignment—really matter. But they are not meant to stand alone. They come together in a single, unified A² HARMONIZE framework, which is about building *with* people, not *for* them. When employees help shape our values in workshops, they feel a sense of ownership, authorship, and accountability. It's not just a top-down rollout."

Rachel interjected.

"Okay. So you believe this will drive a shift in behaviors?"

Clara responded with a smile full of conviction.

"We are helping people connect their personal goals to the company's mission in a real, actionable way. When that alignment clicks, it will re-energize everyone. And to keep it grounded—we will track outcomes with metrics, spotlight real stories, not just polished examples, and tie leadership communications with our core values."

Rachel nodded, clearly pleased—Clara was headed exactly in the same direction she'd envisioned. She now turned to Stan.

"Stan, people are our biggest asset—but let's be real. Initiatives like this can trigger pushback. Some folks might say it conflicts with their beliefs. What are we doing differently this time?"

Stan spoke up.

"When things are vague, people get nervous—we've seen that. So we're keeping this completely voluntary and non-denominational. It's about well-being, not belief systems. Clara and Cathy will help keep it grounded in that."

Rachel raised an eyebrow.

"And if someone still feels alienated?"

Stan shook his head.

"We'll have anonymous reporting channels and HR will act quickly on any issues. Transparency will be critical."

Rachel leaned forward, her tone sharper now.

"What about the quiet skeptics? The ones who roll their eyes when no one's looking, or mock it off-site? They'll go through the motions but never buy in."

Clara answered first.

"You're right. Authenticity matters. If this feels like a checkbox exercise, people will tune out. Leaders at all levels need to actively engage, not just endorse. And we'll share real stories—how people are genuinely benefiting. Once employees see that, the cynicism will start to fade."

Stan added,

"We're not going to police humor—it's part of the culture. But we will encourage open dialogue. Let them voice doubts. That openness is often the first step to shifting mindsets. Plus, we'll highlight wins across the company. When people see results, perspectives change."

Rachel paused briefly and said, "Okay—so this A^2 HARMONIZE thing... it's not just a framework. It's a culture operating model, isn't it?"

Sophia nodded. "Exactly. It weaves purpose into how we lead, plan, measure, and evolve."

Rachel nodded and turned to Cathy.

"During the Green Future rollout, which we considered one of our critical initiatives on sustainability, yet we saw superficial buy-in, especially from middle management. Some supported it in meetings but quietly resisted change. How will we avoid that?"

Cathy didn't hesitate.

"This time, the leadership will go through coaching themselves. They need to internalize the benefits—not just for their teams, but for themselves. And we'll tie their participation to performance metrics."

Rachel pushed further.

"And the skeptics?"

Cathy replied,

"We'll start with pilot groups and measure results—better productivity, reduced burnout. Once leaders see the data, resistance will fade."

Rachel turned to Sophia next.

"Sophia, scalability has always been our Achilles' heel. We start strong at HQ but lose steam globally. What's different now?"

Sophia answered confidently.

"This time, we're taking a phased approach—starting at HQ, learning what works, and adapting as we expand. And we'll make it easy to access, using digital tools like mindfulness apps and virtual workshops, so no one's left out because of time zones."

Rachel asked,

"And how will we stay accountable across the regions?"

Sophia replied,

"We'll appoint local champions in each region. They'll ensure consistency while respecting local cultures. We'll track adoption rates and gather regional feedback to stay on course."

Rachel stood briefly and addressed the room.

"One of the biggest issues with Green Future was momentum. The task force vanished after a year. How do we make sure this initiative lasts?"

Cathy responded,

"We'll rotate task force members regularly to avoid burnout and keep energy fresh. Their work will also tie into career development."

Clara added,

"We'll publicly celebrate milestones. Show how these initiatives are making a difference, inside and outside the company."

Stan chimed in,

"And from a legal and resource standpoint, we'll ensure there's a dedicated budget and support. No one should feel like they're flying solo."

Rachel crossed her arms.

"Okay, but how do we prove success? I don't want this initiative getting criticized for being all feel-good and no impact."

Sophia replied,

"We've built KPIs into every stage—stress levels, engagement, productivity. These results will be reported regularly to maintain visibility."

Rachel paused, then added,

"Let's go deeper. We talk a lot about purpose alignment— but how exactly are we tying individual aspirations to the company's mission? Can we make that real for people at every level?"

Cathy jumped in.

"That's where the A2 Model—Aspire and Align—comes in. We're asking employees to articulate their personal aspirations through structured workshops and digital reflection tools. And to support that, we've refined Zenyra's mission itself to reflect purpose, mindfulness, and well-being. It's not just a new statement—it's a compass for the Integration and Empowerment phases of the A² HARMONIZE journey. Then we map those aspirations to tangible actions that serve both the individual and Zenyra's mission."

Clara followed up,

"It's not one-size-fits-all. For example, if someone wants to reduce workplace stress, they can lead mindfulness circles— directly contributing to our well-being pillar. Someone passionate about sustainability might co-lead a green task force that drives our environmental goals. And those seeking meaning beyond metrics? They can co-create purpose workshops that help others connect values to roles."

David added,

"Even leadership development is included. Employees who want to lead with integrity can enroll in spiritually anchored leadership programs, reinforcing our culture of conscious decision-making."

Cathy concluded,

"The point is: aspiration isn't something we're collecting and shelving—it's the fuel for the culture we want to build. And we'll track this through participation rates, personal growth indicators, and qualitative feedback over time."

Rachel leaned forward slightly, her tone more pointed now.

"That's good for internal morale, but what about the bottom line? How will we track the actual dollar impact this initiative generates—whether in revenue growth, cost savings, or retention?"

David, who had been listening quietly until now, stepped in.

"We're aiming for real, quantifiable, and measurable impact—things like lower attrition, more values-aligned applicants, and a spike in innovation. We'll track submitted ideas and see what gets implemented."

He continued,

"In dollar terms, lower attrition alone could save us millions annually, especially in high-skill functions. We've also linked this to productivity gains from reduced burnout and increased engagement, which translates into improved project turnaround and client satisfaction."

Sophia added,

"And we will be tracking revenue impact as well. With our research, we expect to get a minimum of 8–10% topline growth linked to purpose-driven teams. This isn't just culture transformation—it's performance optimization."

David nodded,

"We'll package these into a quarterly dashboard, aligning with board-level reporting. And for investor communication, we'll pair the financials with human stories—showing not just what changed, but why it mattered."

Rachel nodded slowly.

"And how do we make sure this doesn't just become another program—but something embedded in how we work?"

Clara said,

"We're building it into how we already work—reviews, goal-setting, day-to-day habits. That way, it's not just a side initiative. It becomes the way we lead and operate. Culture, not campaign."

Rachel looked around.

"To make this work, we need more than just enthusiasm—we need ownership. I'll also need a single point of contact. Someone accountable from end to end. This initiative touches every part of our culture, and without clear coordination, it risks getting fragmented or diluted. One person needs to hold the thread, ensure alignment, and keep the momentum alive."

Cathy stepped in.

"I'd like to take that on. HR will anchor this, with full leadership support."

Rachel smiled.

"You've got it. From us, support is a no-brainer. But I'll need two things: One, a detailed plan with milestones—let's move fast, but keep quality high. Two, a clear list of resources you'll need, including a budget."

Cathy nodded.

"I'll pull that together and run it by you tomorrow."

Rachel looked around the room again.

"You've answered most of my concerns. But I want commitment—from all of you. No roadblocks, no half-measures. Let's prove that spirituality can reshape corporate culture. Are we aligned?"

Everyone responded together.

"We're in."

Rachel closed her notebook.

"Fantastic. I'll review the final plan with Samuel and the other execs and circle back with their input. Thanks, everyone."

Two days later, she'd meet with the group again. The plan would go out 24 hours in advance—just enough time for thoughtful review and real feedback.

The Follow-up Meeting with the Peers

The meeting started at the appointed time. A two-minute meditation was followed by the usual greeting of *Om Shanti*. The kickoff was with the group acknowledging the well-thought-out implementation plan shared by Rachel on how to potentially implement.

When Samuel first sought permission to have Rachel join their group, there was a five-minute deliberation—an initial hesitation rooted in doubts about mutual value addition at that stage. It was a moment that now seemed paradoxical, given the spiritual principles they strived to embody. After all, their journey was rooted in selfless service, inclusion, and the collective growth of those around them. As Rachel now stood before them, presenting a meticulously crafted implementation plan that promised to revolutionize their mission, the group couldn't help but reflect on their initial hesitation. Rachel's insights had brought a pragmatic brilliance to their efforts, bridging spirituality with actionable strategies. It was a reminder that spirituality wasn't about judgment or exclusivity but about openness—allowing diverse perspectives to enrich the collective. In Rachel, they had found not just a valuable contributor but a shining example of how blending wisdom and action could create a meaningful impact.

Rachel walked them through some of the pointers her team had given in line with the questions raised by the group. The group listened actively and agreed that they would contribute to improving the implementation plan prepared by

Zenyra's team. The same plan would go as part of the playbook.

Rachel stood, the air charged with quiet anticipation. She offered a brief nod of appreciation before addressing the leadership team gathered before her.

"Thank you all for taking the time to review our proposed implementation plan for integrating spirituality and mindfulness into Zenyra's culture," she began, her voice steady yet warm. "This initiative is designed to enhance well-being, foster inclusivity, and boost productivity—all while staying true to our company's long-term vision. I must say, the initial playbook you shared has been incredibly insightful and laid a solid foundation for what's to come."

Her tone softened as she shifted from strategy to personal experience. "Although I couldn't attend the spiritual retreat with you all, I've personally experienced significant growth over the past few days. Incorporating meditation into my morning ritual has been transformative, and it's deepened my appreciation for the value of mindfulness in both work and life."

She paused, meeting the eyes of each colleague in turn. "That said, I'd truly value your feedback on the proposal. Please be as candid as possible—constructive input is what will help us refine and strengthen this plan. Let's work together to make this meaningful and sustainable for Zenyra."

Samuel was the first to respond. As always, his comments were pragmatic and numbers-focused. He raised the critical issue of return on investment, emphasizing the need for clear financial benchmarks to justify the time and resources being committed. If the company was to secure long-term support from finance and the board, tangible links to core business outcomes—such as employee retention, engagement, and productivity—would be essential.

Rachel acknowledged his point with a nod. "Absolutely, Samuel. We'll establish financial KPIs tied to measurable outcomes—turnover reduction, productivity gains, and other engagement metrics will be monitored throughout."

The conversation flowed easily from there, each leader offering thoughtful contributions. Rather than revisiting the foundational elements Rachel had already laid out, they added valuable layers of nuance and depth.

Leila brought up operational considerations—how the initiative would translate into tangible actions across diverse teams, and the importance of ensuring that spirituality wouldn't be perceived as abstract or disconnected from everyday work realities. Her suggestions around change readiness and communication tone would help shape how the program landed at the ground level.

Meera, always attuned to matters of inclusion, focused on the DEI implications. She praised the alignment between mindfulness and empathy, but urged caution in how the messaging was framed so that employees of all backgrounds and beliefs felt welcomed and respected. It wasn't just about what was introduced—it was about how it made people feel.

Daphne, drawing from her experience implementing cross-functional initiatives, warned of the challenge of sustaining momentum once the novelty wore off. She emphasized the importance of consistent leadership modeling and periodic reflection to ensure the effort didn't become a one-off initiative.

Oliver took the discussion in an exciting new direction. His suggestion to leverage AI for tailoring mindfulness experiences introduced a whole new dimension—real-time personalization, adaptable content, and data-backed insights on engagement. But he also flagged the importance of data privacy and employee trust if such tools were to be adopted meaningfully.

Rachel listened with growing appreciation. "These are exactly the kind of refinements we need," she said. "Many of your points are already shaping the plan, but the specifics you've raised will help us get this right in execution, not just intent."

The mood in the room shifted from evaluative to collaborative. Samuel recommended scheduling periodic financial reviews to track ROI and ensure business alignment. Leila offered her support for pilot programs, especially those involving frontline teams. Meera volunteered to help embed inclusive practices throughout the initiative. Oliver promised to explore tech solutions that could support engagement while protecting privacy. Daphne proposed frequent task force check-ins to monitor progress and adjust as needed.

Rachel smiled, visibly energized by the dialogue. "Thank you, everyone. Your feedback is invaluable, and your support will be instrumental in making this a success. Many of the questions you raised were the same ones I've already been pushing my team to answer—we'll share those insights with you separately for your input. Some of what you've proposed—like the AI angle—is entirely new and exciting, and we'll need to co-create those solutions together. I deeply appreciate your partnership on this journey. What we're building at Zenyra isn't just a program. It's a mindset shift."

She then walked the group through some of the core responses her team had prepared—answers to anticipated concerns and implementation complexities. The leadership team listened attentively, nodding in agreement and adding final thoughts on how to strengthen the proposal further. They agreed to collaborate on refining the implementation strategy, with the revised version forming part of the official organizational playbook moving forward.

As the leadership team concluded its dialogue, what emerged wasn't just a bold initiative or a client solution—it was a realization: real transformation in organizations requires more than just new strategies. It calls for a structure that speaks to the soul and provides meaning.

The A² HARMONIZE model—Aspire and Align—offered that pathway.

It recognized that **aspiration** is more than ambition—it's the internal compass of every employee, grounded in their values, passions, and vision for impact. **Alignment**, then, is the organizational response—how leadership listens, reflects, and constructs roles, rituals, and systems that connect the individual "why" to the organizational "why."

This alignment isn't abstract—it's measurable, motivating, and mutually reinforcing. Research from PwC indicates that 79% of business leaders believe purpose is central to success—but only 34% embed it into decision-making. There is also strong evidence that companies with high purpose alignment enjoy *greater employee engagement* and *faster innovation cycles.*

When implemented with care, the A² HARMONIZE framework turns disengagement into devotion and compliance into creativity. This happens not through mandates, but through a rhythm of reflection, co-creation, and cultural reinforcement—phases that move from individual self-awareness to organizational transformation.

Aspire and Align: Translating Purpose Into Practice

Every aspiration of an individual must be aligned with the organization's mission and initiatives—not superficially, but meaningfully. Below are several use cases that demonstrate this connection in action:

Aspiration	Alignment Example
An employee aspires to reduce workplace stress and create a positive environment	Spearhead stress-reduction workshops through existing mindfulness programs, reinforcing the organization's mission of holistic well-being.
An employee is passionate about environmental sustainability	Join or initiate a green task force aligned with sustainability goals—translating passion into purpose-driven outcomes.
An employee seeks deeper meaning beyond metrics	Co-create purpose workshops with the People & Culture team to help others reflect on values—supporting the culture of spiritual fulfillment at work.
An employee wants to improve collaboration and emotional intelligence	Lead peer support groups or emotional wellness circles rooted in values of empathy and conscious communication.
An employee wants to lead ethically and transparently	Participate in leadership training programs anchored in spiritual values—fostering a culture of integrity and authentic leadership.

These are not "extra" tasks—they are integrated into the flow of work, creating systems where personal growth fuels organizational progress.

Enablers: External Experts and Ethical Safeguards

Supporting this journey is a coalition of **external experts** who lend structure and trust:

- **Consultants** bring neutrality, ensuring confidentiality and psychological safety.

- **Neuroscientists and behavioral psychologists** ground the experience in cognitive science, making it credible to even the most skeptical.

- **Purpose coaches and DEI specialists** tailor the program to individual and cultural diversity—ensuring no aspiration is left unheard or unsupported.

But expertise alone isn't enough. **Ethical guardrails are foundational.**

Participation is always **voluntary** and **confidential**. Employees control what they share and with whom. No aspiration data is used for performance evaluations unless explicitly initiated by the employee. This clarity allows trust to flourish—because **aspirations belong to people, and alignment belongs to leadership.**

Leading with Purpose: Success Indicators

The A² HARMONIZE framework is designed not just to feel meaningful—but to *deliver* meaning with measurable outcomes.

Category	Metric Example
Engagement	% participation in aspiration discovery workshops
Alignment Quality	% of employees who perceive their roles as purpose-aligned
Organizational Impact	Drop in attrition; boost in discretionary effort and Net Promoter Scores (eNPS)
Culture Vitality	Frequency of storytelling, peer recognitions, and regional purpose activations
Innovation Output	% increase in purpose-driven ideas submitted and implemented (target: +20%)

Studies from LinkedIn, Harvard Business Review, McKinsey, NYU, and Gartner consistently show that employees who find a deeper sense of purpose in their work are far more likely to stay with their employers. Purpose is no longer a "nice to have"—it's a strategic imperative. In an April 2021 article, McKinsey emphasized— *"Employees expect their jobs to bring a significant sense of purpose to their lives. Employers need to help meet this need, or be prepared to lose talent to companies that will."* Similarly, Harvard Business Review has highlighted how purpose-driven organizations unlock greater energy, creativity, and commitment from their people. When individuals connect their personal values with their professional contributions, they don't just show up—they bring their full selves to work.

Leadership as Enablers: A Note on Catalytic Management

While the Management as Catalyst framework is explored in the appendix, it is worth noting here that leaders play a pivotal role in embedding this model. Their job is no longer to manage compliance but to enable connection—between individual purpose and the organization's broader mission. It starts with leaders listening differently, coaching with empathy, and modeling purpose-led decisions.

Purpose-driven leadership reduces burnout, strengthens trust, and boosts cross-functional collaboration.

Closing Reflection

The A² HARMONIZE framework is not a program to be launched, but a presence to be lived. It lives in the pause before a meeting. In a Seva hour that touches a life. In the reflection shared quietly between colleagues. In the courage to ask: *What truly matters—to me, to us, to the world we serve?*

Zenyra didn't just survive a business challenge.

It was emerging with a renewed commitment to purpose, a model for meaning, and a roadmap that transforms aspiration into culture.

In a world where companies are rethinking the "how," Zenyra chose to lead with "why."

And in doing so, it offered the rest of us a powerful question to ask—not just as leaders, but as humans:

What am I aspiring toward—and how do I align it with something greater?

CHAPTER FIVE

SIX MONTHS LATER

A few months had passed, and it was now July 2023. As Samuel walked out of the board meeting, he reflected on the various accolades he had received from the board members. The same individuals who had questioned his methods now celebrated the epic transformation of his company. It was a reminder of what he had always known but often felt alone in living: true leadership means having the courage to go against the tide, even when approval is uncertain. Success, after all, has many fathers—but failure rarely finds company. He was thinking to himself about the irony of the corporate world, where the quiet truths of failures are often buried beneath the loud applause of success. Though it is the failure that often reveals the true leaders. He thought back to a Harvard Business Review study that found leaders who had experienced at least one significant failure early in their careers were 23% more likely to succeed in senior executive roles than those who hadn't. Failure, handled with integrity and resilience, builds not only wisdom but credibility. For Samuel, the transformation hadn't been a straight path lined with wins—it had been paved with resistance, difficult decisions, and moments of doubt. And now, as the applause echoed down the corridor behind him, he knew that it was those less-visible failures, those crucibles of growth, that had forged the real victory—just as they had for countless others whose quiet efforts would never make the headlines. And perhaps more importantly, he understood that for real change to thrive, organizations must learn not just to celebrate success—but to respect the failures that made it possible.

It took remarkable courage for Samuel to implement a drastic initiative—something which was unheard of in the technology industry. To ensure the work was conducted only during regular hours, the company stopped email and phone access for employees after 7:30 p.m., and the services were reinstated at 8 a.m. the next morning. During the break, automated messages greeted folks to reach out to a specific colleague (with contact details). Naturally, that colleague was in a different time zone and was only available during their local 8 a.m. to 7:30 p.m. time slot. The company ensured that the globally dispersed teams were able to provide 24/7 coverage and smooth transitions. While this approach faced some initial setbacks, it ultimately proved to be a game-changer.

Samuel also committed to introducing holistic metrics for performance measures for individuals and leaders. They were rooted in the spiritual values of purpose, empathy, employee well-being, and inclusive, ethical leadership. This was being discussed in their weekly meetings and was made part of the weekly and monthly reviews. The outcomes were mapped with due weightage to their appraisal data by the HR team. To address the skepticism of senior managers, they invited a neuroscientist to present the science behind mindfulness and its link to productivity.

Despite initial huge resistance, the results were undeniable.

Engineers found mental space to innovate, and burnout rates declined. Productivity didn't dip—it soared. With structured transitions, work got done without employees feeling chained to their screens 24/7.

The company not only retained its top engineers but also saw an uptick in groundbreaking patents. The approach fostered a healthier, more sustainable innovation culture, proving that moments of stillness can fuel extraordinary breakthroughs. This helped in revenue and margin growth for the organization. The news about the transformed, healthier work environment spread like wildfire. Some of the key engineering leaders who had quit earlier, after reconfirming that these new ways of working were real and well-intentioned, applied and rejoined the organization. After all, the initial AI products had their sweat and blood all over them.

But what surprised everyone even more was what came next. The wave of cultural transformation didn't just resonate internally—it turned heads across the industry. Some of the best minds from competing firms, intrigued by the buzz and driven by a desire to be part of something more meaningful, applied proactively. They weren't just looking for a job—they were seeking an environment where innovation was no longer fueled by burnout, but by purpose. The organization had become more than a workplace—it had become a movement.

Samuel had redefined what it meant to lead in the technology industry—not by chasing endless hustle, but by instilling balance, purpose, and clarity into his company's DNA. What began as an experiment in mindfulness had evolved into a cultural shift, proving that true innovation didn't thrive in exhaustion but in presence and well-being.

As he reflected on the transformation, he couldn't help but recall the conversations he'd had with his fellow leaders from the retreat. Each of them had arrived with their own battles— some fighting dwindling growth, others struggling with disengaged teams, or the suffocating pressure of board expectations. Yet, here they were, daring to challenge the status quo, weaving ancient wisdom into modern leadership.

The shift was undeniable. What had once seemed radical was now a proven strategy, reshaping how employees engaged with their work. As the transformation took root, it became clear that Samuel wasn't alone in this journey. This was not just

Samuel's vision but a shared awakening—one that was taking shape across industries as his fellow collaborators embraced and championed the shift in their own workplaces.

Samuel was also thrilled to see how his fellow collaborators from the retreat had shaken up their organizations by boldly integrating spirituality into corporate workplaces.

Leila Costa faced declining employee engagement despite her consumer goods company's reputation for sustainability. To restore purpose, she launched the *Purpose in Action* initiative and a Seva program, inviting employees to volunteer in local community projects. Initially met with skepticism, especially toward mindfulness practices, the approach soon bridged personal values with corporate goals. By embedding spiritual principles into KPIs and reconnecting employees with beneficiaries, Leila sparked a cultural revival—raising satisfaction scores and making sustainability personal and lived.

At her microfinance institution, Daphne encountered deep mistrust due to top-down decisions that alienated frontline staff and communities. Guided by spiritual tenets of servant leadership and the Guru's teachings, she implemented a *Listening First* strategy, decentralizing authority and rebuilding trust through community co-creation and Seva. The result: a reimagined, high-impact financial model that empowered rural women, inspired internal cultural change, and gained international acclaim for ethical, grassroots finance.

Oliver and Meera had their own interesting journey leveraging spirituality in their part of the world. But the most exciting part was happening at Zenyra, spearheaded by Samuel's friend Rachel. What began as a bold experiment to restore purpose and well-being became a full-blown cultural awakening. Under Rachel's hands-on leadership, Zenyra didn't just integrate spirituality—it reimagined success itself, turning stillness into strategy, and presence into performance.

Samuel thought to himself that their collective efforts were no longer just personal experiments but signals of a larger potential movement—one that challenged the long-held belief that high performance required relentless hustle. What had started as introspective dialogues at the retreat was now reshaping leadership in real time, proving that a new way forward was not only possible but necessary.

The fictional turnaround stories may illustrate how spirituality— far from being an abstract ideal—can serve as a compass guiding leaders to reshape corporate cultures from within. These imagined scenarios were designed to show how leaders, when infused with a higher sense of purpose, might not only weather crises but orchestrate profound transformations, paving the way for enduring, purpose- driven growth.

Each narrative underscores a critical truth: real change begins with uncovering the root causes of challenges and tackling them head- on with empathy, bold experimentation, and unflinching reliance on data-driven insights. From inspiring stakeholders with heartfelt testimonials to refining processes for efficiency, and from piloting innovative programs to delivering undeniable, measurable results, these leaders demonstrated that the fusion of human connection and practical

execution was not just effective—it was revolutionary. Their relentless focus on bridging vision with action dissolved resistance and solidified the foundations for lasting, meaningful change.

Let's explore the concept around *Seva* initiative: embedding purpose through selfless service. How can organizations connect their workforce to its sustainability goals and other values? The fictionalized cases show the human arc of transformation, the underlying principle—that service fosters engagement, purpose, and organizational renewal—is deeply rooted in global research and business practice.

Across the world, organizations are discovering that encouraging employees to serve—whether through local volunteering, mentoring, or skill-based community work—does more than benefit society. It revitalizes people. It builds connection. And, increasingly, it drives business outcomes that metrics alone cannot deliver.

In the modern workplace, Seva represents more than volunteering. It is a philosophy of purpose-in-action, aligning individual fulfillment with collective contribution.

To bring this philosophy into organizational life, progressive companies are beginning to adopt what can be thought of as the SEVA framework—a strategic and time-bound roadmap to integrate service meaningfully into company culture.

The journey begins in Phase 1: Start with Intent, typically unfolding within the first one to two months. This involves aligning the initiative with the company's purpose—not as a box to check but as a genuine cultural shift. A clear internal communication strategy must follow, ideally with a CEO or senior executive championing the effort. The metric at this stage is clarity: measurable through employee awareness surveys and internal campaign engagement (such as open rates or attendance at town hall briefings).

Within the next two months, Phase 2: Engage Employees in Co-Design comes to life. Instead of dictating top-down activities, successful companies empower teams to choose their causes—whether environmental, educational, or community-based—based on what resonates locally. This approach ensures relevance and diversity in engagement. Metrics here include number of employee-submitted project ideas, team enrollment percentages, and even qualitative data through focus groups or listening circles.

By Month 4 or 5, organizations move into Phase 3: Volunteer Programs in Action. This is the pilot phase, where employees begin participating in structured service time—often one hour per week, one day per month, or through impact-focused team events. This phase must be backed by scheduling flexibility and managerial buy-in. Measurement is critical here. Trackable KPIs include total volunteer hours logged, participation rates by department, and correlations with short-term well-being metrics—such as pulse survey scores on meaning and morale.

By Month 6, the shift enters its most crucial phase: Phase 4: Align with Recognition and Reviews. Service is integrated into existing feedback systems. Volunteer contributions are highlighted in performance reviews, newsletters, and company meetings. Managers are encouraged to mention *Seva* impact stories in 1:1s and quarterly check-ins. The culture begins to absorb service not as a "side activity," but as a performance-enhancing input. Metrics at this phase include frequency of service-related mentions in recognition systems, increases in employee Net Promoter Scores (eNPS), and manager-level advocacy scores.

This four-phase journey typically unfolds over six to eight months—but its influence expands far beyond that timeline. In practice, many organizations find value in repeating the cycle annually, allowing fresh causes, new champions, and evolving stories of impact to reinvigorate the cultural momentum. As familiarity with the framework grows, so does the potential to accelerate its implementation. In fact, with effective planning, the entire process can be streamlined to three to five months. These phases, while sequential in theory, are not bound by strict silos in execution. For example, Phase Two—engaging employees in co-design—can begin within weeks of Phase One's initial rollout, while Phase Three may pilot in tandem with early co-designed ideas. Even Phase Four, focused on recognition and integration, can start layering in toward the end of Phase Three, rather than waiting for full completion. This fluid, overlapping approach not only speeds up adoption but also creates a living, breathing rhythm of Seva in the organization—where service is not a campaign, but a continuous practice embedded in leadership, culture, and systems.

Real-world examples illustrate the framework's potential. Salesforce, whose 1-1-1 model has shaped global philanthropic benchmarks, integrates service directly into onboarding and performance conversations. Over 7.5 million volunteer hours later, its culture of service has become inseparable from its brand. CEO Marc Benioff emphasizes that "giving back is part of our DNA," adding in a *Time* interview that employees don't just work for Salesforce—they work for a better world through Salesforce.

Cisco, through its Time2Give program, allocates five paid volunteer days per employee each year. Departments that fully engage in the program report higher collaboration scores and a 13% increase in retention. Meanwhile, Accenture's Skills to Succeed initiative, which taps employee expertise to help underserved communities, has reached over 5 million people globally, while boosting leadership capability ratings in internal 360° assessments.

Of course, no transformation is without challenge. Skepticism, bandwidth limitations, and inconsistent adoption remain common obstacles. Some managers may resist reallocating time to service, fearing loss of focus or output. Others may worry that only a subset of enthusiastic employees will participate, making the program seem fragmented or optional.

These risks are real—but they are also manageable. Transparency and strategic reinforcement are key. Leaders must articulate that *Seva* is not a cost, but a catalyst. Communication should be ongoing, stories should be personal, and involvement must be inclusive. Manager incentives can be tied to engagement rates, and service participation can be framed as a marker of high-performance leadership—not an add-on, but an asset.

The business case continues to grow. According to Deloitte, companies that embed purpose in culture see 40% higher retention and a stronger brand reputation among customers. Great Place to Work notes that employees engaged in employer-sponsored service are four times more likely to feel proud of their workplace—one of the most consistent predictors of engagement and discretionary effort.

In a post-pandemic world where employees are rethinking what matters, *Seva* offers more than a program. It offers a path. A way to bridge what we do with why we do it. A way to help employees experience their own significance—not just in metrics or promotions, but in meaning.

This isn't about building better corporate programs. It's about building better cultures. Cultures that serve—and in doing so, elevate.

In many organizations, leadership has long been equated with authority, control, and decisiveness. Yet, a different model is quietly gaining traction—one that doesn't diminish results but elevates how those results are achieved. This model is known as Servant Leadership, and at its core lies the principle of *Seva*.

Unlike traditional leadership, which starts with the ambition to lead, Servant Leadership begins with a deep desire to serve. The goal is not personal gain or positional power, but to support the growth, well-being, and success of others. In practice, it means leading with empathy, humility, and stewardship—values that align seamlessly with the philosophy of *Seva*.

The concept of Servant Leadership was first formalized by Robert K. Greenleaf in 1970, but its roots run far deeper—in teachings found in ancient Indian, African, and Eastern traditions. Today, it is being revived by leaders who recognize that service is not a sign of weakness but a strategic strength in a complex, human-centered world.

Transitioning to a leadership culture rooted in *Seva*—requires more than good intentions. It demands a shift in how leadership is understood, practiced, and rewarded. The SEVA Leadership Framework™ offers organizations a practical pathway to cultivate Servant Leadership across teams, systems, and culture. It is structured around four foundational phases, each of which aligns with a core leadership principle and unfolds over a realistic timeline of six to nine months.

The *first phase, S* – See the Whole Person, invites leaders to shift their lens: from viewing employees as roles or resources to recognizing them as full human beings. This phase typically spans the first one to two months and involves creating spaces where empathy becomes the norm. Leaders are encouraged to hold listening sessions, practice authentic check-ins, and learn to engage with team members beyond deliverables. At this stage, the goal is to build trust and psychological safety—conditions where people feel seen and heard. Organizations often track early impact through employee sentiment surveys and qualitative feedback during one-on-ones.

By the third month, the organization moves into *E – Empower from Within*. Servant Leadership thrives not on control, but on cultivation. This phase focuses on developing autonomy, voice, and ownership among teams. Leaders begin adopting a coaching mindset, encouraging participation in decisions, and creating growth opportunities that align with individual aspirations. Empowerment becomes the currency of leadership. Internally, metrics such as participation in team-level decisions, internal mobility, and upward feedback quality offer insight into traction.

As trust and empowerment begin to take root, *V – Value Service Over Status* unfolds between months four and six. This phase is where the *Seva* spirit becomes visibly practiced. Leaders model humility by stepping in to serve alongside their teams—not to prove a point, but to share in the experience. Status is de-emphasized; service becomes the badge of honor. Stories are shared where leaders defer credit, lift

170

others, and make collaboration more important than hierarchy. Cultural data begins to reflect a drop in competitive silo behavior and a rise in cross-functional cooperation. Peer recognition increases, and teams begin to notice the tone shift: it feels less about position, more about presence.

Finally, by months seven through nine, organizations arrive at *A – Align Systems with Values*. At this point, the behaviors introduced earlier must be reinforced structurally. Leadership development programs, promotion criteria, feedback loops, and recognition systems are updated to reflect servant values. Service to others—coaching, empathy, support—is no longer considered a "soft skill." It becomes a leadership requirement. Organizations measure alignment through retention data, performance reviews, and alignment between stated values and observed behaviors. The culture begins to codify what was once aspirational: leadership is not about who has power, but about who uses their power to uplift others.

This journey from *seeing* to *serving* doesn't replace existing leadership capability models—it deepens them. It moves leadership from the transactional to the transformational. The SEVA framework enables companies to scale humility, embed empathy, and reframe leadership not as authority to be exercised, but as stewardship to be earned.

Over time, as more leaders adopt this model—not as a technique, but as a way of being—organizations begin to shift. Not through pressure, but through example. Not through mandates, but through meaning. And in that shift, performance doesn't fade—it flourishes.

Satya Nadella, CEO of Microsoft, offers a compelling case. Upon taking the helm in 2014, Nadella shifted Microsoft's leadership tone from combative to collaborative. His first internal memo didn't speak of profit targets, but of empathy. In interviews and public talks, he frequently references how reading *Nonviolent Communication* and practicing mindfulness shaped his leadership. Under his tenure, Microsoft embraced a growth mindset culture, encouraging leaders to listen deeply, empower teams, and serve employees' learning journeys. The result: a nearly tenfold increase in market capitalization over a decade and a cultural renaissance at one of the world's most iconic companies.

Nadella is not alone. Cheryl Bachelder, former CEO of Popeyes Louisiana Kitchen, turned a struggling fast-food brand into a Wall Street success story—not by squeezing performance, but by serving her franchisees. "I had to flip the traditional view of leadership. My job was to serve the people who deliver the results, not demand results from people I barely supported," she wrote in her book *Dare to Serve*. During her tenure, Popeyes saw a 60% increase in profits and became a case study in service-led transformation.

This alignment between *Seva* and Servant Leadership is not just philosophical—it is measurable.

A 2023 meta-analysis published in the *Journal of Occupational and Organizational Psychology* reviewed 130 studies and found that Servant Leadership is positively correlated with employee engagement, psychological safety, and organizational commitment. Employees led by servant leaders were 24% more likely to stay with the company, and teams under servant-style managers reported significantly higher trust and collaboration scores.

Another study by the Greenleaf Center for Servant Leadership showed that companies with servant-leader cultures experienced higher employee retention and fewer HR complaints. The reason is clear: when employees feel respected, heard, and supported, they invest more willingly in their work and in one another.

But implementing Servant Leadership through *Seva* comes with *challenges*. One of the most common is perceived *vulnerability*. In many corporate environments, service can be mistaken for softness, and leaders may hesitate to show empathy or admit uncertainty. To mitigate this, organizations must decouple compassion from weakness in their cultural language. Executive coaching, leadership storytelling, and lived examples from senior leaders can help reframe service as strength.

Another risk is *lack of structure*. Servant Leadership, if not grounded in clear roles and accountability, can lead to ambiguity or slow decision-making. The antidote lies in clarity: being a servant leader does not mean abdicating authority—it means using authority to elevate others. Training programs and leadership frameworks can emphasize this balance between empowerment and responsibility.

There is also the risk of *inconsistency*. A few isolated leaders practicing Servant Leadership will struggle to shift culture if the broader system doesn't reinforce it. Companies that succeed embed *Seva* principles into their leadership competency models, feedback loops, and promotion criteria—ensuring that service is not just praised, but rewarded.

The cultural return on investment is profound. At Whole Foods Market, co-founder John Mackey designed the company's philosophy around *Conscious Capitalism*, drawing deeply from the principles of *Servant Leadership*. Leaders are expected to serve team members, customers, and communities. This service-centric mindset helped build one of the most loyal employee and customer bases in retail, and ultimately led to Whole Foods' $13.7 billion acquisition by Amazon in 2017. Even post-acquisition, Mackey remained vocal about preserving the soul of the company: "A business that only makes money is a poor business."

As these stories show, *Seva* is not an act reserved for volunteer days or CSR campaigns. It is a daily discipline. A mindset that asks, "How can I help others succeed before myself?" It takes courage. It takes clarity. And it takes consistency.

In a leadership landscape increasingly defined by volatility and burnout, Servant Leadership offers something radical: a path to high performance through humility. It doesn't lower standards—it raises consciousness. And when practiced as *Seva*, it reconnects leaders to the very reason leadership exists in the first place—not to command, but to care.

Ultimately, *Seva* as Servant Leadership is not just good leadership. It is *deeply human leadership*. And in the age of quiet quitting, cultural fragmentation, and disengagement, it may be the most quietly powerful force we have.

CHAPTER SIX

ZENYRA'S SPIRITUAL TRANSFORMATION

Zenyra Corporation, a multinational technology powerhouse, was at a crossroads. The company had achieved financial success year after year, but in the last couple of quarters, the growth was muted in their domestic market, which had the lion's share of their revenues. Additional dynamisms were at play—employee burnout, declining morale, and disengagement. To stay competitive, Zenyra needed a bold strategy that would not only address these challenges but also redefine its culture. Under Rachel Sinclair's leadership, Zenyra embarked on a groundbreaking journey: integrating spirituality into the corporate fabric.

The Beginning of Change

Rachel announced the initiative at Zenyra's annual leadership summit. Her vision was clear: spirituality would become a cornerstone of the organization, fostering purpose, mindfulness, and inclusivity. The proposal was met with skepticism. Some executives feared it would be seen as a soft initiative, detracting from the company's performance-driven ethos. Others questioned its feasibility in a fast-paced, profit-centric environment.

To address these concerns, a cross-functional task force was formed, including representatives from HR, operations, legal, customer service, and sales. Several leaders, who became key allies, advocated for the initiative's potential to drive sustainable growth.

Rachel had earlier asked for a single point of contact to lead the initiative end-to-end, and Cathy from HR stepped up to take on that role. However, recognizing the cultural shift required and the need for visible leadership commitment, Rachel decided to go beyond delegation. She chose to work closely with Cathy, adopting a hands-on approach to give the initiative the necessary momentum and credibility from the top.

Rachel personally led a series of discussions with key individuals and smaller groups, ensuring that leaders reporting directly to her fully understood and embraced the new vision. She engaged in in-depth conversations to address concerns, gather feedback, and build alignment within the leadership team.

Post this buy-in, the initiative got rolled out to the entire organization as per the phased-out plan. A pilot program approach was adopted during the initial phase, allowing for quick wins to emerge early. These early successes—supported by concrete data points and compelling employee stories—proved to be a critical success factor. They helped establish organizational confidence and motivated teams across functions to give their full commitment to the initiative.

At the broader organizational level, Rachel spearheaded strategic communications to articulate the initiative's purpose and significance. Through company-wide messages, town halls, and leadership updates, she reinforced the importance of integrating spirituality into Zenyra's culture. By maintaining clarity and consistency, she ensured that every employee, from senior executives to frontline teams, was aware of the initiative's goals and impact. She knew that the success of the spirituality initiative rested on one crucial pillar: clear, continuous, and consistent communication. Rachel and her leadership team prioritized open, transparent communication across the organization through interactive Q&A sessions.

A clear and compelling focus was placed on communicating the deeper purpose behind the initiative. By starting with the "why," the company succeeded in uniting its globally diverse teams around a shared sense of meaning and direction.

The first phase focused on understanding Zenyra's readiness for spirituality. Surveys revealed a staggering 68% of employees felt disconnected from the company's mission, while 52% reported high stress levels. A cultural audit uncovered a lack of inclusivity in decision-making processes and a rigidity in workflows that stifled creativity. Skepticism from different teams emerged, with some voicing concerns that spirituality initiatives might dilute business focus or be perceived as intrusive.

To move forward, the task force carefully analyzed patterns across survey data, cultural audits, and sentiment reports—identifying root causes and common threads. This process enabled them to translate employee feedback into clear, practical recommendations. They recommended starting with training programs and creating spaces for mindfulness. AI-powered sentiment analysis helped identify departments most in need of intervention, ensuring targeted implementation.

During the assessment phase, Zenyra undertook a deep dive into understanding the individual aspirations of employees. This included one-on-one conversations, anonymous surveys, and focus groups, helping to align personal goals with the company's overarching mission. However, this process wasn't without its challenges. A notable difficulty was the persistent focus on material goals, such as making more money or gaining titles, which many employees raised during these sessions. Additionally, some employees were resistant to discussing personal purpose, viewing it as unrelated to their professional roles. Others feared judgment, hesitant to share aspirations that diverged from traditional career paths. Instead of dismissing material goals outright, facilitators encouraged employees to explore the deeper motivations behind them—whether it was security, recognition, or a desire for impact. Interactive storytelling sessions featuring leaders who had successfully integrated personal purpose with business success provided tangible role models. Confidential peer circles were introduced, allowing employees to discuss aspirations in a safe, supportive space. Further coaching sessions and workshops to shift the mindset, emphasizing the importance of purpose, shared values, and long-term fulfillment over individual gains, were introduced. A simple framework was introduced for discovering individual purpose, prompting employees to reflect on key questions:

What activities make you feel alive?

What problems in the world do you feel naturally drawn to solve?

When do you feel most at peace and in flow?

This introspective approach encouraged employees to look beyond conventional success markers and explore deeper motivations that drive personal and professional satisfaction.

By fostering an environment where employees felt seen and understood, Zenyra nurtured a stronger connection between individual aspirations and the organization's greater vision. Over time, resistance softened, and employees began to embrace the idea that aligning with a shared purpose could lead to both personal fulfillment and professional success.

Phase I—Assessment & Awareness—took approximately two and a half months, slightly longer than the original 1–2 month timeframe.

This was due to a combination of factors detailed earlier and the depth of cultural audits across Zenyra's globally diverse teams, extensive one-on-one conversations, and the need to surface nuanced, often unspoken sentiment from employees at all levels.

The extended timeline was intentional and necessary— laying a solid foundation and ensuring that insights gathered were meaningful and actionable, not just surface-level data.

Phase II—Implementation & Integration—unfolded over 3 months.

Although it was originally scoped for 2 months, additional time was required for legal and HR reviews, and for customizing training modules to suit different departments and cultural contexts.

However, by strategically initiating Phase II activities in parallel with the final weeks of Phase I, the team was able to recover nearly a month, sustaining momentum while preserving quality.

Phase III—Adoption & Empowerment—stretched from Month 3½ to Month 8. While this 4½ month timeline may appear long, it allowed for deep cultural embedding of daily mindfulness practices, purpose-aligned KPIs, and peer mentorship structures that required trust-building and behavioral change—not just process rollout.

Phase IV—Sustaining & Scaling—began around Month 6 and continued for several months. Because global expansion and DEI alignment needed localized sensitivity, this phase remained ongoing, driven by a dedicated task force that monitored adoption metrics, cultural resonance, and innovation feedback loops.

Phases V (Measuring Business Impact & ROI) and VI (Evolving and Scaling) progressed largely as planned, encountering only minor issues along the way.

Implementation: Facing Resistance

The rollout began with leadership workshops on mindfulness and ethical decision-making. A lot of technical team members initially resisted. Engineers, data scientists, and product developers—trained to think in binaries and equations—viewed mindfulness with suspicion.

"We're engineers, not monks," one developer scoffed during a session, arms crossed as others around him nodded in agreement. The room buzzed with similar sentiments—this was the world of algorithms and precision, not meditation cushions and deep breathing. Many believed that productivity came from long hours and relentless problem-solving, not from pausing to reflect. Resistance mounted. Attendance at voluntary sessions was sparse, and some employees outright dismissed the initiative as corporate fluff.

Recognizing the skepticism, the task force introduced a new strategy: real-life, peer-led storytelling. Carefully selected employees across departments were invited to share how mindfulness had tangibly impacted their performance.

One of the first to speak was Wendy, a mid-level manager known for her analytical rigor. She shared how stepping away from a problem after a mindfulness session had unexpectedly led to a breakthrough on a stalled product feature—saving both time and cost. Her credibility gave the practice weight; it wasn't about soft skills—it was about solving hard problems more effectively.

Slowly but surely, the perception shifted. Skepticism wasn't erased—it was *engaged*. And that made all the difference. Mindfulness wasn't about becoming monks; it was about equipping minds to solve better.

Amit from Sales had launched weekly peer sessions that focused on applied benefits. Another such story came from Alex Carter, a junior executive who credited mindfulness with helping him close a high-stakes deal. By staying calm and empathetic during tense negotiations, he secured a $35 million contract.

Overcoming Challenges

Despite early wins, challenges persisted. Some employees perceived the initiative as another corporate directive rather than a genuine change. The adoption of spiritual principles being integrated into the corporate world posed challenges, especially the new metrics such as the Empathy Index, Ethical Decision Score, Trust & Psychological Safety Score, Conflict Resolution Effectiveness, and Ethics Training Completion— initially sparked confusion and resistance. Many managers were unsure how to objectively assess traits like empathy or ethical reasoning without seeming vague, subjective, or inconsistent. Others feared these "soft" metrics could dilute focus from performance. To address this, the task force launched targeted training sessions and created structured assessment tools with real-world scenarios, behavioral anchors, and 360° feedback models. Over time, as leaders witnessed improved team cohesion and psychological safety, the skepticism gave way to cautious support—and eventually, broad acceptance.

Leadership modeling also proved challenging. When a senior executive was caught violating ethical standards, Rachel acted decisively and terminated the executive's employment, reinforcing the company's commitment to integrity. Alongside this, she ensured that transparent communication was sent to the entire organization, reaffirming that ethical breaches would not be tolerated, regardless of rank. This move resonated deeply, rebuilding trust and demonstrating that spirituality was more than rhetoric.

Among the skeptics was Adrian, a senior leader who saw the spirituality initiative as a distraction and quietly escalated his concerns to a board member. When the topic surfaced in a tense board meeting, Rachel responded not with defensiveness, but with clarity and data—grounded by the stillness she had cultivated through her daily meditation practice.

Instead of confronting Adrian, she invited him into dialogue, choosing empathy over ego. That conversation—and the calm conviction behind it—sparked a shift. Over time, even the doubters began to see that spirituality wasn't soft; it was strategic.

Rachel's ability to navigate the conflict with grace and integrity became a case study in leadership, demonstrating that even the most challenging situations can be opportunities for growth and connection when approached with mindfulness and compassion.

Critical Turning Points

During leadership interviews, some concerns surfaced, casting shadows over the bold new initiative. Some voiced a sentiment, "Our team's always chasing targets. How do we make time for mindfulness?" These words echoed the struggles of a performance-obsessed culture that saw little room for introspection.

Peter, the Chief Diversity Officer, saw things differently. He recognized the initiative as more than just a corporate endeavor; it was a chance to heal the fractures within Zenyra's global teams. These fractures weren't just emotional—they were structural. In a sprawling organization with operations across continents, each country had evolved its own subculture, often operating in silos. Local teams aligned with regional priorities, but the ability to plug into a shared, unified vision was missing. This disconnect stifled collaboration, diluted purpose, and left many employees feeling like outsiders within their own organization. "This isn't just about mindfulness," he remarked during a critical strategy session. "It's about aligning our personal aspirations with the company's mission. Only then can we truly thrive."

Determined to turn vision into reality, Peter, under the mentorship of Cathy, the company's veteran HR strategist, crafted a program designed to resonate deeply with every individual at Zenyra. They had named it "Harmonize," emphasizing a truth often overlooked: people spend the majority of their lives at work, and it should be more than just a means to a paycheck. Rachel herself took an active role— speaking at town halls, recording personal video messages, and embedding the Harmonize philosophy into leadership training to ensure it wasn't just a program, but a lived belief across the organization.

The program framed work as a canvas where individuals could express their unique aspirations while contributing to a collective mission. This shift reframed the spirituality initiative from being a corporate directive into something deeply personal. Employees first explored their personal purpose through guided reflection exercises and one-on-one coaching. Then, in Purpose Alignment Workshops, they were encouraged to map their personal goals to team and organizational missions. Teams even co-created Shared Purpose Statements, articulating how their collective efforts supported the broader vision of Zenyra.

This shift reframed the spirituality initiative from being a top-down directive to a co-owned movement. Employees no longer saw themselves merely as cogs in a machine but as creators shaping their own paths within a shared ecosystem.

For the first time, many Zenyra employees began looking at the company not just as an employer but as a platform for self-expression and contribution. Through initiatives like *Seva* hours—one hour each week dedicated to community service aligned with personal values—and *dynamic role rotations* based on evolving aspirations, employees found new ways to express who they are through what they do.

Through this lens, they connected their roles with their life's purpose, igniting a wave of creativity and enthusiasm. The results were palpable. This was discussed periodically in a structured manner during the reviews while leaving the doors open for unstructured dialogues and mentorship at any time. Managers held space for these conversations not just during structured reviews, but through informal mentorship and real-time coaching. Recognition programs celebrated not only results, but authenticity, empathy, and creative purpose alignment. The result was a culture that didn't just talk about purpose—it lived it.

For Arun Patel, a quiet and diligent account manager, the initiative had stirred something unexpected. A workshop he'd attended—organized under Rachel's new leadership vision—

left him with a phrase that lingered in his mind long after the session ended: *"Fear blocks creativity. Detach, and you free yourself to act with purpose."*

It wasn't a dramatic revelation—just a quiet shift. But it changed everything.

Days later, while reviewing accounts, Arun paused over OmniTech Solutions—a long-standing client with flat engagement. Normally, he'd push a renewal and move on. But something about that phrase nudged him. What if he stopped selling and started listening?

He reached out to the CTO with no pitch, just a question: *"What challenges are you facing, and how can we help?"* That one conversation unlocked an entirely new opportunity: OmniTech needed a partner for their digital transformation—a role they hadn't even considered Zenyra for until then.

Arun hesitated before escalating it. But this time, he reminded himself—fear wasn't in charge. Rachel responded immediately.

"You saw beyond the transaction," she told him. "That's what this initiative is about."

Rachel personally backed the effort, assembling a cross-functional team and coaching Arun through every step. She guided not just the strategy, but the spirit of the pitch—centered in empathy, stillness under pressure, and service to the customer's deeper goals.

The deal closed quickly—a multi-year partnership worth millions. But for Rachel, the real win was what it revealed: when individuals grow, organizations grow with them.

At the next all-hands, Rachel didn't lead with revenue numbers. She told Arun's story.

"This wasn't just good business—it was conscious business. Arun led with presence, not pressure. That's what we're building."

Meanwhile, in the partnership division, another breakthrough had taken shape. Jeffrey stood at the head of the table, his usual calm replaced by a quiet grin. "It's done," he said, and the room exhaled. They had just signed a $50 million partnership with one of the world's top tech firms—Zenyra's biggest deal of the year. But what made it remarkable wasn't the number. It was the *how*. Unlike their usual reactive role, Jeffrey's team had co-created this deal from scratch. Months earlier, during a spiritual alignment session, someone had posed a question: *What if we shaped partnerships from purpose, not pressure?* Rachel had been in that session. She didn't just approve the experiment—she joined it. She showed up to brainstorming calls, challenged assumptions, and kept the team anchored to their intention: trust, alignment, and shared impact. Now, as she stood beside Jeffrey in the glow of their success, she felt it again—that quiet affirmation. A business built with soul could still win big.

The initiative's success in the headquarters paved the way for global expansion. Dipti, part of Cathy's team in HR, led efforts to adapt programs for regional offices, ensuring cultural relevance. In India, for example, mindfulness was integrated with yoga sessions, while in Europe, reflective leadership workshops took center stage. Rachel collaborated closely with Cathy and Dipti—not as a distant sponsor but as a co-creator, offering strategic input and helping local leaders adapt without diluting the core. Each region brought its own nuances. But the foundation—presence, purpose, and humanity—remained universal.

AI and technology played a crucial role in scaling the initiative. An app was developed to track participation, gather feedback, and suggest personalized mindfulness activities. The app's gamified approach boosted adoption rates to 75%, exceeding initial targets. Rachel personally championed its development, pushing for features that aligned with the initiative's deeper purpose—not just engagement, but genuine inner growth—and regularly reviewed user feedback to ensure the experience stayed human-centered.

In the months that followed, the ripple extended beyond Zenyra's walls. Moved by Rachel's purpose-led pitch, Rahul returned not just with renewed business—but with new opportunity. Catalyst introduced Zenyra to three strategic customer accounts (two in APAC, one in Europe), co-hosted joint solution workshops, and positioned them as a preferred innovation partner. Within five months, these engagements translated into substantial bookings. And Catalyst wasn't alone—other partners, inspired by Zenyra's renewed clarity and spiritual edge, began opening doors of their own. When you lead with presence and purpose, the ecosystem responds.

Results: A Transformed Zenyra

Within a year, the impact was evident:

- Employee stress levels dropped by 22%, while job satisfaction increased by 18%.

- Turnover rates fell by 15%, saving millions in recruitment costs.

- Productivity metrics rose by 12%, and innovation pipelines grew by 20%.

- Customer satisfaction scores improved, with 30% of clients citing Zenyra's values as a reason for loyalty.

- In only five months, Zenyra's purpose-led transformation drove over $350 million in new bookings.

Journey Beyond

Zenyra's spiritual transformation is an ongoing journey. Quarterly reviews and feedback loops ensure continuous improvement. The company's mission statement now proudly reflects its commitment to purpose, mindfulness, and inclusivity.

As Rachel reflected on the journey during the next leadership summit, she said, "Spirituality isn't a destination; it's a way of being. At Zenyra, we've proven that purpose-driven leadership and business success can go hand in hand."

Zenyra's transformation became a case study for other corporations, proving that when purpose and profit align, the possibilities are limitless.

What unfolded at Zenyra may be fictional—but the patterns it represents are strikingly real. Across industries, organizations are awakening to a deeper truth: spiritual intelligence is not a soft virtue; it is strategic capital. It fuels clarity in decision-making, resilience under pressure, and ethical integrity—qualities the modern workplace is desperate for.

What Rachel and her team experienced is increasingly backed by research. Studies consistently show that employees who align their personal values with their work feel more empowered, engaged, and capable of performing at their best. In addition, the American Psychological Association highlights that mindfulness practices—such as Mindfulness-Based Stress Reduction (MBSR) through meditation and yoga, and Mindfulness-Based Cognitive Therapy (MBCT) for depression—offer a wide range of benefits, including reduced anxiety, relief from chronic pain, and support for overcoming smoking and addiction.

Across industries, companies that embed mindfulness, purpose, and spiritual intelligence into their operations consistently report gains not only in employee well-being—but in hard business metrics like productivity, retention, and revenue.

Here are some well-documented examples illustrating the same:

At Google, the "Search Inside Yourself" program (co-founded by Chade-Meng Tan) trained thousands of employees in mindfulness and emotional intelligence. Internal surveys showed higher empathy scores, lower stress, and stronger cross-functional collaboration. Employees reported a 32% increase in emotional intelligence, with improvements in collaboration and leadership readiness as reported at SIYLI (Search Inside Yourself Leadership Institute). This positively contributed to Google's continued success in launching new products.

SAP adopted the same program globally, leading to increased employee satisfaction and lower attrition. SAP also launched a company-wide initiative to help employees discover and align with their personal purpose using self-reflection coaching. SAP reported a 40% increase in employee retention in key talent areas and significantly higher engagement scores in purpose-aligned teams.

At Aetna, 13,000+ employees took part in meditation and yoga-based stress-reduction programs. Employees reported a 28% reduction in stress, a 20% improvement in sleep quality, and a 19% reduction in pain. Aetna saved $2,000 per employee annually in healthcare costs and gained $3,000 per employee per year in productivity. This is as reported in Harvard Business Review, "Proof That Mindfulness Should Be Taken Seriously in Business".

Microsoft integrated mindfulness training across teams and began scheduling intentional "focus time" in calendars. The result? A drop in stress-related absenteeism and increased productivity. At

LinkedIn, former CEO Jeff Weiner publicly advocated for "compassionate management" and restructured meetings to include reflection time—shifting the culture from reactive to intentional.

In Japan, the manufacturing giant Kuraray implemented spiritual leadership principles across its plants. Over five years, the company recorded a 20% increase in employee retention and double-digit innovation growth, attributing this to trust-based leadership and purpose alignment.

General Mills launched a mindful leadership initiative program for 400+ executives. Participants reported increased clarity, better decision-making, and enhanced ability to handle conflict. A study found that 80% of participants felt a positive shift in their ability to lead authentically.

What these examples demonstrate—like the transformation seen in various characters in Zenyra's story—is that spirituality in business is not about mysticism; it's about meaning. It's about showing up whole, making values-based decisions, and fostering psychological safety that fuels high performance.

If you're a reader moved by this journey, ask yourself:

1. What values drive my best work?

2. Do my team members feel psychologically safe to speak, create, and challenge?

3. When was the last time I led from purpose—not pressure?

You don't need to overhaul your organization overnight. Start with reflective pauses. Invite conversations about "why" in meetings. Introduce a pilot mindfulness circle. Recognize ethical courage—not just outcomes.

As the Harmonize program showed, transformation begins with listening—first to ourselves, then to those around us. And when culture aligns with character, results follow.

As Paul Polman, former Unilever CEO, famously said:

"It's no longer about being the best in the world. It's about being the best for the world."

That's what Zenyra's journey exemplifies. And that's what workplaces of the future must aspire to become: places where people don't just work to earn—but to grow, contribute, and flourish.

In the end, as Rachel reflected, spirituality isn't a tactic—it's a way of being. And when organizations adopt this truth at scale, they don't just create better businesses. They create better people, better outcomes, and ultimately, a better world.

CHAPTER SEVEN

WHAT NEXT?

In-person Meeting of the CXO Peer Group

With these successes under their belt, the group decided to meet in person. In the second week of August, the group gathered in a serene conference room overlooking a tranquil lake, a symbolic setting for the profound discussions ahead. Rachel, Samuel, Oliver, Daphne, Leila, and Meera—leaders from diverse industries—were there to reflect on their journey of integrating spirituality into their organizations and to brainstorm ways to scale the movement across the corporate world. The air buzzed with anticipation and the unspoken acknowledgment that they were embarking on something much larger than themselves.

Rachel opened the meeting with gratitude. "First and foremost, I want to take this opportunity to express my heartfelt gratitude to Samuel, my dear friend, for introducing me to this transformative concept that has reshaped my perspective on leadership and life. I am equally grateful to each one of you in this room for your unwavering commitment, insightful contributions, and the courage to embark on this extraordinary journey. Together, we have not only challenged conventional norms but also proven that weaving spirituality into our organizations is not just a radical idea—it is a powerful force for meaningful change. Looking around this room, I'm reminded of how far we've come. Each of us took a leap of faith by embedding spirituality into our organizations. The results speak for themselves—increased revenues and margins, higher employee engagement, reduced attrition, and, most importantly, a palpable sense of purpose among our teams. But this is just the beginning."

As each leader shared updates, the room brimmed with stories—testaments to how spirituality in leadership wasn't just theory but transformative in practice.

Leila spoke first.

"At my company, we always prided ourselves on sustainability—but internally, something was off. People felt disconnected from the very mission we claimed to champion. That's when we launched 'Purpose in Action'—a spiritual re-rooting through Seva. Employees volunteered in their communities, not as a box-ticking CSR activity, but as a soul-connecting exercise. And the results were profound: a 15-point surge in engagement, clearer alignment between purpose and daily work, and most importantly, a return to joy. It wasn't metrics that moved them—it was meaning."

Oliver leaned forward.

"Our EV transition was facing internal mutiny. Veteran engineers felt obsolete. But when we reframed the mission as a spiritual call—to build a cleaner, kinder future—and involved everyone from slogan creation to product testing, the walls crumbled. Meditation sessions, storytelling circles, and servant leadership made the difference. One engineer told me, 'This isn't just a job anymore—it's a cause I believe in.' From ridicule to reinvention, spirituality was our bridge between legacy and future."

Daphne added her voice.

"I was losing touch with the communities we were meant to serve. The top-down model had alienated both employees and borrowers. Inspired by our retreat, I switched to 'Listening First'—decentralizing decisions and trusting frontline wisdom. We introduced guided reflection practices and embedded Seva time into the workweek. Community leaders started partnering with us again. Our microfinance success rate jumped. But beyond numbers, what healed us was humility. Spiritual leadership reminded us to serve before solving."

Meera smiled.

"You all remember the skepticism I faced—introducing mindfulness in a creative agency? People laughed. But after six months of 'Mindful Creativity Labs,' we saw a 30% rise in original ideas and the return of passion to our brainstorming rooms. Our biggest client said, 'You gave us more than a campaign—you gave us soul.' That word—soul—was missing for too long. Now it's our edge. Spirituality didn't just save us— it reawakened our creative spirit."

Rachel listened with pride and humility.

"Each of your stories reinforces what I felt deep down— we're not isolated disruptors. We're part of a rising tide. One that reimagines leadership through stillness, service, and soul. What was once viewed as soft is now our strongest differentiator."

Samuel, known for his visionary ideas, nodded. "It's been transformative. Our developers now start their sprints with mindfulness exercises, and we've seen a surge in creativity and collaboration. A sprint, in our world, is a focused period— usually one to two weeks—where teams tackle specific software development goals. Starting these with intention has changed everything. But as we celebrate these wins, the question is: how do we take this beyond our organizations? How do we make spirituality a cornerstone of corporate culture worldwide?"

Oliver, the automotive pioneer, leaned forward. "This feels like our moral responsibility. We've witnessed firsthand the profound impact spirituality has on people's lives—not just professionally but personally. Imagine if leaders across industries embraced this. The corporate world could become a force for good, addressing profit with purpose and people."

Leila, a renowned advocate for social equity within corporations, added, "It's not just about making workplaces better; it's about setting an example for future generations. If we succeed, we'll redefine success itself. But we need a concrete plan."

Meera leaned forward, speaking with clarity and conviction. "We need to be pragmatic. Here's how we could approach this:

First, create a Universal Playbook—we document best practices and frameworks, much like our original version, but evolve it so it's adaptable across industries."

Samuel raised an eyebrow. "Wait—when you say 'like our original playbook,' you mean the one we all used internally, right? The one that mapped out purpose alignment, leadership storytelling, mindfulness practices..."

Meera nodded. "Exactly. That playbook laid the groundwork. We know it worked—across different geographies, team sizes, and cultures. But now, the idea is to build a more modular, open-source version—one that other organizations can pick up and tailor. It should be practical enough for a startup and scalable enough for a multinational."

Rachel interjected, her tone energized. "Let's also cross-pollinate. We have real-world results—reduced attrition, improved engagement scores, and innovation metrics. That data needs to be part of the playbook. If we want to move industries, not just organizations, we need credibility and proof."

Daphne leaned in, nodding at the enthusiasm in the room. "If we're turning our internal playbook into a universal one, we need to keep it simple, scalable, and smart. This universal playbook won't prescribe, but will act as a guide. To evolve this into a Universal Playbook, here's how organizations and changemakers can proceed:

First, we need to preserve core practices and broaden the scope: Retain high-impact modules from the original playbook—like daily mindfulness practices, leadership alignment rituals, and storytelling circles—but reframe them with industry-agnostic language and flexible implementation pathways.

Secondly, capture cross-industry insights: Collaborate with other organizations that have applied or adapted the original playbook. Document how different sectors (tech, healthcare, manufacturing, education) have integrated these practices uniquely, enriching the universal version.

The third step is critical to reap the maximum benefits for each organization. We need a modular design for customization: Structure the Universal Playbook into adaptable modules—introductory, intermediate, and advanced—so companies can calibrate based on readiness. This ensures that a 50-person startup and a 50,000-person enterprise can both find relevance.

The fourth step will ensure monitoring of metrics by embedding toolkits and KPIs. These include actionable tools: survey templates, onboarding modules, facilitator guides, and KPI trackers that show tangible outcomes like reduced burnout, increased innovation, or improved team cohesion.

Next, we must build a shared platform: Host the playbook on a collaborative, open-source platform where organizations can contribute updates, case studies, and best practices—creating a living document that evolves with the collective experience of its users.

And finally, let's keep it alive. Host it on an open platform where others can contribute and evolve it over time. It becomes a community-built resource, not a static manual."

Oliver leaned in. "This sounds good. And if we build that, why not bring people together to launch it? Think big—a Global Summit for Spiritual Leadership. Invite CEOs, CHROs, policymakers, and thought leaders. We position it not just as an event, but a global call to action."

Leila nodded enthusiastically. "A summit could accelerate adoption. We'd use it to unveil the Universal Playbook, share success stories, run immersive workshops, and forge partnerships. We could even offer a preview of what training and implementation could look like across various sectors."

Samuel, still cautious but intrigued, asked, "And who would drive this? We all have full plates."

Meera replied, "We form a Global Council—a dedicated task force that curates the content, manages the summit, and stewards the rollout. Each of us nominates someone senior, committed, and aligned. And we meet quarterly to track progress."

Rachel added, "We'll also need to bring in academic institutions—especially leadership and MBA programs. If we want this to last beyond us, the next generation needs to be fluent in this way of thinking. Imagine spirituality as a core leadership skill taught alongside strategy and finance."

Daphne nodded thoughtfully. "Curriculum partnerships. That's smart. And it roots the concept in something structured and credible."

Meera continued, "The Universal Playbook becomes the heart of the initiative. The summit gives it voice and visibility.

And the council ensures it's governed, refined, and expanded over time."

Rachel paused for a moment, taking it in. "We're not starting from scratch. We're scaling what already exists. That gives us a head start."

Samuel, always the pragmatist, folded his arms. "If we do this, we do it right. That means funding, metrics, infrastructure."

Oliver smiled. "Which is why we align early on the model. We define success metrics, ROI benchmarks, and partner with organizations that share the vision." He looked around. "This doesn't need to be a side project. It can be the start of something transformative."

Leila leaned in. "Let's also consider coalition funding. If we each bring in partners—foundations, conscious capital funds, maybe even ESG-aligned VCs—we'll have the resources to scale with integrity."

The room fell into thoughtful silence, each leader processing the scale and weight of what was forming.

Daphne, a trailblazer in sustainability, raised a cautionary point. "While these ideas are excellent, we must tread carefully. The word 'spirituality' can be polarizing. We need to frame it as a universal approach to well-being and purpose rather than something tied to specific beliefs. Messaging is critical."

Rachel leaned forward, her voice filled with conviction. "If we get this right, think about what we could achieve. We'll create more humane workplaces, improve mental health and emotional resilience across industries, and enhance innovation and productivity through purposeful leadership."

Samuel folded his arms, shaking his head slightly. "I hear you, Rachel, but let's not underestimate the challenges ahead. Traditionalists will resist this—they'll see it as 'soft' or impractical. Plus, leaders like us already have packed schedules. This will require a serious time commitment. And without measurable metrics, how do we prove it's working?"

Oliver tapped his pen on the table, thinking. "Then we need a dedicated team to drive this forward. What if each of us nominates a senior leader from our organizations to form a task force? They could develop and refine a universal playbook, create training modules for leaders, and plan a global launch event."

He looked around the room. "That way, we don't just talk about it—we make it happen."

Leila added, "Funding will also be key. If we're serious, we'll need resources for research, marketing, and outreach. Perhaps we can pool contributions or seek grants from philanthropic organizations aligned with our vision."

As the discussion deepened, the group realized the scale of their ambition.

Meera emphasized, "This isn't a side project. If we're committing to this, it needs to be a priority. Let's dedicate quarterly meetings like this one to track progress and adapt our strategies. Each of us must also be willing to speak publicly about this initiative, leveraging our platforms to inspire others."

As the meeting drew to a close, Rachel posed a pivotal question. "Are we all in? This isn't just about our organizations anymore. It's about creating a legacy that transcends industries and borders."

One by one, the leaders expressed their agreement, each voice carrying a blend of determination and hope. Samuel summed it up: "This is more than a movement. It's a revolution of the heart in the corporate world. Let's make it happen."

The meeting ended with a unanimous decision to move forward. As they parted ways, the group felt a profound sense of purpose, knowing they were about to embark on a journey that could redefine the future of leadership and business. They didn't just leave with a plan; they left with a mission.

Rachel's Big Decision

The Pull of Purpose

As Rachel walked out of the room, the air felt electric with the weight of the decision they had just made. The energy of the meeting still pulsed through her veins, but as she moved toward the quiet of her office, the magnitude of what lay ahead began to crystallize in her mind.

Sitting by the window overlooking the city skyline, Rachel allowed herself a rare moment of solitude. She gazed at the horizon, the setting sun casting a warm glow that seemed to merge seamlessly with her thoughts. The revolution of the heart in the corporate world—Samuel's words echoed in her mind. Could she truly leave behind the world she had meticulously built over decades to pursue something so intangible yet profound?

Rachel's heart swelled as she envisioned organizations worldwide adopting practices that honored not just profits, but people's souls. A workplace culture that valued mindfulness, compassion, and purpose over relentless competition could transform lives—not just for employees but for their families and communities. She imagined leaders being trained to make decisions rooted in empathy and integrity, cascading positivity across the globe. This vision was compelling, almost magnetic.

And yet, it wasn't without its challenges.

Not only this, but Rachel had also experienced tremendous success by leveraging spirituality in her personal life as well.

Over time, Rachel witnessed a profound transformation not just in the atmosphere of her home, but in its emotional fabric. Her daily meditation practice had brought a sense of calm that softened her once-reactive temperament. Instead of rushing through conversations or multitasking during family dinners, she had learned the art of *sacred presence*—giving her full attention to the moment. Guided journaling helped her process residual resentment and anxiety, while evening gratitude reflections kept her grounded in the blessings she had once overlooked. As her inner peace deepened, so did the harmony around her. The tension that once lingered in the air gave way to laughter, shared silences, and an unspoken sense of safety. Her home was no longer just a place she returned to—it became a sanctuary of connection and renewal.

Rachel's embrace of spirituality redefined what success meant to her. She no longer chased validation through packed schedules or performance metrics; instead, she found fulfillment in alignment—living by her values, not her calendar. Her children began seeking her out, not just for needs, but for comfort and companionship. Her relationship with her husband, once brittle from neglect, began to flourish with shared rituals like morning walks and weekend cookouts. There was less striving, more being. And in those still, sacred moments—reading beside her daughter, laughing over burnt pancakes, meditating under the early sun—Rachel discovered something she hadn't felt in years: wholeness. Through spirituality, she hadn't just repaired her relationships; she had returned to herself.

Her practical mind began to dissect the implications.

Moreover, her personal sacrifices loomed large. Moving away from the corporate sphere meant stepping away from a position of immense influence and financial security. It meant venturing into uncharted territory, where success wasn't guaranteed. Would she be letting down her family? Her employees? Herself?

Rachel reached for her journal, a practice she had embraced for clarity during pivotal moments. She sketched out two columns: one for the potential benefits of this shift, and the other for its risks.

Pros:

1. *Global Impact:* Helping organizations foster humanity and purpose could ripple into creating a better world.

2. *Legacy:* Leaving a meaningful legacy that transcended financial success.

3. *Personal Growth:* A journey that would challenge her to grow spiritually and emotionally.

Cons:

1. *Uncertainty:* The risk of failure in an endeavor so idealistic.

2. *Resistance:* Pushback from skeptics and entrenched systems.

3. *Personal and Financial Sacrifice:* Leaving behind influence and financial security meant risking stability, identity, and the expectations of those who relied on her.

As Rachel reviewed the lists, she felt the familiar pull of doubt. The cons whispered of risk, of stepping into the unknown. But the pros spoke louder—to her spirit, her purpose, her longing to serve.

Seeking clarity beyond the page, she moved to her quiet corner and settled into meditation—something she had begun relying on for every major decision. In stillness, she let the noise of the mind settle. Each breath became an anchor. With eyes closed, she connected inward—past logic, past fear—until a quiet truth surfaced. It wasn't about what she might lose; it was about what she was meant to give.

The collective agreement with the CXO peers to create something larger than themselves felt like a divine sign. Perhaps this was not a question of leaving something behind, but of stepping into something greater. And a smile broke across her face.

A New Chapter

The next morning, Rachel called her executive assistant to clear her schedule for the day. She spent hours drafting a framework for her next steps: establishing partnerships with like-minded organizations, developing a curriculum for spiritual leadership, and connecting with global thought leaders in this space. The work excited her in a way she hadn't felt in years.

By noon, she stood once again by the window, but this time her reflection in the glass bore a look of quiet determination. This wasn't just a career pivot; it was a calling. She realized she didn't have to choose between her corporate experience and her spiritual vision—she could bridge the two to create a more harmonious world.

The path ahead was uncertain, but Rachel felt an unshakable conviction that she was ready to take the first step. Rachel steadied herself before dialing Samuel's number, her fingers trembling slightly. As soon as he answered, she said with a calm resolve, "Samuel, can we meet? I have something important to share."

Later in the afternoon, Rachel and Samuel sat in a quiet corner of a café, the hum of conversations around them providing a soothing backdrop. Rachel took a deep breath and began.

"Samuel, I've been thinking a lot since our meeting. This initiative we've started... it's not just another project for me. It feels like a calling. I'm considering stepping away from my corporate role to dedicate myself to this full-time."

Samuel's eyebrows lifted in surprise, but his expression quickly softened into a smile. "Rachel, that's... extraordinary. I can see how much this means to you. But are you sure? This is a huge step."

"I've weighed the risks," Rachel replied. "It's terrifying, but the potential impact... it's too important to ignore. I've always believed in leading with purpose. This is my chance to live that belief."

Samuel leaned forward, his voice steady and earnest. "Then let me join you. I've been inspired by your vision from the start. If you're taking this leap, I want to take it with you. Together, we can amplify this mission."

Rachel's eyes widened. "You'd really do that? Samuel, you have so much on your plate already."

"And so much of it feels trivial compared to this," Samuel admitted. "This isn't just a cause; it's a movement that could redefine how we live and work. I want to be part of that, and I want to walk with you in making it a reality."

Samuel leaned back, a thoughtful look on his face. "You know, Rachel, I come from a long line of businessmen. The path was laid out—inherit the legacy, grow the empire." He chuckled softly. "It would've been easy. Safe. But I never felt at peace just inheriting success. I needed to build something of my own. To know I could lead and leave a mark that was mine."

He paused, eyes steady on Rachel. "You, on the other hand, carved your path from scratch—breaking barriers I never had to face. While I was stepping out of the shadow of privilege, you were rising despite it. And yet, here we are—different roads, same crossroads. Ready to build something that truly matters."

He continued, "That's why this opportunity, this mission, feels almost intoxicating to me. It's not just about business; it's about impact, about shaping something bigger than ourselves."

With Samuel by her side, Rachel got reassurance that the chosen path is the right one.

Samuel's comment about Rachel carving her path from scratch stayed with her long after they parted ways. As she drove home, his words unlocked something tender and buried—a flood of memories from a time when forging her own path meant walking miles, quite literally.

She thought back to those frostbitten mornings of her childhood in rural America—trudging along frozen dirt roads, worn-out shoes crunching beneath her as she made her way to the nearest bus stop. Her father had already left in their only truck, chasing contracting jobs that barely kept them afloat. There were no school buses for kids like her—only long walks, biting winds, and an ache that was both physical and emotional.

She had known then that they were poor, but it wasn't just the empty lunch pail or the secondhand textbooks—it was the isolation. And yet, she pressed on. Every step, every scraped dollar saved from babysitting or waitressing, every late night under the flickering oil lamp—it all carried her forward, toward a future no one dared dream for her: college.

Now, decades later, on a very different road, that same fire burned within her. Back then, she was walking toward survival. Now, she was walking toward significance.

This mission—this fusion of corporate insight and spiritual vision—wasn't a departure from her past. It was the culmination of it. The girl who once studied by candlelight was still here. Only now, she had a seat at the table—and a voice strong enough to build a new one.

Once she reached back at her office, Rachel knew that the next step was sharing her decision with the board, her team, and the broader group.

Zenyra had always worked on grooming backups for all her leadership positions. This helped in mitigating risks associated with any unplanned attrition. In her case, Rachel had been grooming David to potentially take over the reins from her in the future. She believed he was ready—not just because of his strategic acumen, but because he had consistently demonstrated a calm, level-headed approach in high-stakes negotiations, and communicated with clarity and conviction across all levels of the organization. His ability to unite cross-functional teams and keep them focused during turbulent times reassured her that the company's future would be in capable hands. Most importantly, he understood the flow of dollars. She would offer to stay back as a Vice Chairman on the board as a non-executive leader, subject to the board's approval. This would allow her to contribute strategically from a broader perspective, preserve continuity in leadership, and provide guidance during the transition, without interfering in day-to-day operations. For Rachel, staying on as Vice Chairman was less about holding onto power and more about ensuring that Zenyra Inc.'s long-term vision remained intact as the next generation of leadership stepped in.

She knew the criticality of smooth transition to her successor. It would define their legacy and strengthen the foundation already built to grow further from there.

As Rachel prepared to step down from her role as CEO, she felt a quiet sense of fulfillment rather than finality. This wasn't the end of her journey—it was simply the beginning of a more meaningful one. Her mind returned to the words of Peter Drucker, the father of modern management and a pioneering thinker who emphasized values, purpose, and responsibility in leadership:

"Management is doing things right; leadership is doing the right things."

Unlike many who viewed leadership through the lens of power or process, Drucker understood that true leadership was about impact—about shaping lives, cultures, and the world by choosing what is right over what is merely efficient. His words echoed what Rachel had come to believe: that being a leader isn't just about scaling businesses—it's about creating a legacy that outlives your title.

For years, she had built companies, shaped strategies, and delivered results. But it was time to contribute differently—to give forward, to help the corporate world rediscover its soul through the lens of spirituality. This was not about leaving something behind—it was about sending something meaningful ahead.

She started penning her thoughts in the following headings:

1. Transition & Acceptance: While David was being groomed for the potential CEO role for the future, she did not want to underestimate the criticality of rolling out a new offer to David. She started jotting a few pointers for the compensation team and the board, which might move the needle forward.

2. Inclusivity of Various Stakeholders: Rachel started listing all the relevant stakeholders, internal as well as external, with a timestamp of when and how to reach out to them. The overall readiness of the ecosystem for this transition had to be thought through and planned nicely.

3. Ensuring that the Leadership Team Remains Intact and Views the Transition in a Positive Light: Rachel started jotting individual traits against each leader's name. And next to it, she started noting how this news would be shared with them.

4. Communicate, Communicate, Communicate: This was fundamentally the glue to bring all the pieces together. Listing all the relevant stakeholders (internal and external) and balancing the communication with the right messaging and timing was the key.

5. Realistic Timelines: Apart from the mandated notice period, she was OK to offer her services for an extended period.

6. Onboarding: Support the new CEO

7. Focus on "Go Forward": Under the umbrella of trust and transparency

She drafted a heartfelt message, blending vulnerability with conviction. First, to her organization that stood by her to help scale Zenyra to its pinnacle in the industry:

"After much reflection, I have decided to step away from my role to pursue a mission that aligns deeply with my values. This is not a goodbye, but a shift in focus to contribute to a global movement that fosters purpose and humanity in the workplace. I am grateful for everything we have achieved together and confident in the team's ability to continue driving success."

Her next message was to her CXO peer group, who completely altered the trajectory of her life forever:

"Our meeting ignited a spark in me that I cannot ignore. I believe we have the opportunity to create a profound shift in the corporate world, and I am committing myself fully to this mission. With Samuel's support and the collective strength of this group, I know we can make an extraordinary impact."

The Road Ahead

The next morning, Rachel only retained a couple of critical meetings and spent hours solidifying her next steps: establishing partnerships with like-minded organizations, developing a curriculum for spiritual leadership, and connecting with global thought leaders in this space.

With Samuel at her side, she knew that she had a trusted ally in making things happen. Together, they had witnessed the power of transformation—how mindfulness, purpose, and conscious leadership could breathe life into even the most rigid corporate structures. But this was only the beginning.

Rachel no longer saw boardroom victories as the pinnacle of success. Instead, she felt a deeper calling—to bring this revolution to every organization willing to embrace it. The resistance she had faced, the doubts, the silent battles with skeptics—all of it had only strengthened her resolve. She had spent decades mastering the art of strategy, execution, and leadership; now, it was time to infuse it with something greater.

As she looked out at the horizon, she didn't envision an empire to build, but a movement to ignite. And with Samuel—a kindred spirit who had walked a similar path—she wasn't alone in this mission. They would take this message beyond the walls of their own companies, beyond industries and markets, to create workplaces where success wasn't measured by exhaustion, but by the fulfillment of purpose.

For the first time in a long while, Rachel felt truly free. Not stepping away—but stepping forward, into a future where work and well-being weren't opposing forces, but powerful allies. And this time, she wasn't just leading a company—she was leading a change the world was ready for.

Feeling lighter than she had in weeks, Rachel shut her laptop and let out a deep breath. There would always be more work to do, but she chose presence over planning. She drove home with the windows slightly down, letting the breeze clear her mind. Once inside, she was quickly pulled into a familiar rhythm—her son waving a controller at her with a mischievous grin. She found herself laughing as she battled her son in a video game, both of them fiercely competitive yet equally amused by each other's tactics. Later, she sat by her daughter's side, listening intently as she practiced for her upcoming recital, soaking in the melody and the quiet joy of being in the moment. And before the night ended, she curled up on the couch with her husband, letting herself sink into the comfort of an old favorite movie.

Tomorrow would bring new challenges, but tonight was a reminder of why this journey mattered. Purpose wasn't just something to pursue in the workplace—it was woven into these simple, irreplaceable moments of connection.

To translate the vision of a Universal Playbook into reality, individuals and organizations can begin by anchoring the idea in lived experience. Step one is to gather data and stories—from pilot programs, internal experiments, or grassroots leadership practices that blend performance with purpose. This foundation becomes the raw material for identifying what works across contexts. Once distilled into modules—such as "purpose rituals for teams," "leading with empathy," or "mindful decision-making"—these elements can form the backbone of an adaptable framework. Leaders can host roundtables or working groups to stress-test the content across sectors, gathering feedback from teams at various stages of maturity.

The ultimate goal of the Universal Playbook is not uniformity but *alignment*—a common language and toolkit for embedding spiritual intelligence into business without losing contextual nuance. For readers who wish to get involved, the next step would be to champion pilot implementations in their own organizations or networks. This could look like forming a spirituality-in-business cohort within their company, co-authoring case studies, or co-hosting cross-sector learning circles. The Playbook becomes a shared starting point, not a fixed doctrine—a resource to be localized, iterated, and evolved through collective practice.

To bring wider attention and scale, organizing a Global Summit on Spiritual Leadership in Business can be a powerful accelerant. Readers can contribute by helping convene diverse voices: CEOs, HR leaders, startup founders, academics, and even policymakers. The summit could combine inspirational storytelling with hands-on working sessions—where teams co-create new modules, set bold adoption goals, and explore collaborative funding or research partnerships. More than a conference, it would be a living launchpad for a movement—positioning purpose, not as an HR initiative but as a competitive advantage and moral imperative.

In the opening of Chapter 7, we glimpse a rare yet profound moment—leaders from unrelated industries convening, not to negotiate mergers or outpace competitors, but to co-create something far larger than themselves.

This is not fiction alone. This is a growing real-world phenomenon: altruistic leadership coalitions, where CEOs and changemakers come together to address systemic challenges—climate change, mental health, ethical AI, workplace dignity, and societal inequities—well beyond their traditional spheres of control.

Contrary to what one might assume, these alliances aren't always born of brand strategy or shareholder mandates. More often, they arise from a deeper impulse—a spiritual recognition that leadership today is not just about growth, but about guardianship.

There's a growing expectation for business leaders to look beyond profitability and prioritize long-term societal value. According to EY's 2024 CEO Outlook Pulse Survey, over half (54%) of global CEOs now place greater emphasis on sustainability and broader stakeholder impact than in previous years.

Underlining what's possible when competitors collaborate, BMW, Mercedes-Benz, and Volkswagen recently joined forces with eight suppliers in a landmark open-source software alliance. Signed in June 2025 under the VDA's S-CORE initiative, the project aims to develop essential but non-differentiating vehicle software—such as middleware for diagnostics, secure communication, and over-the-air updates—via a *code-first, open-source approach* managed by the Eclipse Foundation. This pre-competitive cooperation addresses industry-wide challenges: modern vehicles contain over 100 million lines of code, making standalone development prohibitively complex and costly. By pooling resources on the shared digital "underwear" of software-defined vehicles (SDVs), the initiative frees companies to focus individually on innovative, brand-defining features. Led by senior executives from BMW and Mercedes, this group of 11 organizations—including Tier-1 suppliers like Bosch and Continental—has pledged to deliver an MVP of the stack by end-2025, a full reference architecture by 2026, and production-ready deployment in vehicles by 2030.

This kind of forward-thinking leadership—rooted in transparency, shared purpose, and ecosystem collaboration—is increasingly seen as essential to building long-term resilience and public trust.

This data signals more than a trend—it marks a paradigm shift in the consciousness of corporate leadership. As the desire to address shared, systemic challenges grows, so too does the realization that no single organization, however powerful, can solve them alone.

This is a fundamental shift—from transactional capitalism to transcendent responsibility. It's a growing recognition that business leadership today must also be moral, communal, and future-facing. In place of competition as the dominant narrative, we are seeing a movement toward co-creation and stewardship.

And this shift is already playing out in the real world. Below are a few powerful examples where this new spirit of altruistic collaboration and values-led leadership has moved from intention to impact:

- The Business Roundtable (2019 Redefinition of Corporate Purpose)- 181 U.S. CEOs, including leaders from Apple, JPMorgan Chase, and PepsiCo, signed a statement committing to serve not just shareholders, but also employees, communities, and the planet. This marked a landmark move away from the Milton Friedman-era shareholder primacy.

- The B Team- Co-founded by Sir Richard Branson, head of Virgin group, and Jochen Zeitz, CEO of Harley-Davidson. The B Team brings together CEOs, heads of state, and civil society leaders to champion sustainable business. Members include leaders from Unilever, Salesforce, and Natura, united around climate justice, workplace dignity, and inclusive economies.

- The World Economic Forum's "Alliance of CEO Climate Leaders"- This coalition includes more than 120 global CEOs who have pledged to decarbonize their operations and advocate for bold policy reform—an industry-spanning alliance focused on a global public good.

- The Mental Health at Work Commitment (UK)- Major employers like Deloitte, Barclays, and PwC collectively launched a framework to improve mental well-being across corporate Britain—sharing resources, toolkits, and data transparently to benefit competitors and allies alike.

These examples are not isolated incidents—they are signals of a broader awakening. Behind every such initiative lies a convergence of deeper motivations, shared purpose, and an evolving definition of what it means to lead.

To understand the roots of these unlikely yet impactful collaborations, we must look beyond organizational charters and into the hearts of the leaders themselves. What compels them to cross competitive boundaries? What shifts the mindset from market dominance to shared stewardship? What compels them to cross competitive boundaries? What shifts the mindset from market dominance to shared stewardship? The answers lie not in strategy decks, but in lived human experience—where the call to lead transforms into a call to serve.

Here are some of the most profound forces that make such coalitions possible:

- Shared sense of urgency: Whether it's climate, burnout, or inequality, leaders increasingly recognize that no single entity can solve systemic problems alone.

- Values-led leadership: Many modern CEOs are driven not just by KPIs, but by personal convictions—often shaped by their own moments of burnout, loss, or moral awakening.

- Spiritual Capital at play: When leaders operate from a sense of service, not ego, collaboration becomes not just possible— but inevitable.

"It's no longer about being the best in the world. It's about being the best *for* the world." – Paul Polman, former CEO, Unilever.

Yet as noble and necessary as these collaborations are, they are not without friction.

When leaders step outside their industry comfort zones to build something collective and transcendent, they often find themselves navigating uncharted terrain—where old playbooks no longer apply, and new forms of trust must be earned in real time.

Transcendent leadership may begin with shared purpose, but sustaining it requires grappling with the very human challenges of difference, doubt, and structural tension.

Here are some of the most common hurdles these visionary alliances must overcome:

- Cross-industry language gaps: A tech CEO and a supply chain executive may approach the same problem with very different lenses.

- Competing priorities: Balancing fiduciary responsibilities with long-term altruistic goals can invite boardroom skepticism.

- Trust and transparency: True collaboration demands vulnerability—something unfamiliar in hyper-competitive corporate cultures.

Yet, those who persevere report unmatched benefits—shared innovation, greater resilience, employee engagement, and enhanced societal legitimacy.

We are entering a new era where no organization operates in isolation, and no leader can ignore the interconnectedness of people, planet, and performance. The collaborations we saw in fiction—like those initiated by Rachel and her peers—mirror what's both needed and emerging in the real world.

These coalitions don't dilute individual influence—they amplify collective impact.

They prove that Spiritual Capital is not just an internal resource—it's a shared currency. One that allows us to build what no single balance sheet ever could: a regenerative, humane, and purpose-driven world.

But not all transformation begins in boardrooms or multi-stakeholder forums. Sometimes, the most profound shifts happen in solitude—in the quiet reckoning of a leader confronting the limits of success as they've known it. While some executives are collaborating to redesign systems from the top, others are stepping away altogether, drawn by a more personal call. What unites them is the same driving force: the desire to create meaningful change—not just in markets, but in lives.

In a world once enamored with titles, prestige, and corner offices, a quieter revolution is underway. Across industries and continents, successful corporate executives are stepping off the traditional path—not out of failure or fatigue, but out of a deep desire to do something more meaningful.

They are trading stock options for social ventures, conference rooms for classrooms, and quarterly earnings calls for community-building circles. And they are doing so in greater numbers than ever before.

According to a 2023 study by Deloitte, nearly 70% of senior executives surveyed said they were considering leaving their roles in the next 2–5 years to pursue work with greater personal significance. In McKinsey's 2022 "Great Attrition" report, purpose misalignment ranked among the top three reasons for executive departures—right after burnout and toxic culture.

And this isn't just talk. Many former C-suite executives have been leaving their corporate roles to start or join purpose-driven startups and nonprofits. Even though this often means earning less, those who make the switch frequently say they find greater meaning and fulfillment in their work and lives.

So why do they leave? What drives high-performing executives to abandon prestige, compensation, and control?

The answer, it turns out, is both personal and systemic.

It often starts quietly. A question. A pause. A gnawing sense that, despite hitting all the right KPIs, something essential is missing.

"I had everything I was told to chase," said Ruchika, a former retail CEO who now runs a rural education initiative. "But I wasn't building anything I believed in. I was optimizing someone else's dream."

"After 20 years in finance, I realized I could price a derivative in three time zones, but I didn't know my neighbor's name," shared Carlos, now a city-based community housing innovator.

For others, the wake-up call is more abrupt—a layoff, a health scare, or simply the realization that they no longer recognize the person in the mirror during Monday morning meetings.

And then comes the leap. Not always graceful. Not always immediately successful. But almost always irreversible.

Leaving the corporate machine is one thing. Building something new is another.

What does the path forward look like after stepping away from the known? Many begin with pilots—a side project, a foundation, or a prototype. They spend time listening, unlearning, and immersing themselves in the problem they now want to solve.

They often:

- Partner with grassroots organizations to understand real-world needs.

- Go back to school, enroll in design thinking or nonprofit management programs.

- Engage coaches and mentors who've made similar transitions.

- Face skepticism—from family, peers, and even their inner critic.

What helps them persevere is a combination of community, conviction, and clarity of purpose.

"I'd go from speaking on global panels to chasing logistics for food deliveries to schools. But the meaning I felt? Nothing ever matched that," said Nalin, who left a consumer goods conglomerate to build a sustainable nutrition platform for children in India.

The ventures these former executives lead span sectors—education, mental health, sustainability, ethical supply chains, regenerative agriculture, youth empowerment—but the common thread is unmistakable: they build for legacy, not just livelihood.

- Rina Prasad, once a pharma strategy head, now runs a mobile health van network that's reached over 800,000 women in underserved areas across Southeast Asia.

- Alexei Markov, ex-tech VP, created a platform that connects retirees with meaningful volunteer opportunities—redefining aging with dignity and contribution.

- Tariq Dar, a former investment banker, launched a fund that supports refugee entrepreneurs with seed capital and mentorship.

While many of them earn far less than they did in their corporate careers, they report feeling more energized, more alive, and more in tune with their values.

And perhaps the most powerful question of all: what if success was never the destination, but simply the raw material for something deeper? What these journeys reveal is this: meaning is not something you find once you've succeeded. It's something you build as you go.

As organizations struggle to retain top talent and inspire younger generations, the lesson is clear—people want to matter more than they want to win. And increasingly, they are willing to leave behind the illusion of success in pursuit of something real.

"I didn't leave because I failed," said one leader. "I left because I wanted to succeed differently."

In the end, it's not about leaving the world of business behind—it's about reimagining what business is for. Whether through collective movements or quiet personal shifts, a new generation of leaders is choosing to succeed differently. They are trading old scorecards for new forms of significance. Their stories remind us that real transformation doesn't wait for permission—it begins the moment we choose to lead with purpose, not just position. The fiction we opened with is no longer fiction alone. It's a glimpse of what's possible when we honor the truth that leadership, at its highest, is service to something greater than self. The future is not waiting to be predicted—it's waiting to be co-created.

CHAPTER EIGHT

SPIRITUAL CAPITAL—
THE CALLING

In today's evolving workplaces, a quiet revolution is taking root—one that reframes success through the lens of meaning, purpose, and inner well-being. Leaders and teams alike are beginning to recognize that professional achievement and personal fulfillment need not exist in separate spheres. Instead, the two can coexist, enriching one another and transforming the very fabric of organizational culture.

But how does this transformation move beyond the personal? How does spiritual awareness scale from an individual's internal journey to become a shared, strategic force that shapes teams, inspires leadership, and redefines business success? This chapter explores how the concept of spiritual capital—the value created when purpose, values, and inner alignment inform action—can become a powerful, collective asset within organizations.

Levels of Spirituality in an Organization

When individuals start taking ownership of driving spirituality, we can consider organizational spirituality at different levels:

(1) Individual,

(2) Group,

(3) Workplace,

(4) Regional level,

(5) Organizational.

As might be clear, individual spirituality is a personal search for purpose and meaning, with the aim of self-improvement to attain a sense of fulfillment, content, connectedness, and inner peace.

The same general definition can be applied to group spirituality. Typically, this group of people may exchange notes on this topic and spend time with one another after office hours or during breaks. However, this may not directly impact the organization's business in a meaningful way.

It is only when a group of individuals actively practicing spirituality come together within a workplace that the initial ripples begin to emerge—subtle yet powerful shifts in how people interact, make decisions, and show up for one another. These ripples might look like teams starting meetings with a moment of reflection, leaders making space for empathy in performance reviews, or employees openly expressing a sense of purpose in their daily work. Over time, these small practices accumulate, and when adopted by multiple teams or departments, the ripple expands—moving from isolated acts to a visible cultural shift across regions or the entire organization.

The results can be profound. Take Salesforce, for example. The company introduced mindfulness zones, employee well-being programs, and purpose-driven leadership training across its global offices. This wasn't just a wellness perk—it became part of their core management philosophy. Within a year of scaling these initiatives, Salesforce reported increased employee engagement, higher retention rates, and even saw innovation rise significantly, with a marked uptick in cross-functional collaboration. A company-wide survey indicated that over 90% of employees felt their work had meaning, and many credited mindfulness practices for reducing burnout and improving focus.

When ripples like these reach an entire organization, employees begin to experience a deeper sense of fulfillment, contentment, and interconnectedness. A heightened sense of inner peace replaces workplace stress, fostering an environment where individuals are more engaged, empathetic, and purpose-driven. Cynicism begins to fade, especially around job satisfaction and corporate values, laying the foundation for all future positive impacts. And at the heart of this transformation are leaders who champion spiritual leadership across the organization with authenticity, setting the tone for sustainable cultural change.

However, before leaders drive from the front, there is one more critical thing to accomplish. To highlight my point better, let me quote a few lines from the famous story *Alice in Wonderland,* by Lewis Caroll, where Alice asks the Cheshire Cat:

"Would you tell me, please, which way I ought to go from here?"

"That depends a good deal on where you want to get to," said the Cheshire Cat.

"I don't much care where–" said Alice.

"Then it doesn't matter which way you go," said the Cheshire Cat.

This depicts a very powerful lesson applicable to all of us in life—be it professional or personal. The dialogue between Alice and the Cheshire Cat highlights a universal truth about direction and purpose. Without a clear goal or destination in mind, the path one takes becomes irrelevant, as any route will suffice. It reflects the confusion and aimlessness that can arise when one lacks clarity of purpose. Life, like Alice's journey, is full of crossroads, and without intentionality, we risk wandering without fulfillment or growth. The conversation reminds us that understanding *where we want to go* is essential to making meaningful choices. Leaders and individuals alike must recognize their own paths—for only then can they inspire themselves and others to follow with purpose, creating a journey that is positive and fulfilling for all.

Spirituality provides the tools to discover and align with our deeper purpose. Through introspection, meditation, and mindfulness, spirituality helps us identify what truly matters—our values, aspirations, and the essence of who we are. By fostering self-awareness, spirituality empowers us to define our "destination," whether it's personal growth, inner peace, or contributing to a greater good.

Moreover, spirituality teaches detachment from external distractions, allowing us to focus on paths that resonate with our authentic selves. It empowers us to choose with intention, guided by wisdom and clarity, ensuring that our journey through life is purposeful and fulfilling.

As the Cheshire Cat implies, direction is meaningful only when tied to purpose, and spirituality lights the way toward discovering and committing to that purpose.

Stepping beyond Alice's tale and into our own reality, I want to share a belief close to my heart:

I envision a world where spirituality becomes an integral part of our daily lives.

When individuals embrace spirituality with sincerity, they unlock deeper clarity of purpose and direction. Imagine communities where decisions are driven not by fear or ambition alone, but by awareness, compassion, and collective well-being. In such a world, workplaces become more human, relationships more grounded, and society more harmonious.

This is the future I believe we can build—a peaceful and purpose-aligned ecosystem, rooted in spiritual consciousness and sustained by intentional living.

Let's take this vision a step further—not just as a personal hope, but as a shared and achievable possibility.

Imagine a corporate world where every individual's personal purpose is seamlessly aligned with the organization's mission and values. In such an environment, work transforms from routine to resonance. It becomes a channel for personal growth, contribution, and collective success.

When this alignment is real, employees don't just perform—they thrive. They show up with energy, commitment, and a sense of ownership. They go the extra mile not out of obligation, but from a place of inner motivation. Purpose fuels passion, and passion drives performance.

And the business impact? It's not just cultural—it's commercial.

Organizations that nurture purpose-driven, emotionally connected teams experience higher productivity, greater innovation velocity, and significantly stronger financial outcomes. According to Deloitte and Harvard Business Review, purpose-led companies outperform peers by over 40% in revenue growth, enjoy profit margins up to 20% higher, and see markedly higher customer loyalty and brand equity.

Thrilled customers. Empowered teams. Inspired leaders. The result is not just exponential growth in revenues and margins—it's sustainable, values-aligned success that builds a legacy far beyond the balance sheet.

I recently came across an insightful article on organizational development by Michael O'Malley, published in the *Harvard Business Review*, titled "10 Principles of Effective Organizations." His point of view on each principle is as follows:

1. Encourage cooperation - Can you imagine a company that could survive with members having divergent motives and antagonistic goals? The key to a successful organization is to achieve a cooperative institutional order and quash destabilizing self-interest. Companies accomplish this by changing the calculus of the relationship through rewards and punishments. A more effective and lasting strategy, however, is to change the nature of work relationships. Friends cooperate more than strangers, where the allure of self-maximizing behaviors is high.

2. Organize for change - Organizations that need to change often don't. Once-great companies have found their final resting places in an expansive graveyard of slow-movers and has-beens. In effective organizations, leaders build the case for change, create a positive mindset for change, convince others of the value and legitimacy of the change efforts, and battle against systemic forces of institutional inertia that lock companies into their current, misguided trajectories.

3. Anticipate the future - Not every organizational death is avoidable. The preservation of an organization- depends on its leaders having the navigational judgment and skill to prepare their companies for what lies ahead. However, when the future arrives, many companies cannot meet the demands that new markets and consumer tastes require, as long-term aspirations have been thwarted by short-term impulses. No formulaic solution exists for the ability to peer into the future, but leaders can surround themselves with capable, perceptive people who collectively challenge the assumptions on which their current actions are based in order to imagine other possibilities.

4. Remain flexible - Organizations must be at once disciplined and flexible, prudently reacting to the unexpected during turbulent times and flexibly bending when rushes of demand are placed on them—then regaining their shape once the need for transformation has passed. This ability to situationally morph in response to customer/market demands is typically achieved through improved automation and additions to staff in number or function in the attempt to align the technology and people with what customers want, when they want it—while avoiding costly utilization errors like being understaffed at peak times. For example, Singapore's Changi Airport reconceptualized the problem of handling long customer lines by redirecting people directly to their gates for check-in rather than having fliers converge and pile up at a single point like pouring seeds into a funnel.

5. Create distinctive spaces - It is hard to find studies that *don't* support the link between the quality of a work environment and employees' health, satisfaction, and performance. Indeed, the basic dimensions of indoor environmental quality—such as thermal comfort, air quality, lighting, acoustic quality, and the ergonomic furnishings—consistently correlate with

enhanced performance. The quality of the environment is a potential competitor for scarce mental and emotional resources that can either enable or undermine learning and task performance. For example, research consistently finds that employees who have greater contact with nature experience less stress and have better problem-solving skills, impulse control, attention spans, coping abilities, and productivity.

6. Diversify your workforce and create an inclusive environment - Complex tasks require a diverse mix of viewpoints and abilities to satisfactorily complete. Indeed, the wisdom of needing different people to pool their physical, attitudinal, and intellectual assets to solve problems is well established. Studies routinely show that gender and racial diversity, for example, improve the performance of workgroups, top management teams, and boards of directors when conditions of inclusion prevail. Although diversity is necessary, conflicts can arise among dissimilar people that can impair team performance. Without adept leadership and conditions of psychological safety, diversity in groups may create factions and interpersonal frictions called "faultlines" that must be broken down through ongoing efforts that make people feel significant, wanted, and welcome.

7. Promote personal growth - An effective talent management program is one in which a company has a large pool of able, external job candidates, sufficient competent coverage of existing positions, succession plans throughout the organization, and a panoply of support programs: career counseling and development, career planning workshops and vocational assessments, mentoring and coaching programs, and in-house training and educational assistance to augment employees' career objectives. That said, the most notable way organizations expect people to improve is in job-related ways

by honing expertise. The metamorphosis from novice to expert lies along a continuum anchored by two extremes: one representing natural evolution (our physical attributes and temperaments), and the other driven by effort (training and practice).

8. Empower people - The practice of empowerment in organizations is often like a parent handing the keys of a high-performance vehicle to their teenager and hoping, day after day, that the car will return intact. Simply handing over power to another provides little assurance that something positive will come of it. Similarly, a company cannot simply dictate a new operating procedure that shifts decision-making from centralized control to greater delegation and distributed authority. The change entails a significant shift in culture and operations that involves increased information-sharing, technological enhancements, participative decision making, extensive training, collaborative problem solving, and team trust. The only managers that matter are the ones who can support people's confidence and ensure that they have control over their affairs, can cope with disappointments, and achieve goals that matter to them.

9. Reward high performers - Despite the rhetoric of attracting and retaining the best, the aggregate talent within organizations often is mediocre. Why? Decisions regarding hiring, pay, promotions, and retention are based on factors other than merit, such as friendship ties, tenure, petty jealousies (as when threatened managers rid themselves of worthy competitors), favoritism, politics, and discrimination. The consequences to organizations are obvious. In contrast, when executed well, merit-based pay for performance plans increase job satisfaction and motivate action and, when appropriately structured, are instrumental in producing environments in which the best help the rest. Indeed, it is

common in teams that the top members will lift the performance of good, but less capable, members.

10. Foster a leadership culture - Everyone who has worked in an organization understands the power of leadership and its influence on culture—both positive and negative. On one hand, the adverse effects of abusive supervision and incivility on employees' mental and physical health, job satisfaction, and performance are well-documented. On the other hand, supportive, inclusive management practices that provide psychological safety empower people to take reasonable risks, make mistakes, speak up and challenge the status quo, and ask for help or request resources to make improvements.

Each principle was thoughtfully explained, with an emphasis on how organizations must navigate human behavior and institutional practices to thrive. The article aptly notes that fulfilling these 10 principles is a "tall order" because they represent ambitious, ideal goals that organizations often struggle to fully implement.

As I reflected on Michael O'Malley's insightful article on organizational vitality, one thing became clear: while the principles are universally resonant, they need an anchoring mechanism that ensures long-term application.

That anchor, I believe, is *spirituality in the workplace.*

Here's my interpretation of each principle through a spiritual lens. Spirituality is about purpose, empathy, values, interconnectedness, and service. Hence, it nurtures a sense of shared purpose and interdependence. It also fosters openness and courage to appreciate every change as evolution and not disruption. And change suddenly doesn't seem threatening for individuals as well as organizations and anticipates the future to be prepared for it proactively. Spiritual practice heightens intuition and long-range clarity. A purpose-led organization sees beyond quarterly results into generational legacy. Similarly, spiritual environments cultivate adaptability by anchoring people in inner steadiness, not external structure. This helps employees as well as organizations become flexible and adaptable by shunning any rigidity whatsoever. Restoring, inspiring, and reconnecting individuals (and hence organizations) to a greater whole is yet another benefit reaped when spirituality creates distinctive spaces with sacred behaviors. Additionally, spirituality teaches that every soul carries unique gifts. Inclusion isn't a mandate—it's a reverence for difference. Empathy, dignity, and deep listening happen in auto mode. Spiritual workplaces honor not just skill development, but also the deepest form of growth—personal transformation. Empowerment is trust in action. It's recognizing the divine potential in others and giving them room to rise. Spiritual leaders operate with a servant leadership mindset, prioritizing the well-being of their teams and creating safe spaces for open communication, innovation, and creativity. Such leaders are also adaptable, ensuring that organizational processes remain flexible enough to respond to ever-changing needs of the market and customers.

This leads to an empowered organization with empowered employees who are entrusted to make decisions and take actions. True reward honors effort, intent, and alignment with purpose—not just outcomes. Spiritual recognition uplifts the soul and inspires intrinsic motivation. Leadership is not a position—it's a presence. Jeff Bezos remarked on a few occasions that Amazon would inevitably face disruption and eventual decline, but emphasized his role in extending its lifespan. Organizations that integrate spirituality develop resilient teams and leaders who take proactive steps to adapt and evolve, delaying obsolescence and maintaining relevance in the face of challenges.

Spiritual leadership is about modeling wholeness, humility, and higher purpose. When embedded into corporate culture, these qualities *amplify performance*.

O'Malley rightly concludes that fulfilling these principles is a "tall order" as they are "ambitious aims." Many companies try—but fall short due to a lack of consistency, cultural depth, or emotional connection. In the majority of cases, it is due to entrenched silos, short-term business pressures, or a lack of consistent role modeling by leaders. Additionally, without a shared emotional or ethical foundation, these principles risk becoming checkbox initiatives rather than transformative cultural pillars.

Spiritual capital fills that gap. It offers the ethical spine, emotional wisdom, and energetic coherence required to make these principles stick—not as posters in boardrooms, but as lived truths in hallways, meetings, and decisions. By marrying performance with purpose, structure with soul, and leadership with legacy, we can move beyond conventional success—and into significance.

Simplifying complex concepts into actionable strategies is something I value deeply. I offer concrete, actionable strategies to bring each of these ten principles to life—translating intention into implementation, and philosophy into practice. For readers and leaders seeking to embed fulfillment, resilience, and ethical clarity into their workplace culture, the following strategies may offer a practical starting point.

1. Actionable Strategies to Encourage Cooperation

Initiate inter-departmental "value circles" to promote mutual learning and respect. Implement cross-functional collaboration initiatives, such as joint projects or team-building retreats, to break down silos and encourage knowledge sharing. Design rituals (e.g., gratitude circles, peer acknowledgements) that elevate contributions beyond KPIs. Celebrate collective wins and regularly recognize and celebrate collaborative efforts to reinforce the value of teamwork.

2. Actionable Strategies to Organize for Change

Establish a change management framework that includes clear communication plans, training programs, and support structures. Conduct "change story" sessions where leaders share personal transformation journeys. Use mindfulness, guided reflection, and training to reduce fear and resistance. Establish "soulful change ambassadors" across teams to facilitate conscious transitions. Equip leaders at all levels with the tools and resources to guide their teams through transitions effectively.

3. Actionable Strategies to Anticipate the Future

Embed future-sensing practices (e.g., scenario journaling, spiritual trend dialogues) in strategy cycles. Create "Purpose Foresight Labs" to align emerging trends with inner mission. Foster a culture of continuous learning and innovation by encouraging employees to stay informed about industry trends and emerging technologies. Put a framework for employees to share their relevant inputs on the future of these labs. Bring in external futurists and thinkers to challenge current frames. Implement regular strategy sessions to discuss potential future scenarios and prepare proactive responses.

4. Actionable Strategies to Remain Flexible

Create "fluid roles" that allow people to work across functions based on passion and strengths. Develop agile work processes and decision-making structures that allow for quick adaptation to changing circumstances. Encourage a mindset of flexibility and responsiveness across all levels of the organization. Introduce spiritual resilience workshops and champion mindful pausing before action—especially in moments of chaos.

5. Actionable Strategies to Create Distinctive Spaces

Design workspaces that promote creativity and collaboration, such as open-plan areas, rooms for meditation/reflection/prayer, quiet zones, and recreational spaces. Regularly solicit employee feedback to ensure the environment meets their needs and preferences. Incorporate biophilic design: natural light, flowing water, organic materials.

6. Actionable Strategies to Diversify Your Workforce and Create an Inclusive Environment

Implement inclusive hiring practices and provide diversity training programs. Have the recruiting and HR teams well trained on the spiritual aspects to hire and onboard individuals/teams. Offer DEI programs infused with spiritual wisdom. Create employee resource groups and mentorship opportunities to support underrepresented groups and foster an inclusive culture. Use narrative circles to share life stories and dismantle unconscious biases.

7. Actionable Strategies to Promote Personal Growth

Conceptualize and roll out employee development plans to integrate personal purpose mapping with the organization's mission/vision. Conduct regular career development discussions with employees to understand their aspirations and align them with organizational opportunities. Offer training programs, workshops, and access to resources that support personal and professional growth. Provide spiritual coaching as part of leadership programs. Recognize "invisible growth" (e.g., empathy, wisdom, healing influence) alongside performance.

8. Actionable Strategies to Empower People

Redesign roles around autonomy and meaning, just not tasks. Delegate decision-making authority to appropriate levels within the organization. Provide employees with the necessary tools, information, and autonomy to make informed decisions and take ownership of their work. Replace the rigid decision approval system with value-based decision-making guidelines. Create peer-guided accountability structures rooted in mutual respect and shared purpose.

9. Actionable Strategies to Reward High Performers

Introduce "values-based recognition," where individuals are celebrated for embodying core spiritual principles (e.g., compassion, authenticity, service). Establish clear performance metrics and recognition programs that reward outstanding contributions. Create storytelling platforms where teams highlight each other's contributions beyond the numbers. Ensure that rewards are meaningful and aligned with (a) social impact achievements (e.g., *Seva* hours, mentoring impact), (b) individual and organizational goals on values.

10. Actionable Strategies to Foster a Leadership Culture

Run "inner mastery" programs for emerging leaders, covering emotional resilience, spiritual intelligence (SQ), and shadow work. Develop leadership development programs that focus on cultivating critical thinking, problem-solving, and decision-making skills. Pair senior leaders with spiritual mentors or guides. Promote leadership succession based not just on performance, but also on depth of character and culture stewardship. Encourage a culture where leadership is seen as a shared responsibility, and individuals at all levels are empowered to lead.

By integrating these actionable strategies into your organizational practices, you can create an environment where individuals' personal purposes align with the organization's mission, leading to a more engaged, innovative, and high-performing workforce.

In today's evolving business landscape, companies that thrive focus on both financial success and social responsibility. Such organizations not only contribute positively to the world but also reap sustained financial benefits over the long term.

Real-World Example: Starbucks

Starbucks has long emphasized a mission that intertwines business objectives with a commitment to nurturing the human spirit. This approach reflects a form of workplace spirituality aimed at fostering meaningful connections among employees, customers, and communities.

Starbucks updated its mission statement to: *"To inspire and nurture the human spirit – one person, one cup, and one neighborhood at a time."*

This mission underscores the company's dedication to creating a sense of purpose and connection beyond the transactional nature of coffee sales.

It goes on to elaborate on its values:

"With our partners, our coffee, and our customers at our core, we live these values:

- *Creating a culture of warmth and belonging, where everyone is welcome."*

- *Acting with courage, challenging the status quo, and finding new ways to grow our company and each other."*

- *Being present, connecting with transparency, dignity, and respect."*

- *Delivering our very best in all we do, holding ourselves accountable for results."*

"We are performance driven, through the lens of humanity."

Starbucks' statement of mission and values incorporates several practices that align with spiritual principles:

- Employee Empowerment: The company refers to its employees as "partners," fostering a sense of ownership and belonging. This practice encourages personal growth and a deeper connection to the company's mission.

- Community Engagement: Starbucks actively participates in community service and encourages its partners to engage in local initiatives, reinforcing a sense of purpose and contribution to society. Starbucks Partner Networks hosted 23 events in 2023 to address food scarcity, health, and education across the country. Troy James, a licensed store district manager and BPN leader in New Orleans at the time, and now a manager with Starbucks' Inclusion and Diversity team, stated, "The concept of hosting an event to encourage and unite people was compelling, so we engaged."

- Inclusive Environment: By promoting diversity and inclusion, Starbucks creates a workplace where individuals feel valued and respected, aligning with the spiritual principle of honoring the inherent worth of every person.

A study titled *"Spiritual performance from an organizational perspective: The Starbucks way"* explores how Starbucks integrates spiritual values into its business model.

The research highlights that Starbucks' emphasis on human connection, employee well-being, and community involvement contributes to both employee satisfaction and organizational success.

While Starbucks' integration of spirituality into its corporate ethos has been praised, it has also faced scrutiny. Some critics argue that the commercialization of spirituality may lead to superficial practices that serve corporate interests more than genuine employee or community well-being. For instance, discussions around "Starbucks Spirituality" suggest that the company's approach may reflect broader trends in consumer capitalism, where spiritual themes are utilized for brand differentiation.

In response to such criticisms, Starbucks emphasizes that its mission and values are grounded in humanity and giving. CEO Laxman Narasimhan stated, "We are a company with a Mission and Promises grounded in humanity and in giving... Our values deliver performance through the lens of humanity". He further noted that narratives shaped by external voices disconnected from the brand do not accurately reflect Starbucks' commitment to human connection and ethical practices.

Additionally, as mentioned earlier, Starbucks updated its mission statement to better reflect its role in the world. This reaffirmation underscores the company's dedication to integrating ethical values and social responsibility into its core business strategies, aiming to create a workplace where people and principles thrive together.

Starbucks' mission to "inspire and nurture the human spirit" exemplifies an integration of spiritual principles into corporate practice. Through employee empowerment, community engagement, and fostering inclusivity, Starbucks seeks to create a work environment that transcends traditional business objectives. However, the effectiveness and authenticity of such practices continue to be subjects of discussion and analysis.

Apart from all these indicators, I came across an article in *Business Insider* published in August 2024, post the announcement of their new CEO, Brian Niccol, taking over. This article interviewed a few Starbucks employees (or rather partners, as Starbucks prefers calling them) in Singapore and London.

One comment from a partner was, "I would love an increase in pay…I earn slightly more as I've been working for 1.5 years so far…In general, food and beverage salaries aren't that much, for the amount of work we do."

Another partner found the company well organized, particularly when it came to the time for menu changes. Some baristas in Singapore also think their stores lag behind US stores in terms of updated equipment. "In the US, they have more advanced technology in the stores. Ours gets updated a lot later… It would be good for there to be a standardization of technology."

"Sometimes we don't have the ingredients required to make the items they want," one employee said, in response to requests from customers asking for drinks based on US TikTok videos.

The display board could also be digitalized to match those of other coffee chains, such as The Coffee Bean & Tea Leaf. Starbucks, like many food companies, offers different menus in different countries to appeal to local tastes.

"I would love for our special drinks on offer to become regular parts of the menu."

Some of the other thoughts/suggestions shared were around introducing a drink subscription model like the chains, such as Pret a Manger and Blank Street Coffee.

Another employee from the London Starbucks branch said that some of the incentives for customers to return to Starbucks could be improved under the new leadership. By comparison, he said, Starbucks' rewards program is not as generous.

"You have to spend like £50, approximately $64, to get one free drink, which is a lot." In the UK, the program requires you to collect 150 "stars" for a free item; you earn three stars every time you spend £1.

Starbucks can also do more to consider customers' suggestions and feedback, a Starbucks barista in Singapore said. She and one of her colleagues on shift said that Starbucks should run a poll to gauge customers' preferences and update the menu accordingly.

While I trust that Starbucks' leadership is attentive to such feedback, from an outside perspective, there appears to be a disconnect in truly hearing the voices of partners and customers. This kind of feedback deserves open, internal discussion—along with clear, transparent communication about the actions being taken. A recent example underscores this concern. In May 2025, over 1,200 Starbucks baristas across 120 U.S. stores went on strike to protest a newly implemented dress code. The policy mandated solid black shirts and specific-colored bottoms under the green apron, a change that many employees felt was imposed without adequate consultation. Starbucks Workers United, the union representing these employees, criticized the company for not negotiating the dress code changes and for prioritizing brand aesthetics over operational concerns like staffing and wage guarantees.

This incident highlights the importance of transparent communication and genuine engagement with employees. When partners feel their voices are not heard, it can lead to unrest and undermine the company's commitment to its core values. Ensuring that feedback mechanisms are robust and that employees are kept informed about upcoming initiatives can help bridge this gap and foster a more inclusive and responsive organizational culture.

Additionally, the people in the field may also need a periodic update on different upcoming initiatives.

Perhaps it's time to revisit the fictional leadership choices of Daphne and Rachel. Their organizations began to flourish not through top-down control, but by actively listening to the voices on the ground, responding with transparency, and building trust through consistent, hands-on engagement. It's not hard to imagine how a company like Starbucks could benefit from adopting similar principles—especially when tensions arise from perceived gaps in communication and inclusion.

There is also a significant opportunity to apply the A2 model and the Harmonize framework here. When employees align their personal aspirations with the organization's deeper mission and values, they become more than workers—they become believers. This alignment builds positive cultural momentum, where energized, empowered, and engaged partners go the extra mile—not just to grow the business, but to help it thrive holistically. The Harmonize framework, in particular, creates a bridge between inner fulfillment and collective performance—turning everyday roles into meaningful contributions that fuel both purpose and profit.

However, even as Starbucks continues to embed spiritual and humanistic values into its ethos, it is not immune to the complex sociopolitical realities that shape consumer perception. In late 2023 and into 2024, the brand faced significant backlash from Gen Z consumers and pro-Palestinian activists, who accused Starbucks of taking a politically biased stance during the Israel-Palestine conflict. The resulting social media campaigns—many using hashtags like #BoycottStarbucks—led to store protests in cities across the U.S. and the U.K., and a noticeable dip in brand sentiment among younger, socially conscious consumers. As per Business Standard reports, between Nov. 16 and early December, Starbucks' shares dropped 8.96%, equal to losing almost $11 billion in market value and 9.4% of the company's total value. According to a *Morning Consult* report from December 2023, Starbucks' favorability among Gen Z dropped by over 12 percentage points in just one month during the height of the controversy. While the company reiterated its position of neutrality, the episode reaffirmed how sensitive the link is between corporate messaging, perceived values, and public trust.

And yet, despite these flashpoints, Starbucks still offers a strong case study in the pursuit of workplace spirituality—not as a one-time initiative, but as an enduring practice. The company has built mechanisms for partner empowerment and community connection into its operating fabric. For example, its "Third Place" initiative, relaunched in 2024, reimagines store spaces not just as commercial hubs but as welcoming environments where employees and customers alike can feel seen, safe, and connected. Similarly, the company's Mental Health Matters program, launched in partnership with Lyra Health, offers therapy and emotional support to all partners—an extension of Starbucks' long-standing belief that emotional well-being is core to human-centered performance.

In many ways, Starbucks continues to model what a spiritually grounded business can look like at scale. It may stumble in execution or be challenged by perception, but its core aspiration—to nurture the human spirit "one person, one cup, and one neighborhood at a time"—remains a powerful anchor. When paired with stronger listening mechanisms and transparent communication, this foundation positions Starbucks not just to recover from reputational challenges but to evolve into an even more resilient, inclusive, and spiritually intelligent organization.

Ultimately, the question is not whether a company like Starbucks will face criticism or complexity—it's whether it will respond in ways that honor its values and elevate its people. In that regard, the journey of integrating spirituality into business is less about perfection and more about presence, humility, and the willingness to grow through challenge.

Another Real-World Example: Ben & Jerry's

Ben & Jerry's has long stood as a beacon of corporate activism, demonstrating how a company can stay true to its values while maintaining financial success. This commitment starts at the top. Co-founder Ben Cohen has repeatedly shown that his dedication to social justice goes far beyond statements and slogans. On May 14, 2025, Ben Cohen was among seven people arrested during Health Secretary Robert F. Kennedy Jr.'s testimony on Capitol Hill, police confirmed.

As per Ben, "I told Congress they're killing poor kids in Gaza by buying bombs, and they're paying for it by kicking poor kids off Medicaid in the US." Cohen, who, along with the ice cream company, has long engaged in corporate political activism, indicated he was protesting the U.S. response to the Israel-Hamas war in Gaza. In 20121, Ben & Jerry's announced that it would no longer allow its Israeli franchisee to market their ice cream in Israeli settlements in the West Bank, but would continue to sell it within Israel's pre-1967 borders.

Beyond creating premium ice cream flavors, the company has taken an active stance on key social issues, including climate change, racial justice, and fair trade. By embedding these values into its operations—from responsibly sourcing ingredients to supporting grassroots activism—Ben & Jerry's has cultivated a strong brand identity that resonates with socially conscious consumers.

This approach has not only strengthened customer loyalty but also driven profitability. Consumers increasingly prefer brands that align with their values, and Ben & Jerry's has capitalized on this trend by ensuring that its social advocacy is woven into its marketing, supply chain, and corporate policies. As a result, the company has witnessed sustained financial growth while reinforcing its mission of promoting social justice and sustainability.

Ben & Jerry's has consistently demonstrated that corporate social responsibility (CSR) is not just about ethical commitments—it's also a strategic driver of brand loyalty and financial success. By embedding spiritual principles—such as compassion, environmental stewardship, and justice—into its business model, the company has cultivated a passionate consumer base that values purpose as much as product quality. Over the years, its activism has not only reinforced its brand identity but also contributed to revenue and margin growth.

The following examples illustrate how Ben & Jerry's has operationalized these spiritual values across different aspects of its business—from environmental sustainability to ethical sourcing and social justice.

1. Aligning Products with Advocacy: In 1988, Ben & Jerry's launched the Peace Pop to support 1% For Peace, linking brand loyalty to peace advocacy and reinforcing brand identity.

2. Championing Ethical Sourcing: The company took an early stand against Recombinant Bovine Growth Hormone (rBGH), prioritizing ethical dairy sourcing and small-scale farmers, which enhanced credibility and attracted ethically conscious consumers.

3. Environmental Commitments as Spiritual Practice: Reflecting its spiritual commitment to the planet, Ben & Jerry's set an ambitious goal to make all packaging 100% fossil-fuel free, reducing environmental impact and strengthening consumer trust.

4. Balancing Activism with Environmental Action: Through carbon offsets and collaborations with MyClimate and NativeEnergy, the company leads in sustainability, positioning itself as a responsible brand.

5. Grassroots Engagement for Brand Loyalty: Partnering with Farm Aid, Ben & Jerry's promoted sustainable farming, reinforcing its activist image and emotional connection with ethically minded consumers.

6. Social Activism for Brand Trust: The company's work with the Children's Defense Fund and Rock the Vote (registering over 11,000 voters in one day) deepened its social engagement, especially among younger demographics.

7. Creative Advocacy: Bold demonstrations, like serving a 900-pound Baked Alaska on the US Capitol lawn to protest Arctic

drilling, amplified brand awareness and commitment to environmental sustainability.

8. Advocacy to Reinforce Ethical Stance: Protests against cloned animal products and support for Genetically Modified Organism (GMO) labeling legislation highlighted Ben & Jerry's dedication to transparency and ethical food sourcing, enhancing customer trust and retention.

9. Standing with Social Movements: During Occupy Wall Street, active participation by serving ice cream in Zuccotti Park reinforced brand authenticity and loyalty.

By intertwining social responsibility, environmental stewardship, and ethical values with its brand strategy, Ben & Jerry's has cultivated a fiercely loyal customer base, differentiated itself in a competitive market, and ultimately strengthened its financial performance. The company's ability to align activism with product marketing has not only reinforced its brand identity but also contributed to revenue growth by attracting consumers who value ethical business practices. As of its acquisition by Unilever in 2000, the company was valued at $326 million, a testament to how a purpose-driven business can translate into tangible market value. Its continued success under Unilever's ownership—while maintaining its independent board to protect its social mission—illustrates how embedding spiritual principles such as justice, equity, and environmental stewardship can fuel both brand equity and sustained business growth.

Ben & Jerry's case proves that purpose-driven branding is not just an ethical imperative—it's a competitive advantage that fuels long-term profitability and market success.

The success of Ben & Jerry's and Starbucks illustrates that businesses do not have to choose between profitability and purpose—they can achieve both by embedding ethical principles into their core strategies. Companies that genuinely commit to sustainability and social impact are better positioned to attract loyal customers, retain engaged employees, and build long-term resilience in an ever-changing marketplace.

As consumer expectations continue to evolve, businesses that embrace this harmonious coexistence between profits and purpose will not only contribute to a better world but also secure their place in the future of commerce.

More Real-World Examples:

Aetna's transformation under CEO Mark Bertolini offers one of the clearest examples of integrating spiritual well-being into corporate culture—with tangible business results.

After a near-fatal skiing accident in 2004, Bertolini faced intense physical pain and emotional disruption. Traditional medicine offered little relief. In his personal recovery, he turned to yoga, mindfulness, and acupuncture. When he experienced real healing, he decided to bring those same practices into Aetna.

By 2010, Aetna launched a company-wide initiative that included mindfulness programs, yoga classes, and stress reduction training for employees. These were not side perks—they were embedded into Aetna's operational philosophy.

The results were powerful. According to Aetna's internal studies:

1. Stress levels dropped by 28%

2. Sleep quality improved by 20%

3. Employees reported an average 62-minute gain in productivity per week

4. This productivity translated to $3,000 in value per employee per year

What began as a personal exploration turned into a cultural shift—one that showed a health insurer could heal from within.

Bertolini said in interviews: "You can't have a healthy company if you don't have healthy employees."

While Bertolini eventually stepped down, his legacy remained. Aetna became a model for wellness-driven leadership, not just in healthcare, but across industries seeking to bring compassion, presence, and healing into the corporate fold.

Similarly, at *Bridgewater Associates*, the largest hedge fund in the world, you'll find a paradox: one of the most cutthroat financial institutions built on the principles of meditation and radical honesty.

Founder Ray Dalio has practiced Transcendental Meditation (TM) for over 50 years. He credits TM for his clarity, calm under pressure, and decision-making edge. But Dalio didn't keep this to himself—he made it part of Bridgewater's DNA.

Bridgewater introduced:

1. Optional TM courses for all employees

2. Daily meditations and wellness spaces

3. A culture of radical transparency, where feedback is public, direct, and brutally honest

Dalio calls this a form of "corporate mindfulness," where truth overrides ego and clarity trumps comfort. In his bestselling book *Principles*, he argues that "the greatest tragedy of mankind is people holding onto wrong opinions without thoughtful disagreement."

Despite criticism for its intensity, Bridgewater has:

1. Outperformed nearly every peer hedge fund over the past several decades

2. Maintained employee retention in top talent tiers

3. Created a company culture often studied by Ivy League business schools

Dalio's journey proves that spiritual practices like meditation can support high-stakes leadership—even in environments where the pressure is relentless.

Under John Mackey, *Whole Foods* was not just a grocery chain—it was a movement.

Mackey co-founded Whole Foods in 1980 with a vision to bring organic food and ethical business into the mainstream. But his leadership philosophy went beyond profit, and he helped pioneer the framework built on four tenets:

1. Higher purpose

2. Stakeholder orientation

3. Conscious leadership

4. Conscious culture

In practice, this meant:

1. Transparent pay structures (Mackey capped his own salary at $1)

2. No company-wide hierarchy for health benefits—everyone got the same

3. A deep commitment to sustainability, local sourcing, and ethical supply chains

Whole Foods' performance spoke volumes. Before its 2017 acquisition by Amazon for $13.7 billion, the company was consistently profitable, beloved by customers, and respected by employees.

Mackey stated, "We believe in love, care, and trust. Business is not a zero-sum game—it's a value-creation game."

Whole Foods proved that spiritually grounded capitalism could work—not just for boutique brands, but at a national and global scale.

Adobe, best known for its creative software products, is quietly one of the best examples of human-centered leadership in tech.

The company's people philosophy is built on trust, balance, and emotional agility. It replaced traditional performance reviews with "Check-ins"—ongoing, open conversations between employees and managers. Adobe's Chief People Officer explained the change as a way to "treat people like adults"—a deeply humanistic idea.

Adobe has also introduced programs to support the following:

1. Mindfulness and meditation through on-campus classes and digital platforms

2. Emotional resilience through leadership coaching and burnout recovery support

3. Psychological safety by giving all employees access to anonymous mental health resources

The results:

1. Adobe consistently ranks in the Top 10 Best Places to Work (Fortune, Great Place to Work)

2. The company has one of the lowest attrition rates in Silicon Valley

3. Adobe's revenue has more than doubled since 2018, with employee engagement scores rising in parallel

Adobe's story shows that creativity thrives where people feel psychologically safe and spiritually nourished. It's a quiet revolution—but a lasting one.

What it Takes to Make it Happen

The idea that the corporate world and spirituality are mutually exclusive has been challenged and we are experiencing moderate success in pockets. As awareness of mental health, emotional well-being, and ethical leadership grows, there is evidence that the two worlds can co-exist—and even thrive—together.

This coexistence is possible through:

Purpose-Driven Leadership

Organizations that promote a deeper sense of purpose, alongside profit, create more engaged, innovative, and fulfilled employees. Leaders who emphasize spiritual values like compassion, empathy, and ethical decision-making foster a positive work environment.

I was reading an article that stated that approximately 10% of global greenhouse gas emissions are contributed by the apparel industry. Patagonia, a leading apparel manufacturer, has taken a conscious call to improve its environmental footprint. They leveraged (a) an optimized supply chain to reach more than 95% of the USA region in three days without the need for using air shipping, and this drastically reduced their carbon footprint. (b) Zero Emission Maritime Buyers Alliance (ZEMBA), along with other businesses, to purchase zero-emission maritime fuel in bulk. (c) a switch to using only organically grown cotton in all their products, and by 2025, a target to eliminate virgin petroleum and only use preferred materials. All these purpose-driven environmental initiatives to prioritize the planet have made them a popular choice for employees and customers.

These purpose-driven environmental initiatives have not only made Patagonia a popular choice for customers but have also positively impacted employee engagement and retention. The company's commitment to environmental stewardship resonates deeply with its workforce, fostering a sense of pride and purpose. This alignment between personal values and organizational mission has contributed to Patagonia's remarkable employee retention rates. For instance, the company boasts a turnover rate of just 4%, significantly lower than the industry average of 13%.

Furthermore, Patagonia's dedication to work-life balance and family-friendly policies has been instrumental in retaining talent. The company offers on-site childcare, paid maternity and paternity leave, and flexible work schedules, which have led to a 25% lower turnover rate among employees who utilize these benefits.

These examples illustrate how Patagonia's integration of environmental responsibility and employee well-being not only enhances its brand image but also creates a more engaged and loyal workforce.

Purpose-driven leadership draws on spiritual principles like compassion and service. Leaders practicing these values inspire intrinsic motivation in all stakeholders.

Mindfulness in the Workplace

Practices such as meditation and mindfulness have demonstrated tangible benefits in reducing stress, improving focus, and enhancing creativity. Companies that integrate mindfulness training into their cultures, such as Google's Search Inside Yourself (SIY) program, report increased productivity and employee satisfaction. (*See the opening section of Chapter 2 for additional details on SIY.*) Similarly, Salesforce incorporates mindfulness zones in its offices, encouraging employees to recharge and refocus.

There have been scientific neuroscience experiments to show that mindfulness helps improve decision-making, emotional regulation, and resilience. For example, a study conducted at the University of Wisconsin–Madison by neuroscientist Dr. Richard Davidson found that consistent mindfulness practice increases activity in the prefrontal cortex—an area of the brain associated with executive function and rational decision-making. Similarly, research published in *Psychiatry Research: Neuroimaging* (2011) by Sara Lazar and her team at Harvard Medical School showed that individuals who practiced mindfulness meditation for just eight weeks had increased gray matter density in the hippocampus (linked to learning and memory) and reduced density in the amygdala, which plays a role in stress and emotional reactivity. These findings suggest that mindfulness physically reshapes the brain in ways that promote greater focus, emotional balance, and adaptability. These qualities are critical for everyone from entry-level workers to senior executives, equipping them to handle the pressures of a dynamic business environment. This leads to a cohesive, productive, and innovative workforce.

Sustainable Corporate Strategies

The principles of spirituality—such as long-term thinking, ethical action, and emotional resilience—align with sustainable corporate strategies. Companies that prioritize these values are more likely to avoid burnout, foster loyalty, and build lasting success. Companies like LinkedIn promote employee well-being through "InDays," designated times for personal growth, learning, and service. This time is leveraged to "connect, create, and collaborate" by "investing, inspiring, and innovating."

Organizations that leverage and prioritize spiritual principles—ethical leadership, sustainability, and emotional well-being—build lasting, meaningful success.

The fusion of corporate strategies with spiritual principles doesn't dilute ambition or competitiveness. Instead, it humanizes workplaces, strengthens cultures, and redefines success in a way that benefits everyone. As businesses evolve in response to global challenges, this harmonious coexistence between corporate goals and spiritual wisdom could become the foundation of a new era in leadership and enterprise.

Balancing between Profit and Purpose

The idea of creating a corporate culture where profits and purpose, strategy and soul coexist harmoniously is both visionary and increasingly necessary in today's business world. This culture prioritizes both financial success and a deeper sense of responsibility to stakeholders, society, and the environment, integrating purpose into the core of business strategy.

Unilever serves as a compelling example of this balance. Under Paul Polman's leadership, the company launched the Unilever Sustainable Living Plan, aiming to decouple growth from environmental impact while increasing positive social impact. Rather than treat sustainability as a cost center, Unilever made it a driver of innovation, brand value, and long-term financial resilience.

According to a 2020 report by Kantar, Unilever's purpose-driven brands—such as Dove, Lifebuoy, and Ben & Jerry's—grew 69% faster than the rest of the business and accounted for 75% of the company's overall growth. This illustrates how embedding social and environmental purpose into brand identity can directly contribute to commercial success.

From an employee engagement perspective, Unilever ranked consistently high in global employee satisfaction surveys. A 2021 report from LinkedIn listed Unilever among the top 10 companies for professional development and purpose-led leadership, with employees citing the company's commitment to sustainability and ethical practices as a key motivator for staying long term.

Unilever's ability to integrate social impact into its business model—without sacrificing profitability—demonstrates that balancing purpose and profit isn't just a lofty ideal; it's a viable strategy that leads to competitive advantage, talent retention, and brand trust.

Conscious Capitalism: Profit with Purpose

Conscious Capitalism is a movement that recognizes the interdependence of capitalism and a higher purpose. Companies practicing Conscious Capitalism understand that profits are essential, but they are not the sole purpose of the business. Instead, they seek to benefit all stakeholders—customers, employees, suppliers, shareholders, communities, and the environment—creating long-term, sustainable value.

The movement was formally co-founded in 2005 by John Mackey, co-CEO of Whole Foods Market, and Raj Sisodia, a marketing professor and author. It gained significant momentum following the publication of their influential 2013 book, *Conscious Capitalism: Liberating the Heroic Spirit of Business*. Rooted in the United States, the philosophy emerged as a response to growing disillusionment with short-term profit-maximizing practices and corporate scandals in the early 2000s. The Conscious Capitalism organization, headquartered in Austin, Texas, now serves as a global hub for business leaders looking to apply these principles across industries.

The four pillars of Conscious Capitalism potentially could be:

- Higher Purpose: Businesses must define a purpose beyond profit, such as enhancing customer well-being, addressing social issues, or protecting the environment. A clearly articulated higher purpose serves as the moral compass of an organization—it inspires employees, earns customer loyalty, and drives innovation by aligning everyday actions with a meaningful mission. When profit becomes the by-product of purpose-driven action, companies foster deeper trust and long-term resilience.

- Stakeholder Orientation: Instead of focusing solely on shareholders, Conscious Capitalism emphasizes creating value for all stakeholders, building mutually beneficial relationships. While shareholders are individuals or entities that own stock in a company and are primarily concerned with financial returns, stakeholders include a broader group—such as employees, customers, suppliers, communities, and the environment—who are affected by or can affect the company's operations. This approach ensures that business decisions consider long-term impact and shared prosperity, not just short-term profit.

- Conscious Leadership: Leaders in such organizations are driven by purpose, focusing on serving the greater good, fostering an inclusive and empathetic corporate culture. They lead by example, not authority—completely aligned with values, empowering others, practicing emotional intelligence, and building trust through authenticity and transparency. Such leadership inspires loyalty and resilience, especially in times of uncertainty.

- Conscious Culture: A company's culture must be nurturing, inspiring, and deeply connected to its purpose, encouraging collaboration, innovation, and ethical practices. It is the invisible force that shapes behavior and decision-making—when culture aligns with purpose, it becomes a powerful catalyst for sustainable growth and employee fulfillment.

Companies like Patagonia or Whole Foods are often cited as examples of Conscious Capitalism, as they integrate a sense of environmental and social responsibility into their business models while remaining highly profitable.

Servant Leadership: Leading with Empathy and Service

Servant Leadership is a philosophy that flips the traditional leadership hierarchy. Instead of leaders being at the top and subordinates serving them, leaders exist and prioritize the growth, development, and well-being of their teams and communities. This mindset flips the organizational pyramid—placing employees and stakeholders at the center of decision-making and support. This approach fosters a culture of empathy, trust, and empowerment. The key principles of servant leadership:

- Serving Others First: Servant leaders prioritize the growth and well-being of their teams, putting their needs ahead of personal ambition.

- Empathy and Active Listening: Effective servant leaders deeply understand their employees' challenges and aspirations, and they listen to their teams to support their development.

- Building Community: By fostering collaboration and a shared sense of purpose, servant leaders create a culture where individuals feel valued and motivated to contribute.

- Ethical Use of Power: Power in servant leadership is used to uplift and empower others, promoting ethical decision-making and trust.

Leaders like Howard Schultz (former CEO of Starbucks) and Cheryl Bachelder (former CEO of Popeyes) have employed servant leadership to build highly profitable companies while creating positive, people-centered corporate cultures.

Bridging Strategy and Soul

In modern business, bridging the gap between strategy (profits, growth, competitiveness) and soul (ethics, purpose, social responsibility) can create a truly holistic and sustainable approach to success. These organizations pursue profit, but not at the expense of people or the planet. Instead, their business models are designed to create long-term value for all stakeholders—employees, customers, communities, investors, and the environment. Here's how this coexistence can be achieved:

- Holistic and Meaningful Metrics: Instead of measuring success solely by financial performance, companies should use a combination of financial and non-financial metrics. And rather than relying on vague indicators like customer loyalty, purpose-driven companies are increasingly assessed through measurable outcomes—such as reductions in carbon emissions, increased diversity in leadership, or percentage of profits reinvested into community impact programs. As we discussed earlier, a company's social or environmental impact, employee satisfaction, customer loyalty, and financial metrics are all correlated.

- Long-Term Vision: A purpose-driven business strategy is inherently long-term. Rather than chasing short-term profits, these companies invest in the well-being of stakeholders, sustainable practices, and community development, which yield lasting success. This is because the outcomes of such strategies—like environmental regeneration, cultural transformation, or social equity—require consistent, sustained effort over time and don't necessarily produce immediate returns. These companies operate with a clearly articulated purpose that transcends financial gain—whether it's environmental restoration, social justice, or community well-being. This mission shapes decisions across departments and functions.

- Authentic Brand Connection: When strategy and soul are aligned, customers and employees alike develop a strong emotional connection to the brand. Metrics like B Corp Certification, high ESG (Environmental, Social, Governance) scores, and third-party sustainability audits serve as credible indicators of this authenticity. All stakeholders believe in its mission, value its products, and become advocates, helping to drive the company's success.

A good example would be when TOMS pioneered the "One for One" model—donating a pair of shoes for every pair sold. This business model directly linked consumer action to social benefit, positioning the company as an early example of how commercial success can be achieved through a commitment to ethical impact. Over time, TOMS evolved its model to focus on giving grants to grassroots organizations tackling poverty and mental health—further embedding purpose into its strategy.

Conclusion: A New Era of Leadership

The coexistence of profits and purpose, strategy and soul, marks a shift in how companies operate and succeed in a rapidly evolving world. Leaders who embrace Conscious Capitalism, adopt Servant Leadership, and build Purpose-Driven Companies are shaping a future where businesses not only thrive financially but also contribute meaningfully to society.

These companies show that long-term success is not only about outperforming competitors but also about uplifting communities, caring for the planet, and enriching the lives of those they touch. By aligning profits with purpose, strategy with soul, they are paving the way for a more conscious, ethical, and sustainable corporate future.

Who Will Take the Lead?

By now, we may have a deeper appreciation of the rationale, guiding principles, and potential benefits of integrating spirituality into the corporate world. But a pressing question remains: Who will lead this change? While some visionary leaders have made admirable efforts, true transformation requires more than scattered examples—it demands widespread, collective ownership.

It's easy to look outward—toward governments, CEOs, or policy mandates—for action. But the deeper question of who should take the lead points inward. Unlike CSR or ESG regulations that can be externally enforced, spirituality cannot be mandated—its real impact still depends on how wholeheartedly individuals choose to embrace and embody it in their daily work. Systems can enable the environment, but it's people who bring it to life. While systems can support, this is ultimately a personal journey that begins within each of us—not solely in boardrooms or legislation.

Transformation doesn't start in systems—it starts within each individual. Each one of us can lead—by example, through our integrity, compassion, and everyday actions. Rather than wait for formal policies or corporate-wide initiatives, we can begin by living these principles ourselves. This internal commitment brings clarity, connection, and meaning to our work and lives—and in doing so, we naturally inspire others.

When individuals embody these values, cultures shift. Teams become more empathetic. Organizations become more human. We don't need permission to live with purpose—we simply need to take responsibility. That's how we become the very leaders we've been waiting for.

Of course, external support still has a role to play. Governments have demonstrated this through mandated Corporate Social Responsibility (CSR) frameworks. For example, under India's Companies Act of 2013, companies (with a net worth of ₹500 crore or more, turnover of ₹1,000 crore or more, or net profit of ₹5 crore or more during any financial year) must spend 2% of average net profits toward CSR activities. This initiative—being auditable—has created accountability and impact. According to the Indian Institute of Corporate Affairs, approximately 16,352 companies in India are required to comply with this. As per India's National CSR portal, the CSR spending by these companies in FY 2014-2015 to FY 2022-2023 jumped from ₹10,066 crore to ₹29,987 crore—a 2.97x jump in 8 year-period. Another encouraging datapoint is that the share of private companies in total CSR spending increased from 72% in 2014-2015 to 86% in 2022-2023. This shift reflects growing voluntary ownership and initiative within the private sector, indicating that CSR is being viewed less as a compliance burden and more as a strategic lever for long-term value creation and community engagement.

Countries like France, the UK, and South Africa have followed suit. Could similar frameworks be applied to spiritual integration in workplaces? Possibly. For instance, India's Ministry of AYUSH promotes wellness practices like yoga, meditation, and Ayurveda through school programs and national campaigns. Bhutan's Gross National Happiness Index goes even further, embedding spiritual values such as mindfulness and collective well-being into national development policy.

The United Nations offers a global perspective. Built on principles like peace, dignity, human rights, and freedom, the UN has historically aligned its work with spiritual values. The foundational discussions for the UN Charter at the 1944 Dumbarton Oaks Conference included calls for the organization to support not only material progress but also spiritual development. Even today, Rule 62 mandates one minute of silence for prayer or meditation at each General Assembly session.

In 1952, the UN established a Meditation Room—a quiet, symbol-free space for reflection. As Secretary-General Dag Hammarskjöld once said, the space was designed to help people "withdraw into themselves and feel the void," reinforcing the UN's enduring spiritual foundation.

The UN has also launched global initiatives such as International Yoga Day, observed in over 180 countries, and collaborations between its Human Rights Office and faith-based groups to align spiritual teachings with universal values like justice and compassion.

Even UNICEF recognizes the importance of spiritual development in children. Its Convention on the Rights of the Child explicitly promotes spiritual and moral well-being as core to holistic growth. UNICEF's collaborations include creating toolkits for integrating spirituality into early childhood programs and working with religious communities to nurture values like empathy, resilience, and peace.

This emphasis on youth is vital. Today's children are tomorrow's leaders—not just in the corporate world, but across society. And while governments can help by integrating spirituality into school curricula, the most powerful influence begins at home.

Parents play a pivotal role. Children learn more from what we do than what we say. To raise grounded, purpose-driven future leaders, we must model the very spiritual principles we wish to see in them. Shakespeare once wrote, *"It is far easier for me to teach twenty what were right to be done, than be one of the twenty to follow mine own teaching."* Living these principles isn't just beneficial for our children—it transforms us too.

Stories as a Guide

Let me share a few stories to illustrate key points we must consciously keep in mind when embracing spirituality—both personally and within organizations:

1. Self-Responsibility and the Power of Owning One's Path

A once-violent snake transforms its ways after an encounter with a holy man. Embracing gentleness, it refrains from harming others, but the villagers mistake its newfound kindness for weakness. They hurl stones and cruel words, leaving the snake both physically wounded and mentally broken. In a second meeting, the holy man counsels the snake to defend itself without causing harm, teaching it the vital balance between assertiveness and compassion.

This encounter illuminates a profound spiritual lesson: our actions shape our destiny, and self-responsibility lies at the heart of true growth. In the corporate world, self-responsibility means understanding that you shape your own destiny.

Consider a business negotiation where one party continually lowers their prices to maintain goodwill. This can lead to exploitation. Instead, a fair but firm stance—negotiating value rather than price—ensures long-term respect and success.

A leader who follows servant leadership methodology to the core may become overly accommodating; their team might take advantage of them, missing deadlines or undermining authority. True leadership requires setting firm boundaries while maintaining respect. Self-responsibility means that you balance serving your team while ensuring the team puts in 100% of their energy to meet/overachieve the goals and metrics critical for the organization.

During my engineering college days, there was a fellow student from my hometown, Lucknow—a kind-hearted soul who carried an almost saintly patience. He lived just a few rooms down from mine in our hostel wing, and during exams, while most of us burned the midnight oil, he followed a different rhythm. Waking up at an ungodly hour—before 4 a.m.—when others were collapsing into bed, he would rise with unwavering discipline, believing the early morning silence was the best time for focused study.

It wasn't long before a few of us, desperate to make the most of our cramming sessions, started requesting him to knock on our doors and wake us up as he began his day. At first, it was just a handful of requests—friends relying on his punctuality more than their own alarms. But soon, word spread like wildfire. What started as a simple favor snowballed into a full-fledged responsibility. Each morning, he found himself knocking on 25 to 30 doors, each with a different wake-up time. It was as if he had unwillingly become the hostel's human alarm clock.

And yet, irony had a cruel sense of humor. The very people who begged him to wake them up—groggy from barely two hours of sleep—would hurl abuses at him the moment he knocked. Half-asleep curses replaced gratitude, frustration drowned out the initial enthusiasm, and what was once a favor became a burden.

For days, he endured it, sacrificing his own study time in the process. One thing became clear: while he couldn't control how others reacted—whether with gratitude or irritation—he could control how he chose to respond. Each groggy insult became less personal and more like background noise. The real test wasn't their behavior, but his ability to remain anchored in his own values. That clarity became a turning point. He realized that kindness, to be sustainable, must be rooted in self-awareness. And then, something shifted. He realized a truth many fail to grasp—helping others is noble, but not at the cost of self-responsibility. One morning, with a calm but firm resolve, he refused to play the role of the wake-up messenger any longer. The freeloaders of discipline were on their own.

And just like that, order was restored—not just for him, but for those who had leaned too heavily on his generosity. His grades never suffered again, and he walked away with an invaluable lesson: self-responsibility is the cornerstone of true success. No one else can walk the path for you—not even the kindest of friends.

Kindness, when tempered with strength, becomes a powerful tool for conscious leadership—it avoids harm not by appeasing others, but by honoring the deeper principle of cause and effect. Every choice we make—whether in leadership, communication, or personal conduct—sets off a chain of consequences. Strength without kindness can lead to fear and disengagement, while kindness without strength may foster complacency or blurred boundaries. But when these qualities coexist, they create a balanced force that upholds respect, clarity, and trust. For leaders and professionals, aligning actions with spiritual principles—such as accountability, fairness, and integrity— means acknowledging that today's decisions shape tomorrow's reality. Choosing to act with intention and awareness creates ripple effects: fostering loyalty, building resilient cultures, and promoting sustainable success. In this way, self-responsibility is not just a personal virtue but a strategic asset, demonstrating that by owning one's path with both heart and backbone, we actively shape outcomes in both our inner and outer worlds.

2. Ethical Practices and Transparency

One often-repeated story tells of a woodcutter who, in a moment of misfortune, drops his axe into a river. When a water spirit emerges, offering gold and silver axes, he truthfully chooses his own humble tool made of wood and iron. Impressed by his integrity, the spirit reveals that the test was meant to measure his character and rewards him with all three axes—the gold, the silver, and his original tool. The woodcutter's honesty earns him greater rewards than deceit ever could. This timeless tale highlights the profound value of truthfulness in earning trust. Similarly, in the corporate world, trust is the most valuable currency. Ethical companies attract loyal customers, dedicated employees, and long-term investors. Ethical conduct, a cornerstone of spirituality, not only fosters personal integrity but also lays the foundation for sustainable success and transparency in organizations.

Consider Warren Buffett's approach to business—he invests in companies with strong ethical foundations because he believes integrity leads to sustainable success. Companies like Patagonia have built trust through transparent and ethical practices, ensuring customer loyalty.

Take Satya Nadella's leadership at Microsoft—his emphasis on ethical AI, inclusivity, and corporate responsibility has not only elevated Microsoft's reputation but also driven financial success.

In business, unethical shortcuts—fraud, manipulation, or deceit—can bring temporary gains but eventually result in reputational damage and downfall.

Enron's collapse is a classic case. Their dishonest accounting practices inflated financial results, but when exposed, the company crumbled, leading to massive financial losses and legal consequences.

Ethical leaders may not always see immediate benefits, but in the long run, integrity attracts the right opportunities. Ethical brands outperform competitors, attract top talent, and create positive workplace cultures.

3. Vision and Long-Term Thinking

When three masons were asked what they were doing, their responses revealed starkly different perspectives. The first mason replied curtly, "Laying bricks," reflecting a focus on the immediate, mundane task. The second said, "Building a wall," demonstrating a broader understanding but still limited to the immediate structure. The third, with a gleam of pride in his eyes, declared, "Constructing a grand cathedral," capturing a sense of purpose far beyond the task at hand. The third mason's vision not only gave deeper meaning to his work but also likely ensured it was executed with greater care, passion, and dedication. His connection to a higher purpose would make his labor far more fulfilling and content-rich than the narrow perspectives of the first two. This story illustrates how spirituality nurtures a deeper connection to purpose, inspiring individuals to see their work as part of something greater. The third mason's response exemplifies this mindset, showcasing a long-term vision aligned with a higher purpose.

Steve Jobs didn't just see Apple as a company making computers; he envisioned a revolution in how people interact with technology. His long-term vision shaped Apple into an innovation powerhouse, inspiring employees and transforming entire industries. Jobs was deeply influenced by Zen Buddhism, which he explored during his travels to India in the 1970s. His practice of meditation and mindfulness shaped his leadership philosophy, emphasizing simplicity, focus, and intuition. This spiritual perspective guided Apple's minimalist design aesthetic, seen in products like the iPhone and Mac, where less is more. Yet despite his extraordinary vision and spiritual leanings, Jobs was also known for his volatile leadership

266

style. He often yelled at employees, dismissed ideas harshly, and created an intense work environment that some described as emotionally taxing. Former colleagues admired his genius but also acknowledged that his lack of empathy and tendency to micromanage could be deeply demoralizing. His story serves as a reminder that even the most visionary leaders benefit from balancing passion with compassion.

Leaders imbued with such spirituality encourage their teams to pursue meaningful goals that transcend short-term gains, fostering organizational growth, personal fulfillment, and a legacy of lasting impact.

A powerful example of visionary and compassionate leadership in action comes from Ratan Tata during the aftermath of the 2008 Mumbai terrorist attacks, when the Taj Mahal Palace Hotel, owned by the Tata Group, was one of the main targets. Amid the chaos and tragedy, what stood out just as strongly as the violence was the unwavering loyalty and courage of the Taj employees—many of whom risked or even lost their lives to protect guests. This was an outcome of the vision and long-term thinking of the Tata group, imbibed in the five core values of integrity, respect, excellence, pioneering, and unity.

In the months that followed this tragic event, Ratan Tata didn't just rebuild the hotel—he rebuilt trust. He visited the families of all affected employees personally, ensuring their financial and emotional needs were met. The compensation for every employee who was killed ranged from Rs 36 lakh to Rs 85 lakh in addition to the full last salary till the employee's scheduled retirement. The senior management took charge of the education of children and dependents anywhere in the world. They also provided medical facilities to the dependents for the rest of their lives. They also organized a counsellor for life for each person. A psychiatric cell was established in alliance with the Tata Institute of Social Sciences to counsel all those who needed such help. No one was laid off. From janitors to senior managers, everyone received support—not just as employees, but as part of a family.

The exemplary behavior by employees during the attacks became a case study at Harvard. The response was so extraordinary that Harvard University conducted a case study on the organizational culture and employee loyalty at the Taj. Researchers found that this deep-rooted sense of duty and selflessness wasn't spontaneous—it stemmed from years of leadership that emphasized respect, purpose, and empathy. The study highlighted that when employees feel truly cared for, they don't just work for a paycheck—they act with purpose, even in life-threatening situations.

Ratan Tata's approach during this crisis was a masterclass in long-term thinking and compassionate leadership. He didn't just protect a brand; he honored a bond. In doing so, he showed the world that even in the darkest of times, leadership grounded in humanity can illuminate a path forward. Through this crisis, Ratan Tata showed that leadership anchored in empathy and vision can inspire people to face unimaginable challenges together—turning tragedy into a testament of unity, strength, and hope.

Business success isn't just about completing tasks—it's about seeing the grand cathedral. Leaders who embrace long-term vision and purpose build companies that endure, inspire, and create lasting impact. Organizations that integrate spirituality into their leadership ethos foster not only financial success but also a legacy of positive change.

4. Contentment and Self-Awareness

A dissatisfied stonecutter, tired of his humble life, yearned for greater power and status. One day, he voiced his deep desire to be a rich man, and a divine power, hearing his plea, granted his wish. Suddenly, he found himself surrounded by wealth and luxury. Though he could afford grand homes and shaded pavilions, he still felt powerless under the sun's fierce rays whenever he stepped outside. Frustrated, he looked to the sky and envied its unchallenged dominance. If the sun could command the world with its heat, then that was true power. Envious of the sun's power, he wished to become the sun, and again, the divine power transformed him to be the sun.

Yet, even as the sun, he felt powerless against the storm clouds that blocked his rays. So, he pleaded again, and the divine power answered, transforming him into a mighty storm. He thundered across the sky, uprooting trees and flooding rivers, reveling in his newfound strength—until he encountered a massive rock that stood unshaken, unmoved by his fiercest winds. Awed by its unyielding presence, he longed to become the rock. Once more, the divine power granted his wish.

But as a towering stone, proud and immovable, he soon felt a sharp pain—a chisel striking his surface. A stonemason was shaping him, bit by bit. And in that moment of revelation, he understood: all his transformations—wealth, sun, storm, and stone—had been granted by a higher force, yet true power was not in what he became, but in the quiet, purposeful hands of the stonecutter. Without noise or praise, the humble artisan held the power to shape the world.

This timeless parable underscores profound spiritual truths. It reminds us of the futility of seeking fulfillment in external power, validation, status, or transformation. True purpose and strength lie in understanding and embracing one's intrinsic worth. The stonecutter's journey, facilitated by a divine power, illustrates the value of contentment and self-awareness, teaching that we each play a unique role in the grand tapestry of life.

Spirituality encourages us to trust in a higher power while looking inward rather than outward for validation. By aligning our actions with our true nature and purpose, we recognize the significance of our contributions and achieve a deeper sense of fulfillment, balance, and harmony.

This powerful story is highly relevant to the corporate world. Many professionals and leaders fall into the same cycle as the stonecutter—constantly chasing titles, wealth, or influence—only to realize that true fulfillment comes from within. Professionals who understand their true strengths and purpose can unlock far greater potential than those blindly chasing external validation.

CEOs, billionaires, and high achievers often still feel empty despite outward success. Jim Carrey once said:

> *"I wish everyone could get rich and famous so they could see it's not the answer."*

Oprah Winfrey, despite being one of the most influential and wealthy individuals in the world, has openly discussed her early struggles with self-worth and the realization that success without purpose feels hollow. Her journey underscores the idea that true fulfillment stems from alignment with one's values and inner well-being, not just external accolades.

Patagonia's founder, Yvon Chouinard, built a billion-dollar company but donated it all to fight climate change. He said:

"Earth is now our only shareholder."

His deep connection to purpose, rather than wealth, made Patagonia a brand that people trust and admire.

The stonecutter's happiest moment comes when he realizes his own worth rather than constantly chasing external power. Similarly, in business, leaders who cultivate contentment and gratitude avoid burnout, make wiser decisions, and inspire teams.

Companies with strong ethical and spiritual values that focus on their own worth often outperform those solely focused on profit. Why? Because such organizations attract loyal customers, employees, and long-term success. Similarly, the highest-performing leaders are not those who simply chase power, but those who lead with self-awareness, purpose, and contentment.

5. Interconnectedness and Leadership

A curious king, noticing the declining health and happiness of his people, summoned the wise elders of his kingdom. "Why," he asked, "were the people of previous generations so much healthier and happier than they are today?"

After a thoughtful pause, one elder stepped forward and replied, "In those days, people lived in harmony with nature. They took only what they needed and ensured that resources were shared selflessly. They nurtured the earth, and in return, the earth nurtured them. Their lives were guided by balance, empathy, and a sense of collective well-being."

The king reflected on these words, realizing that in his kingdom, unchecked greed and individualism had replaced unity and fairness. The elders' wisdom illuminated the importance of restoring harmony—not just between people and nature but also within communities.

This story carries profound spiritual and leadership lessons. At its heart lies the principle of interconnectedness: just as nature thrives through balance, so too do societies and organizations. True leadership thrives on balance, empathy, and collective prosperity.

Spirituality reminds us of our shared responsibility to care for one another and the world we inhabit. By embracing empathy, fairness, and selflessness, leaders can foster collaboration, trust, and collective growth. Great leadership is not about accumulating power but about empowering others. It calls for a vision that prioritizes harmony and sustainability over short-term gains. Leaders who align with these principles create environments where individuals thrive and organizations flourish, leaving a legacy of positivity and well-being for future generations.

Successful businesses don't just extract value; they create and redistribute it. Leaders who mentor, develop, and uplift their teams build organizations that last beyond them. Richard Branson of Virgin

Group believes in people-first leadership, empowering employees to innovate and grow. He famously said:

"Take care of your employees, and they will take care of your business."

And to take this one step further, businesses do not operate in isolation. They are part of a larger ecosystem that includes employees, customers, communities, and the environment. Organizations that recognize this interconnectedness foster trust, brand loyalty, and long-term growth. When Nadella became CEO, he shifted Microsoft's culture from competition to collaboration, emphasizing empathy, inclusion, and a growth mindset. This transformed Microsoft into a more innovative and people-driven company.

The elder's wisdom highlights the importance of balance—when people take only what they need and give back, everyone thrives. The same applies to corporate decision-making. Short-term gains (like cutting costs at the expense of employee well-being or the environment) often lead to deeper losses over time. Organizations that prioritize sustainability and long-term value over immediate profits build resilient brands. Consumers and investors increasingly prefer companies that act responsibly.

The story teaches that leaders and business, like nature, must strive for harmony, sustainability and focus on interconnectedness. Businesses flourish when they embrace empathy, fairness, and a vision beyond personal gain. True leadership is not about controlling but about nurturing resources (internal or external), for collective success.

6. Unity and Collaboration

Once upon a time, in a peaceful village surrounded by lush hills, lived a wise old farmer with his four sons. Though talented and hardworking, the sons were often at odds with one another, bickering over trivial matters. The farmer, concerned about their future, decided to teach them an enduring lesson.

One morning, he called his sons to the courtyard and showed them a bundle of sticks tied tightly with a rope. "Break this bundle," he said. Each son tried, but despite their strength, none could break it. Then the farmer untied the bundle, handing each son a single stick. "Now break these," he instructed. The sons easily snapped the sticks in their hands.

The farmer smiled and said, "Do you see? Alone, each stick is weak and easily broken, but bound together, they are unbreakable. Such is the strength of unity. If you remain divided, you will falter. But if you stand together, no challenge can defeat you."

He continued, "True unity is not just working together; it is rooted in understanding and compassion. Recognize each other's strengths and respect your differences. When your hearts align, you tap into a power greater than yourselves."

Humbled, the sons vowed to work in harmony. Over time, their unity brought prosperity to their family, and they overcame even the toughest challenges.

This story reminds us that unity is both practical and spiritual. When we connect through empathy and shared purpose, we become resilient and unstoppable. Like the bundle of sticks, we are strongest when bound by compassion, respect, and a common goal. Let us cherish these bonds and create a brighter future together.

In the early 2000s, Disney and Pixar joined forces in what many initially feared would be a fraught acquisition. Critics and insiders alike pointed to stark differences in their corporate cultures—Pixar, known for its fiercely protected creative autonomy and startup-like agility, contrasted sharply with Disney's hierarchical, corporate structure that often prioritized process over experimentation. There were also concerns about whether Disney would stifle Pixar's innovation or dilute its distinct storytelling voice.

However, those concerns were gradually put to rest. The $7.4 billion all-stock acquisition in 2006, led by then-Disney CEO Bob Iger, not only preserved Pixar's unique culture but elevated it. Steve Jobs, then Pixar's CEO, joined Disney's board, and Ed Catmull and John Lasseter took on leadership roles overseeing both Pixar and Disney Animation Studios. The leadership, driven by a shared vision and mutual respect, helped the two entities combine their creative strengths. Under their guidance, the merged entity thrived.

The results were undeniable. Within the first five years post-acquisition, Disney-Pixar released multiple blockbusters, including *Up*, *Toy Story 3*, and *Inside Out*, which collectively grossed over $2.6 billion worldwide. *Toy Story 3* alone brought in more than $1 billion globally and earned multiple Academy Awards. Beyond revenue, the collaboration reinvigorated Disney's animation brand, bringing back critical acclaim and creative excellence that had waned in previous years.

The Disney-Pixar merger stands as a case study in how cultural alignment, when nurtured intentionally, can overcome initial skepticism and unlock exponential value—both creatively and commercially.

Following the devastating 2011 earthquake and tsunami in Japan, Toyota displayed incredible resilience. The company's leadership fostered a unified response by focusing on collaboration between departments, ensuring clear communication, and prioritizing mutual support. The employees worked together to rebuild and recover, and Toyota quickly returned to its position as a global leader in automotive manufacturing, demonstrating the immense power of unity in overcoming crises.

In the corporate world, just like the bundle of sticks, organizations are strongest when they are united. A united team can achieve remarkable things, and it is through spiritual leadership that this unity can be cultivated, making every challenge an opportunity for growth and success. By recognizing that unity is the foundation for sustainable success, the teams remain aligned, compassionate, and resilient, paving the way for growth and a lasting legacy. Leaders who embrace these principles will guide their organizations not only to financial success but to a legacy of positive impact and purpose-driven achievement.

7. Resilience: A strategic imperative

In today's unpredictable world, resilience isn't merely a personal trait—it's a foundational spiritual and corporate capability. True resilience demands more than one story to fully explore its dimensions. Whether through patience and faith, adapting to change, or resourcefulness in crisis, the lessons are multifaceted and deeply relevant to both personal and organizational life.

Below are three powerful parables and their corporate parallels that illustrate the many shades of resilience—each echoing spiritual truths that can guide leaders and institutions through uncertainty and transformation.

- A farmer was eager to cultivate bamboo for the first time in the entire kingdom. He carefully planted the seeds and tended to them daily. He watered the soil, ensured it received sunlight, and protected it from harm.

Yet, as weeks turned to months and months into years, there was no visible sign of growth. By the fifth year, his patience began to waver. Neighbors mocked his efforts, questioning why he continued to toil for something that appeared futile. But the farmer, driven by faith and determination, kept nurturing the seeds. Then, in the sixth year, an extraordinary transformation occurred. The bamboo, which had shown no sign of progress for so long, suddenly began to grow at an astonishing rate, shooting up 90 feet in just six weeks. What the farmer had not seen during those five long years was the bamboo's roots spreading deep into the ground, creating a sturdy foundation capable of supporting such rapid growth.

Spirituality teaches us the value of resilience, patience, and faith in unseen progress. Just as the bamboo needed time to establish its roots, our personal and professional growth often requires a period of quiet preparation. It is during these moments of unseen growth that we cultivate the strength and stability necessary for future success.

In business, as in life, exponential growth is only possible when it rests on a strong foundation. Leaders who understand this principle recognize the importance of investing time and resources into building systems, fostering talent, and cultivating trust—even when immediate results are not apparent. By embracing patience, foresight, and faith in the process, we align with the rhythms of nature and the principles of spirituality, ensuring that when growth does come, it is sustainable and transformative.

Amazon started as an online bookstore in the 1990s, barely making a profit for years. Instead of chasing immediate success, Jeff Bezos invested in infrastructure, customer experience, and technology. It took over a decade, but today, Amazon dominates global e-commerce, cloud computing, and AI—because its roots were firmly in place before growth exploded.

Many groundbreaking ideas initially face resistance or seem impractical. Companies and leaders who remain resilient in the face of criticism often achieve breakthroughs that reshape industries.

For years, Tesla was dismissed as a risky, impractical venture. Elon Musk faced massive financial setbacks and near bankruptcy in 2008. But instead of giving up, he stayed committed to the vision of sustainable energy. Today, Tesla is one of the pioneering car companies, leading the EV revolution worldwide.

Just as the bamboo's years of unseen growth were essential for its eventual towering success, businesses and leaders must invest in foundational work, trust the process, and remain resilient. When the time is right, the results will be exponential and transformative.

One day, a fierce storm swept across a lush forest. Its powerful winds lashed against everything in their path, uprooting mighty oaks and snapping rigid pines. Amid the chaos, the palm tree stood tall, its slender trunk bending and swaying with the gusts. When the storm finally subsided, the forest floor was littered with fallen giants, but the palm tree remained, unharmed and upright. Its strength lay not in resistance but in its ability to adapt and yield to the forces it could not control.

This simple yet profound story illustrates the essence of adaptability, a cornerstone of spiritual resilience. Like the palm tree, individuals who embrace flexibility and maintain inner calm can weather life's storms without breaking. Spirituality teaches us to remain rooted in our values while bending gracefully to the demands of change, allowing us to grow stronger through adversity rather than being defeated by it.

In dynamic business environments, this lesson is equally vital. Rigid strategies and inflexible leadership can falter under the pressure of unexpected challenges, much like the unyielding trees. On the other hand, purpose-driven flexibility—anchored in a clear vision yet open to change—enables leaders and organizations to adapt, innovate, and thrive.

Rigid business models and leadership styles often lead to stagnation or failure when disruption occurs. Companies that embrace change with agility and foresight are the ones that survive and grow. Kodak, once the leader in photography, refused to adapt to the rise of digital technology, ultimately filing for bankruptcy in 2012. Meanwhile, Fujifilm reinvented itself by diversifying into healthcare and imaging technologies, ensuring long-term success. The difference? Fujifilm bent like the palm tree; Kodak remained rigid and fell.

Organizations that remain stuck in their ways, unable to pivot when needed, often face decline. The business landscape is full of once-great companies that fell due to their inability to evolve. Despite the rise of digital streaming, Blockbuster stuck to its outdated model of physical rentals. Netflix, on the other hand, pivoted to streaming early, becoming an industry leader while Blockbuster faded into irrelevance.

Companies that embrace uncertainty, experiment with new ideas, and take calculated risks are the ones that drive industry change. Innovation thrives in organizations that foster a growth mindset rather than clinging to outdated practices. Apple's constant reinvention demonstrates this principle—it doesn't just make great products, it continually evolves, transitioning from Macs to iPods to iPhones to services like iCloud and Apple Pay. By anticipating change rather than merely reacting to it, Apple continues to lead in innovation.

The lesson to learn from the palm tree is that true resilience in leadership and business doesn't come from resisting change—it comes from embracing it with agility, confidence, and wisdom. By staying rooted in core values while adapting to new realities, businesses can weather storms, thrive through adversity, and lead transformation rather than being overtaken by it.

Once upon a time, a clever monkey who lived in a tree by a river befriended a crocodile. The crocodile, however, had an ulterior motive. Tempted by his wife's demand to bring her the monkey's heart as a delicacy, he lured the monkey onto his back under the guise of offering him a ride across the river. Midway, the crocodile revealed his true intentions, gleefully announcing that he planned to eat the monkey's heart.

The monkey, though startled, remained calm. Quickly assessing his dire situation, he responded with ingenuity: "Oh, my dear friend, you should have told me earlier! I don't carry my heart with me. It's safely stored in the tree where I live. If we return to the shore, I'll gladly retrieve it for you." Intrigued by the idea, the crocodile turned back to the riverbank. The moment they reached the shore, the monkey leapt to safety onto the tree and chastised the crocodile: "It seems both of us have our tricks, but remember—deception can be a double-edged sword."

While the story highlights the value of calm and resourceful thinking, it ultimately reminds us that quick thinking can be the difference between survival and surrender. The monkey's ability to remain composed under pressure allowed him to outwit the crocodile and turn a life-threatening situation into a moment of triumph.

From a spiritual perspective, the monkey embodies the principles of mindfulness and presence. Spirituality teaches us to approach challenges with a calm mind and a resourceful spirit. By staying focused and grounded, even in turbulent times, we can uncover solutions that may seem elusive in the heat of the moment.

In leadership and life, this lesson is invaluable. Just as the monkey transformed a crisis into an opportunity, leaders who cultivate spiritual resilience can navigate uncertainty with creativity and poise. By fostering clarity of thought and adaptive problem-solving, they can overcome obstacles and guide their teams toward success. Ultimately, this tale reminds us that inner calm and ingenuity, when guided by spiritual principles, are powerful tools for navigating life's challenges. Spirituality instills resourcefulness and the ability to focus under pressure—qualities essential for navigating crises and seizing opportunities.

In business, moments of crisis are inevitable—whether it's a financial downturn, a PR disaster, or a high-stakes negotiation. Leaders who remain calm and composed during such times are more likely to make rational, effective decisions.

Each of these stories offers valuable insights into integrating spirituality into corporate practices. By embracing these lessons, organizations and leaders can inspire purpose, resilience, and meaningful growth — while creating a legacy of lasting impact.

Personal Spiritual Journey

In a world often defined by relentless ambition and external achievements, many high-performing professionals find themselves grappling with an inner void—quiet questions about meaning, balance, and true success. My journey is not shared to seek sympathy or admiration, but to offer a mirror—one that reflects the possibility of transformation through loss, introspection, and spiritual awakening. By sharing how a personal tragedy became the catalyst for redefining my purpose, I hope to invite readers to pause, reflect, and explore their own inner compass. This story is not just about me—it's about all of us who are searching for a deeper, more fulfilling way to live and lead. If you've ever wondered whether there's more to success than titles and targets, I believe you'll find resonance—and perhaps inspiration—in the path I discovered.

Right from my early childhood, I had brushed against spirituality in different forms and fashions. Initially, it was through the moral values instilled at home and school. Being part of a North Indian Brahmin family, there was a deep emphasis on the wisdom embedded in the Hindu religion and its scriptures, along with the enchanting moral stories and tales from the *Panchatantra* and *Hitopadesha*. These stories sparked curiosity, leading to spirited discussions with friends about their practicality in the real world. Yet, over time, spirituality became more of an intellectual indulgence—a topic for occasional debates rather than a guiding force in my life.

That changed in 2021.

It was a defining year for me—both professionally and personally. I had just stepped into the role of Global Head at a rapidly growing IT services firm with 18,000 employees. My mandate was clear yet ambitious: to accelerate exponential growth by strengthening the company's alliances with all technology giants and niche players, private equity firms, venture capitalists, analysts, and advisors. Reporting directly to the CEO, I was at the heart of the company's strategic expansion, where success hinged on the performance of my team.

The stakes were high. The organization was already one of the fastest-growing Indian IT services firms, consistently delivering industry-leading quarter-over-quarter growth. My role wasn't just about maintaining momentum—it was about amplifying, adding another layer of intensity to an already high-octane environment already defined by relentless pace and ambition.

As we often say in the corporate world, I was "drinking from the firehose" in those initial weeks—absorbing vast amounts of information, navigating relationships, and strategizing for the future. Then, out of nowhere, life delivered a blow that shattered everything.

I received a call from India. My mother had met with a terrible accident. She was in a coma.

The moment I heard those words, the air felt sucked out of my lungs. A deep, numbing silence followed. My hands trembled as I booked my flight. Everything else—work, responsibilities, the bustling corporate world—faded into irrelevance. My boss and the company were extremely supportive during this entire journey.

When I landed in Lucknow, I rushed to the hospital, my heart pounding in fear and desperation. The sterile smell of antiseptics, the beeping of machines, the sight of my mother lying motionless in the ICU—all of it felt unreal. My schoolmate, now a renowned neurosurgeon, was leading her treatment, which gave me a sliver of hope. But hope is a fragile thing.

For thirteen nights, I parked myself in the hospital, refusing to leave. Sleep was scarce, meals were an afterthought, and in the oddest hours, I made sporadic attempts to keep up with work. My boss was incredibly supportive throughout this ordeal. He urged me to focus on my personal situation, assuring me that work could wait. Yet, despite his kindness, I still felt compelled to do my part.

In parallel, I consulted every specialist I could, desperately seeking a glimmer of optimism in their words. I prayed as well as pleaded with fate—anything to bring her back to me. Hour after hour, I sat by her bedside, talking to her, recounting childhood memories, whispering words of love and reassurance. With the doctor's permission, I played her favorite hymns and songs, hoping—praying—that some familiar note would stir her soul, that she would hear me and find her way back. Music was her essence, the very rhythm of her being. A renowned vocalist on local television and radio, she had once filled countless hearts with her voice.

But this time, there was only silence. She never stirred, never opened her eyes. Not even once.

And then, she was gone.

I lost my mother without even getting to say goodbye.

The finality of it was crushing—an unbearable weight pressing down on my chest. There was no closure, no parting words, no lingering touch—just a hollow, unbearable silence. The woman who had been my anchor—my source of unconditional love—was suddenly... nowhere. The air felt heavier, the world suddenly emptier. There was so much left unsaid—so many conversations we would never have, so many moments stolen in the blink of an eye. I felt unmoored, adrift in a sea of grief, like a traveler caught in a relentless storm with no compass, no map—just a suffocating void. The world moved forward, indifferent to my pain. But I stood frozen, trapped in the echoes of what was and what would never be.

Losing my mother was a shattering experience—one that left me devastated, disoriented, and searching for meaning in the unbearable void she left behind. Grief is an unforgiving teacher—it breaks you, strips you of all illusions, and forces you to confront the rawest truths of life. In my darkest hours, when everything felt meaningless, my wife sent me a few videos on spirituality—on coping with loss, on the eternal nature of the soul. At first, I resisted. What could mere words do against the weight of such profound loss? But grief has a way of making you listen — and slowly, its messages began to seep in.

Little did I know that this tragedy would mark the turning point in my spiritual journey. But now, it has become my lifeline, a means to navigate pain, loss, and the very essence of life itself.

One of the most profound lessons I learned was about accepting the departure of a soul with the same grace as bidding farewell to a loved one embarking on a long journey. While the loss of a life can never be undone, the way we perceive and cope with it can transform entirely. I came across a perspective that encouraged wishing the departing soul well, reassuring it that we are doing fine and hoping for the same on its onward journey. The analogy struck deep—just as we wouldn't want a loved one to leave for a journey burdened by our tears, a soul should not depart weighed down by our grief. If we cling to sorrow, we make their transition harder, just as a traveler would struggle to enjoy their trip knowing their family is in distress.

Perhaps the most striking realization was the urgency of closing karmic accounts in real time—of leaving no words unspoken, no emotions unresolved. My mother's sudden passing left me with the painful regret of unexpressed thoughts, a lesson that now shapes how I approach every relationship. Life offers no guarantees of a second chance, and I now understand the importance of making peace in the present rather than waiting for an uncertain tomorrow.

This newfound perspective on life and loss didn't just change how I coped with grief—it awakened something deeper within me. It made me question everything I had prioritized until that moment. Was I truly living with purpose, or merely existing, caught in the relentless pursuit of success?

Like most, I had always seen spirituality as an abstract idea— something associated with peace, fulfillment, or perhaps an escape from life's harsh realities. But as I stood at this crossroads, I realized spirituality wasn't about retreating from the world. It was about redefining my place in it.

For me, spirituality became a force of clarity, a guiding light cutting through the fog of routine existence. It wasn't passive contemplation—it was an active transformation, reshaping my priorities, my ambitions, and the very essence of how I wanted to live the rest of my life.

At first, it was nothing elaborate—just a couple of minutes of meditation. Like many professionals, my mind was conditioned to chase productivity, always to stay engaged with work, commitments, and responsibilities. Sitting in silence felt unfamiliar, even uncomfortable. My thoughts would wander, jumping from task lists to pending emails, from past worries to future uncertainties.

I struggled to focus. The inertia was real. But something within me whispered that persistence was key.

As days turned into weeks, I felt the need for deeper discipline. What began as a few minutes of meditation evolved into a sacred morning practice—a commitment that would soon reshape my life. I made a firm decision: every single morning, regardless of whichever time zone I was in, I would wake up at 3:30 a.m. for my 4 a.m. meditation. This wasn't just about habit-building; it was about disciplining the mind, detaching from distractions, and training myself to operate from a place of inner strength rather than external noise. Whether I was traveling across time zones or managing a packed schedule, I never allowed excuses to interfere with this sacred commitment.

And something incredible happened.

The very inertia that once made meditation feel difficult began to dissolve. My focus improved. My ability to sit in stillness increased. The clarity of thought that emerged from these silent hours was unlike anything I had experienced before. The restless energy of the corporate world, the constant need to achieve, the subconscious weight of societal expectations—everything started to lose its grip on me.

As my practice deepened, I felt drawn toward structured guidance. I began pursuing my spiritual journey with an organization, where ancient wisdom met practical application. This wasn't about renouncing life—it was about weaving deeper awareness and purpose into life.

Through this path, my perspectives on success, purpose, and fulfillment transformed. I realized that true success isn't about how much we accumulate, but about how much peace, clarity, and joy we cultivate within ourselves.

With newfound clarity, the distractions that once occupied my mind started fading. I no longer felt the need to prove anything to the world. Instead, I became more focused on a deeper purpose—a calling that extended beyond personal ambitions.

One of the most profound shifts happened when I asked myself: "What do I truly want to do in life?"

This wasn't a surface-level question about career growth or financial milestones. It was a deep, introspective inquiry. What was my highest contribution to the world? What legacy did I want to leave behind?

The answers did not come from external validation, but from within.

It was then that the often-quoted saying took on a new meaning for me: "The two most important days in your life are the day you are born and the day you find out why."

Until that moment, I had been running—chasing success, achievements, and external validation, assuming that purpose was something to be earned through ambition. I believed that if I just climbed high enough or achieved enough, the sense of "why" would eventually reveal itself. But it never did. Climbing higher in the corporate ladder, earning more, and receiving accolades never brought a sense of fulfillment. That quote suddenly felt less like a motivational phrase and more like a piercing truth. It revealed a stark gap between the life I was building and the life I truly longed to live. My mother's passing shattered the illusion that success alone could be my purpose—and forced me to ask: Why am I here? What truly matters?

That inner questioning had become impossible to ignore. Something deep within me was stirring, pushing me to seek answers beyond the surface of daily existence. They say that when you truly seek an answer, it finds you. And in my case, it did—through an unexpected source.

A close friend recommended a 21-day course from www.ubuntuverse.org, designed to help individuals uncover their personal *"why."* It wasn't just another self-help program; it was an introspective journey that demanded nothing but my commitment to complete each exercise with honesty and diligence. There was no monetary cost—only the price of sincerity and effort.

As Abhinav Ubuntu, the founder of Ubuntuverse, puts it, the course is *"priceless"*—so he couldn't possibly charge for it. And he was right. Through thought-provoking exercises and guided self-reflection, the program helped me crystallize my thoughts, peeling away layers of doubt and distraction. By the end of those 21 days, my *"why"* wasn't just an abstract idea—it was a revelation.

Through those 21 days of self-reflection, I found myself peeling away layers- years of conditioning, ambition, and societal expectations. The more I searched within, the clearer it became—for too long, my identity had been shaped by achievements, external validation, and the relentless pursuit of societal-defined success. But beneath it all, what I truly craved was something deeper: *meaning.*

That was when I realized that my search wasn't just for a purpose—it was for a foundation, a philosophy, a guiding light to anchor my life upon. And that search led me straight to spirituality.

It was in this journey of introspection that I uncovered my true *why—to bring smiles across the world*. This realization was profound, and it reshaped everything I had once believed about success. No longer was it just about climbing corporate ladders or accumulating accolades. True success, I realized, was about impact—about touching lives, about leaving the world a little brighter than I found it.

With this newfound clarity, I made a bold decision. In 2025, I stepped away from my full-time corporate role to dedicate myself entirely to this mission—as an author, consultant, mentor, and coach. I channeled my experiences, my insights, and my life's learnings into my first book, *BEYOND SUCCESS Unleash the New You*. A book not just about professional excellence, but also about holistic success—one that blends corporate growth with inner transformation, balance, and fulfillment. In this world weighed down by stress and relentless competition, if I could help even one soul find happiness, contentment, and purpose, I would know my journey was worthwhile. This book is more than a compilation of insights—it is a blueprint for success as a way of life, one that transcends societal definitions.

My mission is clear: to bring smiles across the globe. I do this by helping individuals and organizations unlock their best selves—embracing a life of balanced success that harmonizes achievements with personal fulfillment, and where purpose is not a luxury but a necessity. Because *true success isn't just measured by what you accomplish—it's about who you become along the way.*

In just one year, I had not only gained profound clarity but also discovered the courage to act on it. As of April 2025, I haven't missed a single day of my early morning 45-minute meditation ritual. Looking back, I can see how deeply this practice—and the spiritual discipline behind it—has reshaped my life. The impact has been far-reaching and transformative:

1. Mental Clarity and Focus

- The fog of indecision and doubt gradually lifted.
- My ability to prioritize what truly matters became sharper.

2. Emotional Resilience

- Challenges—both personal and professional—did not shake me the way they once did.
- I learned to operate from inner stability rather than external turbulence.

3. Purpose-Driven Action

- Every decision, every project, every goal became aligned with a deeper sense of meaning.
- I was no longer just achieving; I was creating with intention.

4. Detachment from Distractions

- The endless cycle of comparison, the pressure of societal expectations—these began to dissolve.
- My energy shifted from seeking external validation to internal fulfillment.

5. A Renewed Definition of Success

- Success was no longer about titles or wealth. It became about peace, impact, and the ability to uplift others.
- I realized that when you lead from a place of stillness, success follows naturally.

In the world of business, we speak of financial capital, human capital, and intellectual capital. But what about Spiritual Capital—the one asset that fuels all others?

The greatest leaders are not those who simply outperform the competition, but those who operate from a place of clarity, balance, and purpose.

My journey has taught me this: Spiritual Capital is the foundation of true, sustainable success. Without it, ambition feels hollow. With it, even the most ambitious goals become meaningful and fulfilling.

My journey is far from over. Spirituality is not a destination; it is a continuous unfolding.

Every morning at 4 a.m., when I sit in stillness, I remind myself:

- This journey is about inner mastery.

- This path is about contributing to a world that craves conscious, purpose-driven leadership.

- True success isn't measured by what we accumulate, but by who we become in the process—and how we uplift those around us.

And so, I continue—committed, disciplined, and deeply grateful for the calling that has given my life its highest meaning.

Parting Thoughts

As we conclude this exploration into the power of spirituality, it's clear that a paradigm shift is not only desirable but necessary. The thoughts presented here reflect the transformative potential of spiritual capital when embraced by individuals and organizations.

The journey to incorporate spirituality into leadership is not a mere trend or abstract ideal—it's a pragmatic call to action for those who seek a sustainable and purpose-driven future. Today's complex challenges require leaders who can balance the scales of profit and purpose, embedding ethics, empathy, and vision into their decision-making processes.

Leadership for a New Era

The new era of leadership is not defined by titles or power but by the ability to inspire, uplift, and create meaningful change. This is the blueprint for a future where companies thrive not just by delivering products or services but by leaving a lasting, positive impact on their stakeholders and the world.

The pointers and stories shared earlier serve as timeless reminders of the principles that guide spiritual leadership—resilience, empathy, collaboration, and long-term vision. These values are not only applicable but essential for navigating the complexities of the modern corporate world.

Who Will Make it Happen?

So, who will take the lead? The answer lies within each of us. Leadership is no longer confined to boardrooms or executive titles; it is an opportunity available to everyone who chooses to live with intention, authenticity, and a higher purpose. Whether you are a CEO steering a multinational organization or an individual contributing to a team, the principles of spiritual capital can guide you toward a life of fulfillment and impact.

As you reflect on this journey, consider this: true leadership is not measured by what you accomplish for yourself but by what you inspire others to achieve and how you contribute to a greater good. The balance between profit and purpose is not a compromise; it's a harmony waiting to be discovered.

Carving Your Path Forward

The journey toward purpose-driven leadership does not end here—it begins with you. True transformation starts with self-awareness, a commitment to higher principles, and the courage to lead from within.

Embrace the spiritual foundations of kindness, resilience, and vision, weaving them into every decision you make. Create spaces where people feel valued, empowered, and inspired to bring their whole selves to work.

This is more than a shift in leadership—it is a movement. A movement that calls upon individuals, not just organizations, to step forward and embody the change they wish to see. It is about recognizing that spiritual capital is not a concept for tomorrow; it is a force waiting to be unleashed today. The world does not need permission to evolve—it needs bold individuals willing to take the lead.

So, will you wait for change, or will you be the catalyst? Will you rise to the challenge, step into your power, and ignite the spark that transforms workplaces and lives?

The time is now. The choice is yours. The world is waiting. **Lead the way.**

APPENDIX

FRAMEWORKS

The three frameworks outlined below are designed to be both **structured and adaptive**, *recognizing that transformation is not always linear. While each follows a phased approach, some phases may begin in parallel to accelerate impact or accommodate organizational rhythms. Depending on leadership commitment, business readiness, or cultural context, organizations may choose to* **prepone, postpone, or customize** *the sequence of certain phases. These frameworks are also* **interconnected**—*advancement in one area often enriches progress in another. Built-in* **feedback loops** *allow for ongoing recalibration, and leaders are encouraged to tailor the rollout based on the* **needs of different regions, business units, or teams**. *This flexibility ensures that purpose, well-being, and spiritual alignment are woven into the organization in a way that is* **authentic, actionable, and sustainable**.

Spirituality, Mindfulness, and Purpose Alignment in Organizations

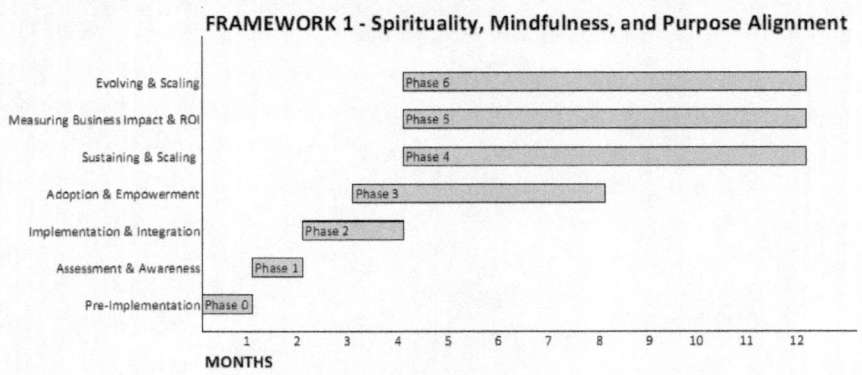

FRAMEWORK 1 - Spirituality, Mindfulness, and Purpose Alignment

Evolving & Scaling	Phase 6
Measuring Business Impact & ROI	Phase 5
Sustaining & Scaling	Phase 4
Adoption & Empowerment	Phase 3
Implementation & Integration	Phase 2
Assessment & Awareness	Phase 1
Pre-Implementation	Phase 0

MONTHS — 1 2 3 4 5 6 7 8 9 10 11 12

Phase 0: Pre-Implementation:

Before initiating this framework, organizations must consult with their Legal and HR departments to ensure that all implementations are compliant with applicable statutory and regulatory frameworks. It is also essential to assess local cultural sensitivities to avoid unintentional exclusion or legal risk. HR and Legal teams should co-design or vet policies and training materials to maintain alignment with labor laws, inclusivity mandates, and workplace equity norms.

Phase 1: Assessment & Awareness (Months 1-2)

Objectives: Evaluate organizational readiness, individual purpose, and its alignment with business goals.

- **Organizational Climate Survey:** Assess stress levels, job satisfaction, and openness to spirituality.
    - **Metric:** 70% employee alignment with company purpose, 20% stress reduction.
- **Leadership & Employee Interviews:** Gauge support and identify expectations.
    - **Metric:** 80% of leaders endorsing spirituality initiatives as beneficial.
- **Personal Purpose Discovery:** Employee surveys & workshops to uncover personal goals.
    - **Metric:** 60% of employees reporting increased clarity on purpose.
- **Cultural & Policy Audit:** Identify gaps in inclusivity, fairness, and values.
    - **Metric:** Benchmark against global corporate mindfulness standards.

> *Include HR and Legal consultation at this stage to ensure policy updates do not conflict with existing compliance obligations or employee rights.*

- **Baseline Business Metrics:** Measure productivity, engagement, and turnover.

  - **Metric:** eNPS score, turnover rate, innovation index.

- **Gratitude & Reflection Baseline:** Assess the current frequency of gratitude expression and team-level reflection practices (e.g., journaling, mindful pauses).

  - **Metric:** ≥ 50% of employees report currently practicing reflection/gratitude at least once a week (baseline for growth tracking).

Phase 2: Implementation & Integration Stage (Months 2-4)

Objectives: Develop structured spiritual and purpose-driven initiatives.

- **Mission & Value Alignment:** Update company mission with spiritual & mindfulness principles.

  - **Metric:** 100% participation in value alignment workshops.

    Ensure HR/legal vetting of revised mission/value statements for legal defensibility and inclusivity.

- **Mindfulness & Emotional Intelligence Training:** AI-driven tools & workshops for all employees.

  - **Metric:** 60% of workforce trained in 3 months, 90% satisfaction rate.

- **Spaces for Reflection:** Physical meditation rooms, virtual mindfulness platforms.

- **Metric:** 70% utilization of spiritual spaces, 85% satisfaction.

- **Purpose-Driven Leadership Training:** Embed spirituality in decision-making & communication.

  - **Metric:** 100% leadership training completion, +15% employee perception of leadership integrity.

- **Decision-Making with Integrity:** Introduce values-based decision framework as a tool for ethical, mindful leadership. Use reflective prompts during key decisions (e.g., who benefits? Unintended harm?).

  - **Metric:** 70% of leaders apply framework in decision-making.

- **Connecting Individual Purpose to Organizational Goals:**

  - **Metric:** 70% of employees articulating purpose alignment.

Phase 3: Adoption & Empowerment Stage (Months 3-8)

Objectives: Ensure active participation and long-term commitment.

- **Daily Mindfulness Practices including Meetings:** Encourage reflection, short silence, gratitude before meetings & key tasks. Instill presence-oriented, reflective culture.

  - **Metric:** 60% employee participation daily & in meetings.

- **Peer Support & Mentoring:** Create purpose-driven peer networks.

  - **Metric:** 50% participation in peer accountability groups.

- **Performance Reviews with Purpose Metrics:** Integrate purpose, empathy, and ethical decision-making into KPIs.

  - **Metric:** 80% of performance reviews incorporate purpose-driven metrics.

    Review updated KPIs and review structures with HR to confirm alignment with formal appraisal policies and labor laws.

  - **Empathy Index:** Peer/360° feedback on listening, compassion, and inclusion.

  - **Ethical Decision Score:** Scenario-based evaluations of values-driven decisions.

  - **Trust & Psychological Safety Score:** Pulse survey results on openness and honesty.

  - **Conflict Resolution Effectiveness:** Case audits reflecting ethical problem-solving outcomes.

  - **Ethics Training Completion:** 90% training completion rate across leadership teams.

Phase 4: Sustaining & Scaling Stage (Months 4-12 & Beyond)

Objectives: Embed spirituality into company culture for long-term growth.

- **Spirituality Task Force:** Monitor, adapt, and innovate purpose-alignment initiatives.

  - **Metric:** 80% task force retention rate.

- **Localized Spirituality Design:** Co-create spirituality practices that reflect local cultural norms ("Kaizen circles" in Japan, Ubuntu in Africa).

  - **Metric:** All regions have localized programs by month 6.

- **Monthly and Quarterly Program Updates:** Revise and enhance based on feedback.

  - **Metric:** 100% completion of quarterly updates.

- **Recognition Programs:** Celebrate employees who embody purpose-aligned values.

  - **Metric:** 10% of employees are recognized annually.

- **Global Rollout & DEI Alignment:** Expand spirituality integration across offices & diversity initiatives.

  - **Metric:** 75% adoption rate, +20% DEI engagement. *Before global rollouts, conduct a cross-cultural compliance review in collaboration with regional Legal and HR teams.*

- **Technology & AI-Driven Enhancements:** Leverage digital tools for scale and personalization.

  - **Metric:** 60% participation in AI-enabled mindfulness programs.

Phase 5: Measuring Business Impact & ROI (Month 4 onwards)

Objectives: Establish clear business value from spirituality-driven initiatives.

- **Employee Well-Being & Engagement:**

  - **Metric:** 20% stress reduction, 15% increase in job satisfaction by the end of month 6.

- **Retention & Talent Attraction:**

  - **Metric:** 10% turnover reduction, 15% increase in culture-driven job applications by the end of month 4.

- **Productivity & Innovation:**

- **Metric:** 20% increase in new ideas from mindfulness programs by the end of month 4.

- **Customer Satisfaction & Business Growth:**

  - **Metric:** 10% customer satisfaction increase linked to employee well-being by the end of month 6.

- **Inner ROI metrics:** Track non-financial indicators like gratitude expression frequency, resilience scores, and spiritual well-being (via optional pulse surveys).

  - **Metric:** $\geq$ 25% YoY improvement in "sense of meaning at work".

- **Financial Performance:**

  - **Metric:** 8-10% margin growth attributed directly to enhanced productivity & retention by the end of month 6.

Phase 6: Evolving and Scaling (ongoing basis from Month 4 onwards)

Objectives: Expand and innovate the program to ensure scalability and relevance.

- **Extend initiatives to global offices or other departments:**

  - **Metric:** 50% of the regions and departments in the first 4 months.

- **Integrate spirituality with diversity, equity, and inclusion (DEI) efforts:**

  - **Metric:** 80% involvement from the DEI teams.

- **Use technology (e.g., apps, platforms) to enhance accessibility:**

  - **Metric:** 80% participation rates in tech-enabled initiatives.

- **Collaborate with external partners for new insights and tools:**

  - **Metric:** 3-4 external collaborators established.

    Legal and HR must remain part of any new partnership assessments to vet data privacy, labor implications, and equity risks.

A² HARMONIZE Framework

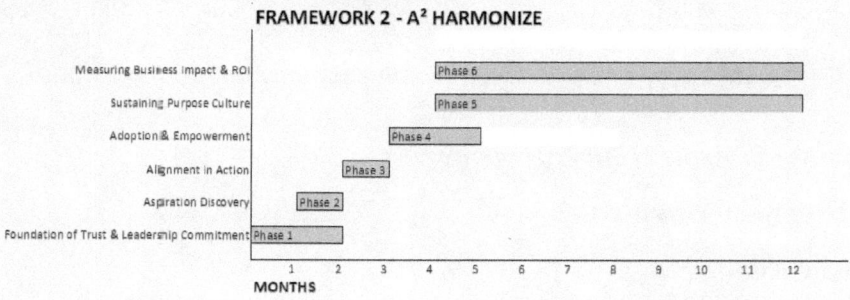

FRAMEWORK 2 - A² HARMONIZE

Before rolling out individual-level programs, all leaders will undergo structured training focused on personal growth, mindfulness, and spiritual leadership practices.

(Total Duration: 6 Months to Institutionalize | Supported by Leadership, HR, and External Experts)

Phase 1: Foundation of Trust & Leadership Readiness

Timeline: Months 0–1

Key Actions:

- **Leadership Bootcamps** on spiritual alignment and empathetic decision-making

- **Neuroscience Briefings** on motivation, habit formation, and psychological safety

- **Mission Re-Evaluation Workshops** to embed spirituality into organizational purpose

- **Org-Wide Launch and Ethics Briefing** to explain confidentiality and intent

Metrics & Targets:

- 100% of senior leadership trained in purpose-based leadership

- Revised mission statement completed and endorsed by Week 4

- 75% employees report feeling inspired by the updated mission

- 85% employee attendance in orientation/launch sessions

Phase 2: Aspiration Discovery

Timeline: Months 1–2

Key Actions:

- **Purpose Discovery Workshops**, journaling, and story circles

  Guided sessions that help individuals reflect on their values, formative life experiences, and aspirations.

- **Digital Tools** (Ikigai, Golden Circle, AI-based assessments)

  Ikigai helps employees find the intersection of what they love, what they're good at, what the world needs, and what they can be paid for—bringing personal clarity.

Simon Sinek's Golden Circle prompts reflection on "Why" (purpose), "How" (process), and "What" (action), offering a simple but powerful lens to frame one's work.

AI-based tools can analyze sentiment, language patterns, and themes from journaling or survey inputs to suggest emerging purpose profiles, strengths, and potential areas of alignment—at scale.

- **1:1 Coaching Sessions** or anonymous entries via a "Purpose Vault"

Safe spaces for deeper reflection, where employees can articulate personal aspirations confidentially.

Metrics & Targets:

- 80% employees complete aspiration profiles
- 90% positive sentiment in workshop feedback
- Minimum 50 anonymous purpose submissions (for trend mapping)

Phase 3: Alignment in Action

Timeline: Months 2–3

Key Actions:

Create Aspiration-Aligned IDPs

Develop Individual Development Plans (IDPs) that reflect employees' personal aspirations while aligning them with business objectives and team goals.

Launch Role-Purpose Mapping Exercises

Help employees analyze how their daily responsibilities connect to their personal purpose and the organization's mission, encouraging role clarity and meaning.

Develop Shared Purpose Statements at the Team Level

Facilitate team discussions to co-create purpose statements that represent how their collective work contributes to the broader organizational vision.

- Add a 3rd dimension to OKRs (e.g., "Impact on Others")

Reflect on how team goals are serving broader values.

Conduct Co-Design Labs to align team goals with individual aspirations

Interactive sessions where team members collaboratively reframe work structures and deliverables to integrate both organizational priorities and individual growth goals.

Metrics & Targets:

- 70% employees with updated IDPs by Week 12

- 50% of teams publish Shared Purpose Statements

- $\geq$ 50% of team-level OKRs include a values-based or personal-purpose component by Month 3

- 65% employees report seeing a clear connection between their goals and the company's mission

Phase 4: Empowerment & Expression

Timeline: Months 3-5

Key Actions:

- **Enable Seva Programs (1 hour per week of community service)**

  Institutionalize time for employees to contribute to causes they care about, promoting selfless service as part of work-life integration.

- **Launch Peer Mentoring & Purpose Coaches network**

  Pair employees with mentors or certified purpose coaches who guide them in applying their personal values and strengths to workplace challenges.

- **Provide Custom Learning Paths (DEI, mindfulness, emotional intelligence)**

Offer personalized training options that reflect each employee's development interests while reinforcing the organization's core values and cultural goals.

- **Introduce Mindfulness Checkpoints in meetings**

  Build in short moments of reflection or grounding practices at the start or close of meetings to reinforce presence, empathy, and intentional communication.

- **Spiritual Story Telling circles**

  Monthly sessions or content submissions where employees share short reflections on moments of meaning, gratitude, or ethical challenge.

Metrics & Targets:

- 50% employee participation in Seva by Week 18

- Mentorship participation rate: ≥10% of employees actively engaged in purpose mentorship (as mentor or mentee); 90%– satisfaction with mentor experience (survey-based).

- 60% employees engaged in custom learning journeys

- 25% of teams implement mindfulness rituals in regular meetings

- ≥ 100 stories shared in internal forums annually

Phase 5: Sustaining Purpose Culture

Timeline: Months 4–6 (then ongoing)

Key Actions:

- **Add Quarterly Aspiration Check-Ins to reviews**

Integrate structured prompts into performance reviews that encourage reflection on whether employees feel purpose-aligned and how they're evolving.

- **Publish Purpose Wall (anonymous stories, recognitions)**

  Create a digital or physical space to share real stories of personal purpose in action, reinforcing social proof and cultural momentum.

- **Launch Recognition Programs (e.g., "Seva Champion", "Purpose Builder")**

  Celebrate those who embody and promote values of spiritual leadership, empathy, and service—beyond performance metrics.

- **Enable Flexible Role Redesigns as aspirations evolve**

  Allow employees to shift responsibilities, take on new roles, or participate in short-term projects that better align with their evolving sense of purpose.

Metrics & Targets:

- 70% employees report feeling "purpose-aligned" in pulse surveys

- eNPS improvement: +20 points by Week 24

- Attrition rate reduced by 10% compared to the pre-program baseline.

- 100+ purpose-aligned recognitions logged on internal platforms

Phase 6: Measuring Business Impact and ROI

Timeline: Months 4–6 (then ongoing)

Key Actions:

- **Map qualitative outcomes to financial impact:** Translate improvements like reduced attrition, increased engagement, or innovation contributions into dollar values (e.g., cost savings, revenue lift, or margin impact).

- **Collaborate with Finance & Analytics teams:** Assign proxies (e.g., dollar value of 5% reduction in burnout-related absenteeism or 10-point engagement increase).

- **Incorporate metrics into executive dashboards:** Report on impact at leadership meetings to ensure visibility, accountability, and budget support.

- **Conduct Before/After Case Studies:** Track cultural, emotional, and business outcomes for key teams (e.g., productivity, client retention, innovation speed, idea generation).

- **Track momentum post-program:** Conduct 6-month and 12-month pulse reviews to track the durability of impact and identify areas for course correction.

Metrics & Target (End of 6 Months)

Category	Metric	Target
Mission Inspiration	*% of employees inspired by revised mission*	*75%*
Aspiration Participation	*% of employees who completed aspiration discovery*	*80%*
Purpose Alignment	*% of employees with aligned IDPs or team purpose statements*	*70%*

Seva Engagement	% of employees actively volunteering	50%
Mentorship Engagement	# active mentor/mentee pairs	100
Learning Journeys	% of employees in custom development pathways	60%
eNPS Score	Net promoter score improvement	+20 points
Attrition Rate	Reduction in voluntary attrition	-10%
Culture Vitality	# purpose recognitions and stories shared	>100

SEVA Culture Integration in Organizations

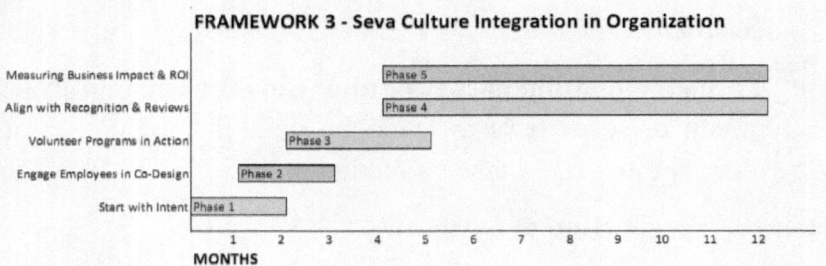

FRAMEWORK 3 - Seva Culture Integration in Organization

Phase 1: Start with Intent (Months 0–2)

Objectives: Align the Seva initiative with the company's purpose and leadership support.

Key Components:

- **Internal Communication Strategy:** The CEO or senior executive announces and models the initiative.

- **Purpose Anchoring:** Align Seva goals with the organization's mission.

- **Employee Awareness Campaigns:** Use emails, town halls, and videos to convey intent.

Outcome Metrics:

- 70% employee awareness via internal surveys

- Town hall/event attendance exceeds 60% participation

- Campaign open/click-through rates above 50%

Phase 2: Engage Employees in Co-Design (Months 1–3)

Objectives: Empower employees to choose locally resonant causes and projects.

Key Components:

- **Cause Discovery Sessions:** Workshops, surveys, or team huddles to identify focus areas.

- **Idea Submissions:** Channels created for submitting community or purpose-aligned projects.

- **Co-Design Labs:** Selected ideas co-developed into implementable projects.

Outcome Metrics:

- Minimum 25 employee project submissions

- 50% department participation in co-design

- Qualitative feedback from focus groups

Phase 3: Volunteer Programs in Action (Months 2–5)

Objectives: Execute service-based programs with structural and managerial support.

Key Components:

- **Service Time Scheduling:** Allow 1 hour/week or 1 day/month for volunteering.

- **Pilot Events Launch:** Organize departmental or team-based initiatives.

- **Leadership Support:** Managers ensure participation without penalizing output.

Outcome Metrics:

- 80% of planned volunteer hours utilized

- At least 60% team participation in pilots

- Well-being scores improve by 10% in pulse surveys

Phase 4: Align with Recognition and Reviews (Months 4+ and ongoing)

Objectives: Institutionalize Seva through performance, recognition, and cultural rituals.

Key Components:

- **Recognition Integration:** Include Seva stories in all-hands, newsletters, and peer awards.

- **Performance Linkages:** Review forms include reflection on service and impact.

- **Manager Engagement:** Managers are recognized for advocacy and integration of Seva.

- **Inner Alignment Reflection Prompt:** Add a spiritual alignment question in performance reviews, e.g., "How did your Seva/role reflect your deeper values this quarter?".

Outcome Metrics:

- Service mentioned in 50% of quarterly reviews

- eNPS improves by +10 points over 2 quarters

- 20% rise in manager-led recognition for Seva

- ≥ 70% of performance reviews include a values-alignment reflection item

Phase 5: Measuring Business Impact & ROI (Months 4+ and ongoing)

Objectives: Quantify the impact of Seva on employee engagement, retention, productivity, and external brand value. Demonstrate the financial and cultural return on investment to ensure long-term sustainability and leadership endorsement.

Key Components:

- **Define ROI Metrics:** Link Seva participation to shifts in employee retention, client engagement, innovation rates, and absenteeism.

- **Collaborate with HR & Finance:** Use analytics teams to assign financial proxies to qualitative outcomes (e.g., cost savings from lower attrition, productivity gains from increased engagement).

- **Pulse Surveys & Focus Groups:** Collect feedback on emotional resonance, team connection, and perceived organizational care.

- **Case Studies:** Document department-level Seva success stories with clear business impact to scale across the organization.

- **Leadership Reporting:** Integrate ROI updates into executive dashboards or quarterly business reviews to maintain visibility and alignment.

Outcome Metrics:

- 10–15% improvement in engagement and purpose-alignment scores in Seva-participating teams

- Reduction in voluntary attrition by 8–10% in departments with high Seva involvement

- At least 3 case studies are documented and used to influence future rollouts

- Financial proxies established for at least 3 Seva-linked performance metrics (e.g., retention, absenteeism, team productivity)

BEST PRACTICES

Management as Catalysts for a Purpose-Driven Culture

Leadership Commitment

Act as champions of spirituality by actively participating in initiatives, modeling behavior, and advocating for purpose-driven practices.

> **Metric:** Leadership participation rate in spirituality-related initiatives (Target: 100% of senior leaders complete spiritual alignment training by the end of Month 1).

Revisit and Elevate Alignment to Organizational Mission and Values

Once the organization's mission and values are revised to reflect a higher purpose, regularly review the alignment with individual and collective aspirations (A2 model).

Foster deeper connections between employees' personal purposes and the organization's goals.

> **Metric:** 70% of employees who feel connected to the organization's purpose (via periodic surveys). Quarterly leadership review of mission alignment with team goals (completion rate ≥ 90%)

Transparent and Inclusive Communication

Create platforms for regular updates on spirituality-related programs, sharing progress, success stories, and insights to foster open dialogue. These platforms may include "Purpose Pulse" newsletters, Slack channels, or MS Teams groups to share spirituality, well-being, and anonymous tools for surveys and/or feedback. These online portals will be best supplemented by in-person or virtual quarterly town halls where leadership transparently discusses progress, listens to employee feedback, and recognizes contributors.

Launch a 'Gratitude Friday' initiative or digital thank-you board to foster a culture of appreciation. Actively encourage monthly gratitude circles or reflections within teams.

Actively encourage feedback to ensure inclusivity and adaptability of initiatives.

Metric:

- $\geq$ 75% employee satisfaction with leadership communication and openness (survey-based).

- $\geq$ 1 spirituality/purpose communication per month from leadership (e.g., newsletter, town hall, Slack update)

- 50% of employees share gratitude messages by month 3.

Strategic Resource Allocation

Dedicate sufficient budget, time, and human resources to implement and sustain spirituality and wellness programs effectively.

Implement emotional resilience curriculum with training around mindfulness resilience, EQ coaching, and silent reflection breaks for stress-heavy functions (like sales, ops).

Ensure these resources are integrated into the organization's strategic priorities.

Metric:

- Percentage of annual budget (0.5%-3% of annual HR budget) and employee hours (0.5% to 4% of employee working hours) allocated to Seva, wellness, and spirituality programs.

- Better stress handling by 75% participants by month 3.

- Annual review shows $\geq$90% utilization of allocated resources.

Recognition and Incentivization

Design systems to recognize and reward employees who exemplify spiritual values, such as empathy, integrity, and purpose-driven leadership, in their work.

Create awards, appreciation events, or bonuses to celebrate these contributions.

Metric:

- At least 10% of employees are rewarded or recognized for embodying spiritual values (tracked quarterly).

- Recognition events are held quarterly across all business units.

Lead by Example: The "Show and Tell" Approach

Demonstrate spirituality in action by integrating its principles into decision-making, conflict resolution, and day-to-day operations.

Publish monthly case studies or reports highlighting real-life examples of spirituality influencing business outcomes and workplace culture.

Introduce a simple reflection checklist around value-based, high-impact decisions with empathy, ethics, & long-term impact.

Publish monthly 'living our values' stories (written or video).

Metric:

- ≥ 1 story or case study published per month showcasing purpose-based leadership in action.

- $\geq 70\%$ of employees report that "leaders walk the talk" (culture survey item)

- 80% leaders adopt checklists by month 4.

- ≥ 12 authentic stories published annually

Create Supportive Infrastructure

Provide spaces (physical or virtual) for meditation, mindfulness, and reflection to nurture spiritual growth.

Begin or end team meetings with 1-3 minute guided reflection/meditation.

Establish mentorship programs where senior leaders guide employees in integrating spiritual principles into their work.

Adapt spiritual programs to regional norms (e.g., Japan's "Kaizen circles," Ubuntu in Africa, etc.)

Metric:

- Mindfulness rooms or virtual hubs are active across 100% of major office locations
- ≥60% teams' recurring adoption of this by month 4
- 80% satisfaction rate from users of spiritual spaces or platforms
- All regions have localized programs by month 6

Integrating

Encourage ongoing education in spirituality through workshops, guest lectures, and book clubs.

Support certifications or training programs that build spiritual intelligence and emotional resilience.

Organize bi-annual offsites and virtual retreats focused on introspection, ethical reflection, and mindful leadership.

Metric:

- 4+ spiritual intelligence or well-being training sessions offered per quarter
- 60% of managers attend at least one session per 6-month cycle

- 80% learner satisfaction across training events. Number of learning sessions conducted annually, and employee participation rates

- 100% leadership participation with ≥80% satisfaction score

Continuous Learning and Development

Encourage ongoing education in spirituality through workshops, guest lectures, and book clubs.

Support certifications or training programs that build spiritual intelligence and emotional resilience.

Organize bi-annual offsites and virtual retreats focused on introspection, ethical reflection, and mindful leadership.

Metric:

- 4+ spiritual intelligence or well-being training sessions offered per quarter

- 60% of managers attend at least one session per 6-month cycle

- 80% learner satisfaction across training events. Number of learning sessions conducted annually, and employee participation rates

- 100% leadership participation with ≥80% satisfaction score

Organizational Mission Alignment with Individual Purpose

The following helps revisit the organizational mission with structured processes to align individual aspirations—creating a purpose-driven culture that is authentic, actionable, and sustainable.

Phase 1: Listen & Discover—Surfacing Individual Purpose

Anonymous Purpose Discovery Surveys

Explore what fulfills employees via reflective, values-based questions. **Metric:** 80% response rate; 70% report increased clarity on personal values

Facilitated Purpose-Discovery Workshops

Use tools like journaling, Ikigai, and Sinek's Golden Circle for deeper introspection.

> **Metric:** 90% positive feedback from participants; 75% workshop attendance rate

One-on-One Coaching Conversations

Trained internal coaches help translate aspirations into personal growth maps.

> **Metric:** 65% of participants complete at least one coaching session

Phase 2: Co-Create—Shaping the Collective Mission

Engage Diverse Stakeholders

Form a cross-functional co-creation group (HR, business leaders, employee reps, external experts) to revisit the mission.

> **Metric:** 100% representation from all business units and HR in the co-creation group

Expand Mission Beyond Profit

Integrate language around purpose, inclusivity, well-being, and spiritual values (e.g., clarity, empathy, mindfulness) in a non-denominational, universal tone.

Metric: Final mission includes ≥3 purpose- or spirituality-aligned themes (e.g., compassion, well-being, inclusivity)

Test & Validate

Present the revised mission to broader teams via town halls or focus groups for authentic feedback and refinement.

Metric: 75% employee agreement that the revised mission "feels authentic" via post-validation survey

Phase 3: Align—Connecting Individual and Organizational Purpose

Purpose Alignment Workshops

Teams align their individual "why" to organizational goals and team charters.

Metric: 70% of employees complete alignment sessions; 65% report a clear connection to team or org goals

Create Confidential Purpose Profiles

Document aspirations privately for development, while using aggregated insights for strategic HR planning.

Metric: 80% profile completion rate; 100% data privacy compliance

Values-Aligned OKRs

Add a 3rd dimension to OKRs focused on ethical contribution or impact on others, enabling teams to reflect purpose in goal-setting.

Metric: ≥ 50% of teams adopt values/purpose-based OKRs by Month 3.

Develop Shared Purpose Statements

Encourage departments to craft statements that reflect how their work drives the broader mission.

Metric: 50% of teams publish a shared purpose statement by Month 3

Phase 4: Activate—Living the Mission through Daily Work

Seva Hours / Purpose Projects

Dedicate time to community service or personal impact aligned with company values.

Metric: 50% employee participation within the first 3 months

Dynamic Role Rotations

Enable cross-functional projects and role flexibility based on evolving aspirations.

Metric: 30% of participating employees shift or rotate roles/projects within 6 months

Embed in Performance Conversations

Include purpose prompts in reviews: "How did your work this quarter reflect your values?"

Metric: 80% of performance reviews include a purpose-reflection prompt

Decision Reflection Checklist

Use a simple reflection tool during decision-making processes to evaluate alignment with empathy, well-being, and organizational values.

Metric: $\geq 70\%$ leadership decisions reviewed with this tool by Month 4

Phase 5: Celebrate & Evolve—Sustaining the Culture

Purpose-Driven Recognition Programs

Celebrate behaviors that reflect both values and impact—e.g., empathy, courage, creativity.

Metric: 10% of employees recognized for purpose-aligned behavior per year

Storytelling & Peer Sharing

Share authentic stories of alignment wins to inspire and normalize purpose expression.

Metric: 100+ peer stories submitted/shared across org platforms annually

Leadership as Purpose Mentors

Equip managers to act as guides—not just evaluators—of personal alignment journeys.

Metric: Mentorship participation rate: ≥70% of employees actively engaged in purpose mentorship (as mentor or mentee); 90%+ satisfaction with mentor experience (survey-based).

Spiritual Impact Dashboard

Track emotional resilience, gratitude frequency, values-aligned behavior.

Metric: Dashboard published quarterly; metrics improve 15-20% YoY.

Adaptive Role Design

Review and adapt roles as aspirations evolve, enabling organic growth.

Metric: 40% of roles evolve or flex within a year based on employee aspirations

Metrics to Monitor Impact

Category	Example Metric
Engagement	% participation in purpose discovery workshops
Alignment Quality	% of employees who feel their roles are purpose-aligned
Culture Vitality	Frequency of peer recognitions & storytelling
Strategic Impact	Attrition drop, engagement lift, innovation rates
Mission Resonance	Employee sentiment score on the revised mission

Thought:

Rather than treating the mission and purpose alignment as two separate initiatives, the A2 Harmonize Alignment Framework recognizes them as interdependent: a mission without personal meaning is forgettable; a purpose without organizational grounding is unscalable.

WORKBOOK EXERCISES – TRANSFORMING CHALLENGES WITH SPIRITUAL PRINCIPLES

These exercises are designed to help you move from insight to implementation. Each one draws upon the frameworks shared in the book and guides you through applying them to your unique context. Use these as leadership reflection tools, team workshop guides, or organizational planning blueprints.

Exercise 1: Reigniting Employee Engagement in a Sustainability-Focused Organization

Context

You work in a consumer goods company operating in one of the most environmentally impactful industries. While the company enjoys a strong eco-conscious reputation, employee engagement has declined—particularly among operational teams. Many feel their daily work is disconnected from the company's sustainability mission. An excessive focus on metrics has eroded emotional connection, leading to lower productivity, dissatisfaction among employees, partners, and customers, and a negative impact on financial performance.

⚠ Challenge Prompt

How can you rebuild the emotional connection between the globally diverse employee base and the organization's sustainability-driven purpose?

🔥 STEP 1: Define the Purpose-Engagement Vision

What transformation do you want to see in employee connection to sustainability goals? What would success look like?

🖊 Your response:

_____

_____

_____

_____

❄ STEP 2: Apply Core Frameworks from the Book

Leverage the following frameworks/ best practices:

- A² HARMONIZE Framework (special focus on Phases 1–5: from trust and aspiration discovery to expression and sustainability)

- Spirituality, Mindfulness & Purpose Alignment (special focus on Phases 1–5: from assessment through inner ROI tracking)

- Management as catalysts for a purpose-driven culture (focus on Phases 1–6: covering leadership alignment, infrastructure, and recognition)

- Seva Culture, Mindfulness Checkpoints, Leadership Communication (focus on Phases 1–5: especially in recognition, alignment, and community impact)

These frameworks are intentionally extended beyond early implementation to include later phases (4–6) to ensure sustainability, measurement, and global adaptability—critical given the emotional disconnect and cultural complexity of the engagement challenge.

To address the disconnect between operational work and sustainability goals, we will integrate the following enhancements:

- Establish peer mentoring and purpose coaches to provide ongoing guidance and personal alignment.

- Use values-based decision checklists to reconnect everyday choices with ethical and long-term sustainability goals.

- Include quarterly aspiration check-ins for employees to reflect on purpose alignment.

- Expand recognition systems to include Seva-linked impact stories and community contributions.

✎ How will you apply these in your initiative?

_____

_____

_____

_____

🏭 STEP 3: Customize for Your Industry, Region, & Organization

What unique aspects of your company or industry must this initiative address? – Given the global footprint, it is vital that purpose and sustainability are communicated in culturally resonant ways. For example, Asia-based teams may align more with spiritual terms like *dharma* or *seva*, while European or North American offices may prefer language rooted in mindfulness, values, or ethics. This ensures universal inclusion without uniformity. Incorporate culturally adaptive expressions of purpose (e.g., Ubuntu in Africa, Kaizen Circles in Japan) to honor regional contexts.

✎ Your response:

_____

_____

_____

☸ STEP 4: Brand the Initiative

Create a name and message for your initiative.

    ✎ Initiative Name: _____

    ✎ Slogan or Message: _____

Visual or Symbolic Ideas:

_____

_____

_____

_____

STEP 5: Design Key Components

Purpose Discovery & Alignment

[ ] Facilitate personal purpose discovery sessions

[ ] Hire external expert coaches to help in this discovery and alignment with the organization's mission (which, if needed, may be modified/elevated in consultation with management)

[ ] Conduct values co-creation workshops and shared purpose statements by the team

[ ] Create Individual Plans (IDPs) aligning aspirations with mission and business objectives

[ ] Leverage digital tools for purpose identification and 1:1 coaching sessions

[ ] Establish peer mentoring and purpose coach networks to support alignment journeys

[ ] Enable flexible role redesigns that evolve with changing employee aspirations and sustainability commitments

Learning, Engagement & Development

[ ] Provide custom learning paths

[ ] Leadership hands-on involvement with regular transparent & inclusive communications, bootcamps, briefings, discussions, and lead by example with "Show & Tell" approach

[ ] Create real-world connection moments with sustainability beneficiaries

Recognition, Culture & Communication

[ ] Launch regular employee surveys to monitor progress

[ ] Allocate resources strategically and empower the team

[ ] Launch storytelling platforms (town halls, videos, articles) and ensure early success is broadcast across the organization

[ ] Launch a "Sustainability Seva Champions" recognition program to reward contributions to internal and external sustainability impact

Mindfulness & Decision Making

[ ] Introduce 5-minute mindfulness checkpoints before meetings

[ ] Introduce quarterly purpose check-ins to help employees reflect on alignment and fulfillment

[ ] Use a values-based decision framework to embed empathy, long-term thinking, and impact awareness into key decisions

Performance, Measurement & KPIs

[ ] Redesign KPIs to include purpose-driven impact and spiritual parameters

[ ] Create a structured program for recognition and incentivization

Your response:

_____

_____

_____

▥ STEP 6: Plan Phased Implementation

Phase	Key Actions	Start-End	Owner(s)	Notes
Pre-Implementation	Align with HR, Legal, and Leadership on Spiritual language, Seva integration, and cultural sensitivities	Week 0-2	HR, Legal, Executive Leaders, Communications	Ensure Cultural/Legal Nuance is included in Baseline Survey & Toolkit Design
	Conduct baseline survey (Engagement, Purpose/Clarity)			
	Develop Communication Toolkits and Change Readiness Assets			
Pilot Phase	Run pilots with 2-3 diverse Teams and/or Regions	Week 3-6	Pilot Sponsors, Learning & Development (L&D), Local HR	Use Insights to refine Messaging and Rollout Plans
	Test Storytelling Formats and Values-Based Decision Checklists			
	Trial Seva recognition and feedback loops			
Phase 1: Awareness	Launch purpose discovery workshops	Month 1-2	CEO Office, Culture team, Communications Team	Emphasize Emotional Resonance over Strategy
	The CEO sends the launch message, with a personal reflection			
	Begin storytelling campaign (internal "why")			

Phase 2: Implementation	Implement IDPs with coaching support	Month 2- Mid Month 3	Learning & Development, HR Biz Partners, Seva Task Force	Prioritize Operational Teams for Early Adoption
	Launch Seva pilot projects linked to sustainability			
	Begin structured story collection and sharing			
Phase 3: Adoption & Empowerment	Redesign OKRs to include purpose impact	Mid-Month 3 - Month 4	HR Biz Partners, People Analytics, Coaches	Tie Reflections to Quarterly Reviews and Performance Conversations
	Activate the peer mentor network for guidance			
Phase 4: Sustaining & Scaling	Launching cultural adaptation kits (region-specific)	Month 4- Month 6	DEI, Executive Leadership, Global HR, Communications	Ensure Accessibility Across All Employee Levels and Geographies
	Begin Quarterly aspiration check-ins			
	Recognize "Sustainability Seva Champions" at org-wide forums			
Phase 5: Measuring Business Impact	Launch Inner ROI dashboard (gratitude, clarity, ethical behavior)	Month 4- Ongoing	HR Analytics, Finance, Executive Leadership	Blend Qualitative and Quantitative Metrics for Executive Visibility
	Link to business metrics: productivity, attrition, innovation, CSATs			
	Work with Finance to assign monetary proxies			
	Expand regionally/global	Month 4-	Environmental Sustainability	Stay Aligned with

328

Phase 6: Evolving & Scaling	ly and across all functions	ongoing	Group (ESG), L&D, Strategic Partners	Emerging Sustainability and Workforce Engagement Trends
	Refresh storytelling and learning content every 6-9 months			
	Collaborate with external experts for innovation & inner development			

Please fill in the above table, ensuring that each action includes the name of a responsible person and specific dates for each timeline.

STEP 7: Measure and Reflect

What metrics will you use to track success?

(e.g., % aspiration profiles, % IDPs for alignment, % employees inspired by revised mission, engagement scores, eNPS, mindfulness participation, productivity, attrition rate, innovation index, culture vitality, KPI shifts, stories shared, Seva contributions & engagement, CSATs, Revenues & Margins at team level, etc.).

In addition to standard metrics, track "inner ROI" such as employee-reported clarity of purpose, gratitude journaling frequency, ethical decision-making usage, and participation in peer-led reflection circles. These qualitative insights can be captured via quarterly pulse surveys or journaling prompts.

Work with Finance and HR analytics teams to assign proxies for emotional well-being, such as the estimated financial impact of a 10% increase in spiritual alignment or a 15-point improvement in ethical trust score (e.g., lower burnout-related absenteeism, higher Seva-led engagement).

In addition to qualitative and behavioral metrics, ensure that the dollar impact is measured wherever feasible—such as cost savings from reduced attrition, productivity gains, improved client retention, or innovation-driven revenue. For greater clarity, consider working with Finance or HR analytics teams to assign financial proxies to each outcome area (e.g., estimating the monetary value of a 10-point increase in engagement or a 5% drop in turnover or burnout-related absenteeism). This reinforces the strategic value of the initiative and strengthens leadership buy-in.

✎ Your response:

....

....

♀ *Final Thought:*

"A role without meaning creates burnout. A purpose-connected role creates energy."

Reignite your culture by reminding every employee—no matter their location, role, or background—that they are a vital contributor to a shared mission.

Continue with Exercises 2, 3, and 4

As demonstrated in Exercise 1, readers are encouraged to create a detailed and customized engagement blueprint using the structured guidance provided. For Exercises 2, 3, and 4, please refer back to the 7-step format in Exercise 1 to guide detailed design and execution for this exercise. You must customize the outcomes of the 7-step process for each context and challenge prompt.

- Start by examining the context and challenge prompt,

- Apply relevant frameworks and principles from the book,

- Customize your solutions based on your industry dynamics and organizational culture, and

- Design a meaningful internal brand to drive ownership, visibility, and inspire buy-in.

Be intentional about linking initiatives to both personal and organizational purpose—and be sure to define key metrics that reflect business, human, and cultural impact.

Exercise 2. Leading Cultural Shifts in Legacy-Driven Teams

Context: A traditional automotive company faces strong internal resistance to its electric vehicle (EV) transformation strategy. Veteran engineers fear becoming obsolete, and investors doubt the financial viability of the transition with high upfront investments. Initial enthusiasm is limited to younger employees. Meanwhile, market trends and regulatory shifts indicate that delaying this transformation could significantly erode future revenues and margins, threatening the company's long-term competitiveness.

> **Challenge Prompt:** How can leaders preserve dignity, address fear, and align legacy talent with innovation—while clearly communicating the business risks of inaction and making a compelling case for sustainable growth through EV adoption?

Exercise 3. Healing Mistrust in Community-Centric Finance

Context: A microfinance initiative intended to serve rural women by a leading microfinance organization offering loans to underserved communities collapses due to impractical loan conditions and exclusion of community voices. Field staff feel unheard, and local leaders grow suspicious of the organization's intentions. As trust deteriorates, loan repayment rates fall, revenues and margins decline, and both employee morale and community engagement suffer.

> **Challenge Prompt:** How do you transform mistrust into co-ownership, reignite passion in the field officers, and design finance models that both restore trust and unlock scalable community impact—while restoring financial performance and

rebuilding credibility through authentic participation and purpose-driven redesign?

Exercise 4. Reviving Creativity in a Burned-Out Media Team

Context: A creative agency known for innovation is losing clients and morale due to overwork and creative exhaustion. Employees no longer felt like creators; they felt like content machines churning out like clockwork. A new mindfulness initiative, intended to restore balance, is ridiculed by the Chief Creative Officer and team. Leaders face internal backlash for promoting practices perceived as unproductive. As creative energy declines, innovation quotient and output quality suffer—leading to falling revenues, shrinking margins, and eroding satisfaction among both employees and clients.

Challenge Prompt: How can leaders balance performance pressure with mindful creativity—to reignite innovation, rebuild employee morale, and reverse the decline in client satisfaction, quality, and financial performance?

BIBLIOGRAPHY

Relevant Links

Source / Title	Link (Full URL)	Book Page(s)	Claim / Usage
Inc., quoting The Wall Street Journal	Dying to Reach the Top? Research Shows Most CEOs Face Exhaustion, Burnout, and Even Early Death--but Small-Business Owners Don't How to Survive Being a 24/7 Boss - WSJ	Preface	CEOs burn out and die on the job
Benefits Canada, quoting Deloitte and LifeWorks Inc	82% of senior leaders experiencing exhaustion indicative of burnout: survey | Benefits Canada.com	Preface	Senior leaders facing exhaustion
Great Place To Work	https://www.greatplacetowork.com/best-workplaces/100-best/2024	Preface	Fortune 100 Best companies to work for
World Health Organization	https://www.who.int/news/item/13-04-2016-investing-in-treatment-for-depression-and-anxiety-leads-to-fourfold-return	2	$1 trillion is lost annually due to depression and anxiety
Gallup	https://www.gallup.com/workplace/288539/employee-burnout-biggest-myth.aspx	2	76% employees face burnout at least sometimes
Modern Health, quoting the Center for Prevention and Health Services	https://www.modernhealth.com/post/cost-of-poor-mental-health-in-workplace	3	Poor mental health costs employers more than they think

333

PMC (PubMed Central), quoting the National Health Interview Survey	https://pmc.ncbi.nlm.nih.gov/articles/PMC11217305/	20	Increase in the number of Americans leveraging meditation
The McKinsey report in 2021	https://www.mckinsey.com/featured-insights/sustainable-inclusive-growth/charts/the-great-attrition-stems-from-a-great-disconnect	20	The great attrition stems from a great disconnect
Brand Hopper Feature	https://thebrandhopper.com/2025/07/14/calm-headspace-driving-the-mindfulness-app-boom/	20	Meditation app downloads soared during the pandemic
Finance Online - Meditation statistics	https://financesonline.com/meditation-statistics/	21	Meditation helping individuals
Meditation statistics from Thegoodbody.com	https://www.thegoodbody.com/meditation-statistics/	22	200 and 500 million people around the world are practicing meditation
Search Inside Yourself Leadership Institute	https://siyli.org/search-inside-yourself	24, 190	SIYLI promotes mental well-being globally
The Global Wellness Institute	https://globalwellnessinstitute.org/press-room/press-releases/globalwellnesseconomymonitor2023/	25	Growth in the total wellness economy
Truworth Wellness	https://www.truworthwellness.com/blog/the-corporate-wellness-hype-v-s-reality/	25	Corporate Wellness- Hype vs. Reality

Harvard Business Review	https://www.health.harvard.edu/blog/yoga-and-meditation-offer-health-care-savings-and-you-can-do-them-at-home-201511188616	26	Aetna leverages Mindfulness to improve productivity by $3000 per employee
McKinsey Health Institute 2023	https://www.livemint.com/news/india/india-tops-in-workplace-burnout-survey-with-59-reporting-symptoms-mckinsey-health-institute-11698999238983.html	42	Global workplace burnout survey
World Health Organization	https://www.npr.org/2021/05/17/997462169/thousands-of-people-are-dying-from-working-long-hours-a-new-who-study-finds	43	Global deaths due to long working hours
	https://www.who.int/news-room/questions-and-answers/item/global-regional-and-national-burdens-of-ischemic-heart-disease-and-stroke-attributable-to-exposure-to-long-working-hours-for-194-countries-2000-2016		
Atlassian	https://www.atlassian.com/blog/state-of-teams-2022	43	Improvements in productivity, innovation, etc., due to an environment for well-being
Wharton	https://knowledge.wharton.upenn.edu/article/what-our-brain-activity-reveals-about-improving-workplace-culture/	44	What our brain activities reveal about improving workplace culture

Atlassian Blog	https://www.atlassian.com/blog/state-of-teams-2022	45	The state of Teams at Atlassian
Microsoft	https://www.microsoft.com/en-us/worklab/work-trend-index/brain-research?msockid=2bde6eae073062a4342b7883061d634c	45	Research proves your brain needs a break
Shoes Consulting	https://shoesoffconsulting.com/blog/digital-marketing-services/the-unilever-case-study-how-they-predicted-remote-work-5-years-early/	45	Remote working done the right way by Unilever
Mindfulworkplace community	https://siyli.org/resources/press/case-study-sap-shows-how-employee-well-being-boosts-the-bottom-line	46	SAP employees benefit from using mindfulness
Danah Zohar	https://www.danahzohar.com/books/spiritual	48	Spiritual Intelligence: The Ultimate Intelligence
Ideas quoting Journal of Business Ethics	https://ideas.repec.org/a/kap/jbuset/v168y2021i1d10.1007_s10551-019-04258-w.html?utm_source=chatgpt.com	49	Spirituality, moral intensity, and ethical decision making
Mercer	https://www.mercer.com/en-us/insights/us-health-news/the-connection-between-purpose-and-resiliency/	99	The connection between purpose and resiliency
Ethics & Compliance Initiative (ECI)	https://www.ethics.org/wp-content/uploads/2018-ECI-GBES-State-of-Ethics-Compliance-in-Workplace.pdf	100	The state of Ethics and Compliance in the workplace

PwC	https://www.pwc.com/us/en/purpose-workplace-study.html	155	Putting purpose to work
McKinsey	https://www.mckinsey.com/featured-insights/mckinsey-on-books/help-your-employees-find-purpose-or-watch-them-leave	158	Help your employees find purpose - or watch them leave
Harvard Business Review	https://hbr.org/2018/07/creating-a-purpose-driven-organization	158	Purpose-Driven Organizations for Employee Engagement
Robert Greenleaf	https://greenleaf.org/what-is-servant-leadership/	169	What is Servant Leadership
British Psychological Society	https://bpspsychub.onlinelibrary.wiley.com/doi/10.1111/joop.12265	172	Servant Leadership and Employee Engagement
American Psychological Association	https://www.apa.org/topics/mindfulness/meditation	189	Mindfulness and meditation impact our brain & biology in a positive way
Harvard Business Review	https://hbr.org/2022/11/revitalizing-culture-in-the-world-of-hybrid-work	190	Revitalizing culture in the world of hybrid work
Ernst & Young	https://www.ey.com/en_us/ceo/ceos-juggle-transformation-priorities?utm_source=chatgpt.com	214	The CEO's top priority around sustainability
German Autopreneur	https://germanautopreneur.com/p/bmw-mercedes-vw-software-alliance	214	Top auto players collaborate for shared infrastructure for SDVs

Business Round Table	https://www.businessroundta ble.org/business-roundtable-redefines-the-purpose-of-a-corporation-to-promote-an-economy-that-serves-all-americans	215	Redefines the purpose of corporations to promote an economy that serves all Americans
Virgin Group	https://unite.virgin.com/our-work/the-b-team/index.html?region=us	216	The B team, and what does it do
World Economic Forum	https://initiatives.weforum.or g/alliance-of-ceo-climate-leaders/home	216	The biggest CEO Alliance is committed to Net Zero Emissions
The Gazette UK	https://www.thegazette.co.uk/ all-notices/content/103417	216	Leading companies sign up for mental health and well-being commitment
Harvard Business Review	https://hbr.org/2022/08/10-principles-of-effective-organizations	227	10 Principles of Effective Organizations by Michael O'Malley
Yahoo Finance	https://finance.yahoo.com/ne ws/jeff-bezos-predicting-amazons-inevitable-180219107.html	232	Inevitable death of Amazon
Starbucks	https://www.businessinsider.c om/starbucks-baristas-what-new-ceo-should-do-pricing-drinks-menu-2024-8	239	5 Starbucks baristas highlight what they want the new CEO to do
Business Standard	https://www.business-standard.com/world-news/starbucks-loses-11-billion-market-value-due-to-	242	The Starbucks boycott led to a loss of $11

	poor-sales-boycotts-123120700054_1.html		billion in market value
Ben & Jerry	https://www.benjerry.com/whats-new/2014/corporate-social-responsibility-history	244	Ben & Jerry's corporate social responsibility
National Library of Medicine	https://pubmed.ncbi.nlm.nih.gov/29990584/	252	Impact of mindfulness and meditation on the amygdala
The Harvard Gazette	https://news.harvard.edu/gazette/story/2011/01/eight-weeks-to-a-better-brain/	252	Meditation study shows changes associated with awareness
Business Brainz	https://businessbrainz.com/wp-content/uploads/2020/09/Unilever.pdf	254	Slide 11 titled Unilever Business Strategy (4/18)
Amazon	https://www.amazon.com/Conscious-Capitalism-Liberating-Heroic-Business/dp/1422144208	259	Conscious Capitalism: Liberating the Heroic Spirit of Business
TOMS	https://www.toms.com/en-nl/about-toms?srsltid=AfmBOooPWpSuiJQ2zga8tmGWeUHpeXY0krGc1K8yqsvR1gKtJBZsgySa	267	One for One model by TOMS
Government of India	https://www.indiacode.nic.in/bitstream/123456789/2114/5/A2013-18.pdf	260	Indian government's Act to mandate CSR for Corporations
Government of India	https://www.csrxchange.gov.in/	260	India CSR portal
Government of India	https://yoga.ayush.gov.in/	261	Yoga promotion by the Indian

			Government, AYUSH
United Nations	https://www.un.org/en/ga/abo ut/ropga/ropga_invte.shtml#:~:text=Immediately%20after %20the%20opening%20of% 20the%20first%20plenary,mi nute%20of%20silence%20de dicated%20to%20prayer%20 or%20meditation.	261	UN 1 min mediation, prayer before every General Assembly meeting
United Nations	https://www.un.org/en/observ ances/yoga-day	261	International Yoga Day by the UN
UNICEF	https://www.unicef.org/child-rights-convention/convention-text	261	UNICEF recognizes the importance of spiritual & moral well-being for children
Disney	Disney To Acquire Pixar - The Walt Disney Company	274	Disney acquired Pixar for $7.4 billion
ineak.com	Case Study: Toyota's Response to the 2011 Earthquake and Tsunami	274	Resilience of Toyota after the 2011 earthquake and tsunami
Computer World	https://www.computerworld.c om/article/1325643/amazon-records-first-profitable-year-in-its-history.html	276	2003 was Amazon's first profitable year, 8 years after its inception
Medium	https://medium.com/@26shru ti.kaushik/how-apple-revived-itself-through-innovation-a-story-of-reviving-the-brand-the-company-apple-inc-ea3194ea5b1d	278	Apple revives through innovation

Ubuntuverse	www.ubuntuverse.org	286	Finding your why
Amazon	https://www.amazon.com/BEYOND-SUCCESS-Unleash-New-You-ebook/dp/B0DM9NRDV8/ref=sr_1_1?crid=ATYUURZYRB5X&dib=eyJ2IjoiMSJ9.n30l9Sh1P5Mm0i2qXU2riASzVmrRKfmDZk0cATBFDg8vyrXXWYnK4kD1YClNaNbDKsfjS6PGtqCmN1gdj2OZwSFM5KQ5VpVBDFoBTvjzi89FpqI9wWC4YjsH1Xnibe8tP2zqA1qgh7AMMBMwzZbGqMnkzSHRnX6XIKM7ybm9j8W9uhHOzhtBjSpv9hpJRGnmX5Tjya1n9dWeOIH-Ou2xA9SspdI5nwttsK2oVcY4TWI.BP-DqcjtIv8UMdqWxPknaukc6PRG5EXD6VuZFC5k6-w&dib_tag=se&keywords=beyond+success+unleash+the+new+you&qid=1750900609&sprefix=beyond+success%2Caps%2C142&sr=8-1	287	Author's previous book 'Beyond Success Unleash the New You'
TED Talk (Simon Sinek)	https://www.ted.com/talks/simon_sinek_how_great_leaders_inspire_action	300, 316	Simon Sinek's Golden Circle and reflection on Why (purpose)
Positive Psychology	https://positivepsychology.com/ikigai/	300, 316	Ikigai - Japanese concept of finding one's true purpose

Disclaimer: The links and resources cited below are owned by third-party sources who retain all intellectual property rights and may modify or remove the content at any time without notice.